The Collaborative Podcast Series; Book 4

Unlocking the Possible

By David B. Savage

Table of Contents

Guests on the Collaborative Podcast Series

In order of appearance on the podcasts, I thank these friends, mentors and collaborative leaders;

Chuck Rose, Denise Chartrand, Kathy Porter, Duncan Autrey, Jeanne McPherson, Allan Davis, Patricia Morgan, Don Loney, David Gouthro, Ken Cloke, Cheryl Cardinal, Ryan Robb, Esther Bleuel, Jeff Cohen, Joan Goldsmith, Amy Fox, Richard Schultz, Laura Hummelle, Colin Campbell, Donna Hastings, Rob McKay, Art Korpach, Tara Russell, Linda Matthie, Viki Winterton, Stephen Smith, Dee Ann Turner, Doreen Liberto, Dana Meise, Teresa de Grosbois, David Milia, Don Simmons, Bruce McIntyre, James Armstrong, Michael Hill, Johanne Lavoie, Atul Tandon, Prabha Sankaranarayan, Bob Anderson, Ginger Lapid- Bogda, Dan Savage, Sarah Daitch, India Sherri, Kevin Brown, David Milia, AnnaMarie McHargue, Bob Acton, David Mitchell, Tristen Chernove, Martin Parnell, Mike Thompson, Stephen Hobbs, Julie Murray, Doreen Liberto, Chuck Rose, Elisabeth Delaygue Bevan, Florian Wackermann, Lance Kadatz, Cliff Wiebe, Amy Schabacker Dufrane, Japman Bajaj, Kate McKenzie, Shawn Anderson, Martin Parnell, Jim Gibson, Jeff Cohen, Barry Wilson, Doreen Liberto, Jeff Cohen, Deva Premal and Miten, Klara Fenlof, Robert Stewart, Sara Amos and Quinn Amos, Ken Cloke, and Duncan Autrey.

This is Break Through To Yes: The Collaborative Podcast Series by David B. Savage

Book 4: Unlocking the Possible with Collaboration provides you with 14 podcasts originally aired on Voice America in 2017.

Let's work together better for our shared future.

Imagine the peaks we will reach together.

Collaboration is the path.

Foreword

If You Want to Go Fast, Go Alone. If You Want to Go Far, Go Together- African proverb

I've been asked many times, why have I done this podcast series. Why have I written Break Through to Yes: Unlocking the Possible within a Culture of Collaboration? Why is collaboration so important?

I'll tell you why. We need it. I need it. Our future needs it. Business is forced into silos and must give up to an open and agile system that better suits today's world and our shared future. We must create shared value. We must think critically. The costs of command and control leadership are getting higher.

During my 42-year career in business, I've held titles including director, president, and chief operating officer. I have seen many and repeated failures, sometimes with the cost of billions. These failures affect organizations and their capital projects and operations. When a company starts making mistakes, tries to force its agenda on others, or conflicts with its own stakeholders, the consequences are significant. People revolt, and profit margins are destroyed. Projects get delayed in regulatory and community review for extended lengths of time. Employees simply don't give their best because they do not trust the systems they work in especially when they have little influence in the processes or programs in which they are involved.

The cost to organizations can be both internal and external disengagement, rejection by regulatory bodies and governments, rejection by impacted communities, and damage to the environment. Add to that a wide range of negative human impacts including everything from depression, conflict, suicide, marital breakdown and career paralysis to the loss of intelligence and vision of the brightest people in your business, simply because they mentally and spiritually check out when they come to work.

All this means lost productivity, lost opportunities to grow and prosper, and distracted leaders and workers who no longer feel able to do good work. Leaders and organizations however can gain a strategic advantage by avoiding all this energy and revenue-zapping negativity simply by working together to build a culture of collaboration.

The soul killing command and control, also, damages families. What if you mattered? What if we mattered. And it was more valuable to explore together than be seen to be right.

Collaboration is not an event, it's a culture. It's the way we work together. I am a lifelong student of how to get the right people in the right place with the right information in the right mindset to figure out how to conquer challenges and solve conflicts together.

Collaboration is a new field of study and success. Collaboration must evolve. Let's learn together and make our world, communities and families better.

Google collaboration in 2012 and you will get 278 million results. Google collaboration today and you will get 550 million results. We are seeking wisdom, skills and systems for collaboration. With this series, I want to build that together.

This is a quote from an OpEd article By Thomas L. Freidman in the New York Times September 27, 2017;

"When work was predictable, and the change rate was relatively constant, preparation for work merely required the codification and transfer of existing knowledge and predetermined skills to create a stable and deployable work force," explains education consultant Heather McGowan. "Now that the velocity of change has accelerated, due to a combination of exponential growth in technology and globalization, learning can no longer be a set dose of education consumed in the first third of one's life." In this age of accelerations, "the new killer skill set is an agile mind-set that values learning over knowing."

Today's increasing speed of change and increasing complexity make collaboration more important now than ever before. No one person can know it all, solve it all or be it all. Together we are better. Together we go far.

Welcome. I am David B. Savage. This compilation of my podcasts is created to provide you, in one source, the deep look at how we work together and how we can do that better. I offer you this compilation of 41 podcasts for your enjoyment, education, and leadership.

When I started writing my book Break Through to Yes: Unlocking the Possible within a Culture of Collaboration, I realized in 2012 that there were few books on collaboration and none of them were collaborative books. This series of podcasts, 41 podcasts, is not about me. It's about "we". It's about "we" and how to create shared value.

In my books and podcasts, I offer you insights from my 42+ years of business leadership, plus the wisdom from over 175 leaders from eight countries around the world. Yes, my book and podcasts have over 175 other voices.

I hope you'll add yours. You may email me at David@DavidBSavage to share your learning and insights. Let's collaborate. I believe that through leadership, excellence and collaboration, we can make our personal and professional lives far better together.

In this compilation, you will experience many perspectives and dreams. It's divided in four easy to read / listen to books.

I)   Book 1: The Foundations for Collaboration

offers you eight 15-minute podcasts originally aired on the Tenacious Living Network, a quick hit, a series of eight 15-minute podcasts.

II)   Book 2: The Collaborative Guest Podcasts

offers you three podcasts where I had been a guest on Barry Wilson, Bob Acton and Duncan Autrey's podcasts. The subjects are collaboration and negotiation, leadership and cumulative environmental effects on our landscape.

III)   Book 3: The 10 Essential Steps of Collaboration

provides you with 16 podcasts originally aired on Voice America. In addition to the 10 Essential Steps, this Book includes the Next Generation of Leaders and our Shared Future.

IV)   Book 4: Unlocking the Possible with Collaboration

provides you with a further 14 podcasts originally aired on Voice America. These podcasts feature collaboration and Disruptive Technology, Organizational Assessments, Critical Thinking, Sports, Leadership and combating human Sexual trafficking with collaboration.

Plus, there's a bonus in our podcasts. You will hear the beautiful music of Chuck Rose, Deva Premal and Miten, and Led to Sea.

Note; The chapters and books are transcripts from the podcasts. These are minimally edited and are not re-written for the Collaborative Podcast Series. These are the brilliant unpolished conversations.

Here is a quote from the podcasts by my friend Ken Cloke, founder of Mediators Beyond Borders and author of many books including The Dance of Opposites.

"The first thing that's misleading is that there is a single thing that is known as collaboration. We can certainly think of it as singular, but we can also think of it as having a kind of infinite number of manifestations. There are small- scale collaborations, which we engage in every time we have a conversation. There are larger collaborations that we engage in in communities and families. "What we have a hard time I think imagining is how far exactly this can go. What is the deepest level of our collaboration? What's the highest achievement that we can make in this field? I think when we begin to think in those terms, we begin to see all of life completely differently,"

Welcome to our Collaborative Podcast Series. Let's collaborate for a better shared future for our people, planet, and communities. You matter. We matter. We are better together.

What is Creating Shared Value, Critical Thinking and Collaboration?

In my talks, writing and consulting, I focus on Creating Shared Value and Critical Thinking. Along with collaboration, critical thinking and leadership, Creating Shared Value is our path to our shared future.

What is Creating Shared Value?

The Harvard Business Review says it best in the January – February 2011 issue How To Fix Capitalism, Michael E. Porter and Mark R. Kramer write;

"The capitalist system is under siege. In recent years business has been criticized as a major cause of social, environmental, and economic problems. Companies are widely thought to be prospering at the expense of their communities. Trust in business has fallen to new lows, leading government officials to set policies that undermine competitiveness and sap economic growth. Business is caught in a vicious circle.

A big part of the problem lies with companies themselves, which remain trapped in an outdated, narrow approach to value creation. Focused on optimizing short-term financial performance, they overlook the greatest unmet needs in the market as well as broader influences on their long-term success. Why else would companies ignore the well-being of their customers, the depletion of natural resources vital to their businesses, the viability of suppliers, and the economic distress of the communities in which they produce and sell?

It doesn't have to be this way, say Porter, of Harvard Business School, and Kramer, the managing director of the social impact advisory firm FSG. Companies could bring business and society back together if they redefined their purpose as creating "shared value"—generating economic value in a way that also produces value for society by addressing its challenges. A shared value approach reconnects company success with social progress.

Firms can do this in three distinct ways: by reconceiving products and markets, redefining productivity in the value chain, and building supportive industry clusters at the company's locations. A number of companies known for their hard-nosed approach to business—including GE, Wal-Mart, Nestlé, Johnson & Johnson, and Unilever—have already embarked on important initiatives in these areas. Nestlé, for example, redesigned its coffee procurement processes, working intensively with small farmers in impoverished areas who were trapped in a cycle of low productivity, poor quality, and environmental degradation. Nestlé provided advice on farming practices; helped growers secure plant stock, fertilizers, and pesticides; and began directly paying them a premium for better beans. Higher yields and quality increased the growers' incomes, the environmental impact of farms shrank, and Nestlé's reliable supply of good coffee grew significantly. Shared value was created.

Shared value could reshape capitalism and its relationship to society. It could also drive the next wave of innovation and productivity growth in the global economy as it opens managers' eyes to immense human needs that must be met, large new markets to be served, and the internal costs of social deficits—as well as the competitive advantages available from addressing them. But our understanding of shared value is still in its genesis. Attaining it will require managers to develop new skills and knowledge and governments to learn how to regulate in ways that enable shared value, rather than work against it."

What is Critical Thinking?

"Critical thinking is self-guided, self-disciplined thinking which attempts to reason at the highest level of quality in a fair-minded way. People who think critically consistently attempt to live rationally, reasonably, empathically. They are keenly aware of the inherently flawed nature of human thinking when left unchecked. They strive to diminish the power of their egocentric and sociocentric tendencies. They use the intellectual tools that critical thinking offers – concepts and principles that enable them to analyze, assess, and improve thinking. They work diligently to develop the intellectual virtues of intellectual integrity, intellectual humility, intellectual civility, intellectual empathy, intellectual sense of justice and confidence in reason. They realize that no matter how skilled they are as thinkers, they can always improve their reasoning abilities and they will at times fall prey to mistakes in reasoning, human irrationality, prejudices, biases, distortions, uncritically accepted social rules and taboos, self-interest, and vested interest. They strive to improve the world in whatever ways they can and contribute to a more rational, civilized society. At the same time, they recognize the complexities often inherent in doing so. They avoid thinking simplistically about complicated issues and strive to appropriately consider the rights and needs of relevant others. They recognize the complexities in developing as thinkers, and commit themselves to life-long practice toward self-improvement. They embody the Socratic principle: The unexamined life is not worth living, because they realize that many unexamined lives together result in an uncritical, unjust, dangerous world." Linda Elder, September 2007 as reported by the Critical Thinking Community website.

"A well cultivated critical thinker:

- ✓ raises vital questions and problems, formulating them clearly and precisely;
- ✓ gathers and assesses relevant information, using abstract ideas to interpret it effectively comes to well-reasoned conclusions and solutions, testing them against relevant criteria and standards;
- ✓ thinks open-mindedly within alternative systems of thought, recognizing and assessing, as need be, their assumptions, implications, and practical consequences; and
- ✓ communicates effectively with others in figuring out solutions to complex problems.

Critical thinking is, in short, self-directed, self-disciplined, self-monitored, and self-corrective thinking. It presupposes assent to rigorous standards of excellence and mindful command of their use. It entails effective communication and problem-solving abilities and a commitment to overcome our native egocentrism and sociocentrism."

Richard Paul and Linda Elder, The Miniature Guide to Critical Thinking Concepts and Tools, Foundation for Critical Thinking Press, 2008.

What is Collaboration?

Here is an except from Break Through To Yes: Unlocking the Possible within a Culture of Collaboration.

"When you Google "collaboration" you get at least 278,000,000 results. [Note if you searched Collaboration on Google in October 2017, you would have received

530,000,000,000 results. This is almost a double in just two years. Will we reach a billion in 2018? There is a significant and growing interest in collaboration.]

Seems there is a lot of interest in learning about collaboration. But what is collaboration represented as?

Merriam Webster defines collaborate as "to work with another person or group in order to achieve or do something." This could be the definition of a meeting or what a football team does. I prefer this definition:

"Collaboration is highly diversified teams working together inside and outside a company with the purpose to create value by improving innovation, customer relationships and efficiency while leveraging technology for effective interactions in the virtual and physical space."

Let's make a joint proclamation that we value collaboration as a powerful way of leading. Collaboration isn't an act, it is the way we lead. To collaborate isn't simply to work together, it is an organizational culture."

And from What Is Collaboration at Work? By Bruce Mayhew, HuffPost July 24, 2014;

"Collaboration is the successful structure of the future - not a single conversation between two employees. A diverse and collaborative culture is a powerful competitive advantage. A well-implemented, trained and supported high-performance team will better align their outcomes around both their objective and company mission.

Tomorrow's successful organizations recognize that in today's complex professional environment that collaboration is critical.

Collaborative leaders recognize there will be challenges and that their greatest responsibility is to guide change and future success by preparing their employees to overcoming these challenges in a respectful and mindful way."

Define your personal values as a successful collaborative leader

Name five values: (for example, integrity, transparency, fairness, innovative, inclusive, curiosity, accountability, intelligence, courageous, perfection, altruism, loyalty, respect, family, humility, truth, determination, independence, ...

1)
2)
3)
4)
5)

How do you choose to lead?

_____

_____

_____

What resources do you need (human, technology, networks, financial, environmental, social)?

_____

_____

_____

What do you choose to let go of to make this so?

_____

_____

_____

What else?

_____

_____

_____

_____

Chapter 1 Collaboration and Leadership featuring Bob Acton and David Mitchell

David: Welcome to our very first show in our 2017 Voice America radio show podcast series. Our executive producer Camille Nash and I are just delighted to collaborate with our listeners in England, France, Canada, Scotland, America, Ukraine, China and many more places.

I was excited to hear that we have 1600 listeners in London, England; 1600 listeners, according to our last analytics. Those listeners contact me, david@davidbsavage.com. I'd love to have one or more of you on a future show.

Today's theme is collaboration and leadership. For the first show in our 2017 series, we have Bob Acton, Obair Leadership; and David Mitchell of Bow Valley College. Both, I think you'll really enjoy and we'll interview during this hour.

Now, let's start with you. Do you wonder whether you are going anywhere? I'll say it again. Do you wonder whether you are going anywhere? Do you sometimes feel like you are doing the same thing over and over? Where is exploration in your life? Where is innovation? Or is leadership repeating the same thing over and over, and over and over? Or might leadership also be innovation through collaboration?

In my 2016 book, *Break Through to Yes: Unlocking the Possible within a Culture of Collaboration*, I provide 10 Essential Steps to collaborate. Step 8 to collaborate is collaborate with vision. In collaboration, we are looking to break out of normal. We're looking to break out of normal and Break Through to fresh and exciting insights and possibilities. We are. Collaboration is much more than doing the same thing better.

In a section called Skating Beyond, I talk about what I do in some of my workshops. I invite you to do it right now. If you've got a piece of paper or pencil, or your tablet handy, just draw what you believe is a skating rink. Yeah, sketch out a skating rink.

I'll tell you, when workshop participants are invited to do this, almost always they draw a hockey rink. Why do we do that? Because most often, we skate on hockey rinks; therefore, skating rink is a hockey rink.

But sometimes, we skate on frozen rivers, ponds and lakes. Sometimes we clear a long and winding path around a lake for skaters to have a larger area and a more interesting activity.

Now, go back to your paper or your tablet. Draw a place that would be magical for your family to skate on. Think of that. What's possible? Unlock that.

Now, hopefully you and workshop participants start drawing long winding pathways that go through forests, go up and down slightly, curves of creative places for you to sit. It might have a canopy overhead. It may have musicians playing nearby and it looks and feels nothing like a hockey rink.

This fresh concept of a wonderful place to skate is nothing like what we first drew. To collaborate with vision, let go of what you think things should be like or what they are like today. Vision invites creativity. Trust and presence encourages our mind to create possibilities beyond what is currently the norm. Vision allows us to Break Through our limiting perspectives.

Let's think about limiting perspectives. Can we see beyond the problem? Too often, organizations get stuck, leaders get stuck. The reason they get stuck is they do not allow themselves to dream big. They tend to focus on the little, and most achievable and safest. Or they get so focused on the problem, they never get beyond that problem.

Now visualize again. Collaborate with Vision. Think about sports. Think about shooting to score a goal in sports. If you focus on the goalie, most often you will not score. If you focus on the net behind the goalie, that is the target. Seeing the target instead of the problem allows you to achieve and to score. Shoot for the net, not the goalie.

Another way of thinking of this is high-performance driving. Some of you are high-performance drivers. Some of you drive on the Autobahn. Some of you drive on 401 in Toronto. Wherever you drive, if there's a collision at high speeds and that collision happens in front of you, you must see past the problem. You must look past the collision.

You see the way through. Get your car there and go to the finish line. If you only see the crash or hit the brakes, you will be part of the crash.

Now here's a technique. Dream big and work back to now. When truly opening to the ideas of others in collaboration, my friend Richard Schultz told me, we have the opportunity to go beyond our own rules and beliefs, and explore ideas and possibilities that we alone cannot see or even choose not to see.

How do we define collaboration? According to Richard Schultz of Collaborative Ways, at its root, collaboration is to co-labor with another or to work together. The simple idea of working together may be the basis of a collaboration, but it also conjures up the idea of something more, something of a higher vibration. It is this higher vibration of the world and the word 'collaborate' that we may want to stretch towards and embrace.

He's talking about collective wisdom. Be bold in your vision. Look at where you wish to be. Dream about how that feels. What is the air like? What do you see? How do you feel?

When I'm coaching executives and I often do in organization, often I must shift them from their day-to-day tension, challenge and frustrations. When we go back to their values and their vision of themselves and their company, oftentimes I'll take them to a place of 5 years in the future. They look beyond the collisions in front of them. They became more strongly motivated.

Setting the strategic plan is far, far easier, looking back from success than looking forward past obstacles. Say it again. Setting the strategic plan is far easier looking back from success than looking forward past obstacles.

What's your finish line? What do you feel when you're there? Who's there with you? What are you doing? What's the setting? What's the sound? What's the motion? What's the energy? What do you want to do to start building that future?

In my 10 Essential Steps, step 9 is, Now Lead and leadership is the theme of this radio show. Effective collaboration requires the strong leadership brought about by such dimensions as clarity of vision, decision-making capabilities, emotional intelligence and engendering of trust. A strong leader demands accountability from his whole team, regardless of who is on that team. Yeah, accountability.

Collaboration is not, let's have a group think. It's finding the collective wisdom with accountability and purpose. What is the essential why that you and your organization are answering? If you and the organization failed, what would be lost to the outside world? Think about that. What's your why and if you didn't fill that space, how would the world suffer?

We've talked about how and why collaboration fails and succeeds in my book. But think about your collaboration. Do you want to be a bystander, a facilitator or a leader?

I want to take this metaphor a little further. Let's look at skiing. Downhill skiing, cross-country skiing, backcountry skiing, I love them all. I do them all. It's wintertime in Canada. When downhill skiing, the chairlift takes me to the top of the hill and I ski down the hill. With cross-country skiing, I follow on the tracks of others. My new passion this winter is backcountry skiing where I head into the mountains and explore new valleys, new vistas, new ridges, create my own trail.

In leadership, much of our lives are like cross-country skiing with our organizations, on the pre-set tracks. Sometimes, we are carried to a peak and ski down in celebration. Sometimes we do that.

How often do you, as a leader, backcountry ski in new valleys? How often do you create new trails? What percentage of your time do you dedicate to innovation and collaboration? Or are you too busy? Are you thinking about this approach to leadership, thinking about backcountry skiing where the fresh snow is, the clean air where nobody else is? If you yelled your name out loud in that mountain valley, would there be an echo or would there be a call in return?

Let's be courageous. Let's get out there. Let's get out in that fresh snow. How often are you leading people on the same path and how often are you exploring and innovating?

Let's think about your future. I talked about bringing my coaching clients, executives to 5 years out. Let's see even go a couple of years out. Imagine yourself as a leader in 2020. You and your organization are celebrating a huge Break Through. Together, you've accomplished what no one had dreamed possible.

What are you expecting? What are you feeling? What's the energy? What's the place? Who's with you?

You're celebrating. Just get that feeling in you and get addicted to that feeling of celebrating your success from your Break Throughs that you're about to create.

So here are some steps, a call-to-action in fact, three things that I would encourage you to write down now and think about. Think about where you need to be, about that feeling of 2020, what your Break Through was. Please do these and send me a note, give me a call, share on social media. Share most importantly with your team, your family, your community.

1) What is the possible you dream of unlocking? That's right, what is the possible you dream of unlocking? What is it? We have many dreams. Let's make them so. What is the possible you dream of unlocking?

2) who are three people that have the expertise to help you? Who are three people that have the expertise to help you? You know who they are. If you don't know who they are, what's the expertise that you need to find out?

3) what will you do right now to start? Right now; what will you do right now to start, to activate this dream fulfillment towards your 2020 celebration?

Now if you want to look at my 10 Essential Steps to collaboration, YouTube videos, videos on creating shared value, some of the coaching work I do, go to my website davidbsavage.com. Contact me. I'll be delighted to have an initial conversation with you, answer any questions that you have.

You have the network. You are developing a stronger network. You will unlock. You will find 3, then 30 people to help you if you start right now.

So, after the break, we're going to come back and talk to Dr. Bob Acton and then later, we will talk to David Mitchell.

David: Listeners around the world, I am so delighted to have my friend and mentor and coach Dr. Bob Acton as our guest today, our very first guest in our 2017 series. Bob is a consulting psychologist and leadership coach who helps people be highly successful in their workplace. Bob leads people, teams and projects themselves, so he knows how hard it can be to get results by working with others.

He helps people achieve peak performance at work by increasing their energy and focus, helping them achieve what's most important to them personally and professionally. Yeah, I'll say that again, most important to them both personally and professionally.

Bob can be found through his business at, www.obairleadership.com and on Twitter @obairleadership or LinkedIn, under Bob Acton.

Bob, welcome today. Thank you so much for joining us and sharing some of your thoughts today with our listeners across the globe. We've got listeners in 31 countries so far, and that's growing; so, welcome.

Bob: Thanks very much for having me, David.

David: With you, Bob, I want to talk about collaborative leadership. With your many years' experience working with peak performers and working with some of the best professionals in Canada, and some of the best coaches in the world, I want to open with a question of, how can people achieve peak performance in their life? It's a pretty broad question, but let's start there Bob. How do people achieve peak performance in their life?

Bob: Yeah, that is a big question. I guess I think that there's many facets or aspects to peak performance. It includes, for example, having the right amount of physical energy or emotional energy, or mental energy to be able to take to that performance. But probably one thing that I think is most important is to really be clear with why you're doing what you're doing, to attach what I might call your personal meaning, what's meaningful for you in your life, to the values that you hold about how you achieve that in your life; and to be really clear about that because that clarity helps you focus in on what's most important.

David: I'm hearing values, purpose, clarity. So that's foundational. When we hear leaders say, I'm not sure who I am as a leader, you're helping them clarify that just to say, okay what's your building foundation here? What's the concrete under everything you do?

Bob: Yeah and that's a great metaphor. I use that all the time, the notion of building a house and what does the foundation of our house look like for you? Everybody's got a different design of their house, of course, and some people want more rooms than others. But we all need a basement or some sort of foundation to the house to hold it in place when the winds blow.

Often in the workplace or in our lives, we have adversity come along and that's the wind that's blowing. And for our house to be solid and stay there and help us stay warm and house our family, it needs to be solid.

David: If we're not clear on our values, then we have little guidance systems, self-guidance systems or ability to say no to what crosses boundaries.

Bob: One of the things that happens to us all is that we often can get trapped into agreeing to somebody else's values. So, if I have a job, let's say, and I have a boss and that boss has a set of goals that they're trying to achieve for themselves and the business. They may have a set of values that are quite critical to them.

It's easy for us to get trapped into the values that others hold rather than being clear about what's important for you. And I'll give you an example of what happened to me this morning.

I was on a conference call and the big boss came on the conference call and never said hello to anybody, never said welcome to the conference call or set an agenda of what we were talking about and just launched into starting to talk about some of the content. That was a good example of how that wouldn't fit for how I would like to work because I have a value that I want to respect people and I want to collaborate with people and doing something simple like saying hello or welcome to the conference call is really an important part of that. So that's like a simple example, but one that I think holds true for all of us.

David: What are a few of your key values? Help people understand whether your values and their values are similar or what you mean by values?

Bob: Yeah. So, I have a few key ones that are important for me. One of them is continuous learning. So, for me, I'm always trying to learn something new. I'm reading books. I'm taking courses. I'm doing those things. So that's something that's important for me.

Another value that's important for me is that I like to create new things. I'm really interested in new projects, innovative things.

So, on the opposite side of that, to put me into a position or a job or a task where it's repetitive, then I can get bored quite easily. So, the values help me figure out what I should be doing, what's going to give me the energy to keep me going when the winds blow, and what I should not be doing.

For example, you and I have connected a lot because we both have, as a value, the notion of collaborating with others. If I'm in a situation where somebody is not collaborative, that's not a place where I'm going to have a lot of positive energy. That's not a place where I want to sit. Does that make sense?

David: Yes. I think you would agree that not sitting there for you and I is our value. That doesn't make it wrong for other people. I used the example earlier in this show about the difference between backcountry skiing, cross-country skiing, and downhill skiing where I'm using that as a metaphor that with downhill skiing, somebody else gets me up to the top of the mountain and I simply ski down. With cross-country skiing, I'm following other people's tracks. But if it's backcountry skiing, I find my own fresh powder, my own fresh snow. I go places in the mountains where nobody's there today.

And to me, that's what I'm hearing from you, Bob, you like to find the new tracks. You like to discover new ways of skiing that you haven't before.

Bob: Yes, absolutely. So that's true for me and as you've said, a value doesn't necessarily have to be wrong or right. It's just what's important for me and I think your original question was how do we help people with peak performance. I think people are performing at a high level or at that peak when they are doing things that are in line with what's important to them.

David: Yeah. Now we talked about the big guy that got on the conference call this morning and just launched into the doing part as opposed to the relating part. Sometimes, collaboration and performance can get really confusing. The boss doesn't want me to be a collaborator. He just wants me to be a messenger or just cross-country ski, stay behind him in his tracks.

So, I'm wondering from your belief in collaboration and I've seen it for a decade now, Bob, is it possible to be collaborative and a peak performer?

Bob: Absolutely. I think that as you and I both know, collaboration takes a set of skills to be able to do that well. And I think they go hand-in-hand with somebody who is a peak performer. I think often we get off-track because we think that peak performers mean that they are individuals and they're not interested in somebody else. They're only out for themselves.

And in fact, I think being a collaborative person really helps you be a peak performer. You must have the right attitude to be able to simply even listen to people.

David: I know in my career, I know I can't do it by myself. I don't have the expertise. I don't have the breadth of knowledge. I must collaborate to be successful.

Bob: Yes. And you asked about my values. I love working with people because I think you end up with a better product. I don't feel all alone out there. So that notion of collaboration, of working with people to create a great thing, whatever that might be, is something that helps people perform at a high level.

One of the people that works with me on my team is an Olympic coach for the Canadian Olympic team. He and I often talk about how does he help his athletes achieve a gold medal. It's not just that particular athlete doing it by themselves. They've got a variety of people working with them, coaches, sports psychologists, nutritionists, finance people, all sorts of people behind the scenes collaborating to help that person achieve that gold medal.

So yes, we watch T.V. and we see the person getting that gold medal and we think about them as an individual or as part of a team. But really, there is a whole variety of people working together behind the scenes to make that happen.

David: Yeah, wonderful metaphor right there, that we seem to celebrate heroes without often enough recognizing that the person that prepares the equipment, the person that prepares the nutrition, the person that prepares the mindset. People like you that prepare their entire performance culture as a coach are also important. Without you, it just can't be as successful.

Bob: Absolutely.

David: Now, how is this collaboration and peak performance helpful to the business itself? It's not – talk about collaboration. Let's talk about peak performance collaboration and what it means to business.

Bob: A good way to think about this is to think about what would happen if you didn't have collaboration. So, when I think about people and I think about people I've worked with or people I've seen in the workplace who are not collaborative, they tend to create conflict around them. They tend to have people not want to work with them, so they leave the team, or they leave the group to go somewhere else, because often people who are not collaborative create tension in others. That tension pulls away from the opportunity to be creative or to be innovative, to be healthy in the workplace.

So, the non-collaborative person creates a lot of problems for an organization and then on the opposite side of that, if you can create an environment with your team, where people are happy to be there or are energized to be there, are focused on the thing they're trying to create for the group, you're going to get a higher production level.

David: Yes. I'm just thinking about some of the pushback in some of our listener's minds might be and I want to go back to your analogy of talking about the Olympic performance. For example, an Olympic athlete in whatever their sport is, collaboration in business, in that business is – not everybody on the team is running the marathon together, or aiming the same rifle or shooting the same puck. It is the team. There can be peak performers but they're there because of the collaborative, right?

Bob: Absolutely.

David: Now as we close Bob, one thing that you will challenge our listeners too, I love this question because you offer so much wisdom and let's just leave them with one thing that you would challenge our listeners to do to improve their peak performance and collaboration.

Bob: It may sound awful simple, David, but I would challenge people to listen more. I think that if we listen to people more, we'll find out what they need. We'll find out their ideas and we'll find out and dive down into their creativity, and out of that will come a better product.

Really, all the people who are probably listening to you are trying to create something. They're trying to create a business product or service, or something. And by listening to the people, listening to your customers, listening to your clients, listening to your own people and really, as I call it listen hard, then by doing that, you can really gather more information. That person feels listened to more, and still wants to be more part of your team. Does that make sense?

David: Yeah. Underneath that, I hear respect.

Bob: Absolutely.

David: Respect and inclusion and learning together.

Bob: Yeah. So, we're back to those values, again. It becomes full circle, the behavior that we exist out in the workplace, the listening is tied into the values that we hold about how we create a business or create whatever it is that we're focused on.

David: And how we want to be valued and treated.

Bob: Absolutely. The old golden rule, right?

David: Yes. Thank you so much Dr. Bob Acton of Obair Leadership. I value your values, your wisdom and every time we collaborate. Thanks Bob.

Bob: Thanks for having me David.

David: Hello again. This is David B. Savage, Break Through to Yes with Collaboration. We have an amazing guest – well, all my guests are amazing. On this first radio show of 2017, my friend David Mitchell. David and I met about 25 years ago. I've been following him, his successful career and now he's in Calgary, Alberta, in a very important role.

I want to introduce David in his current role as Vice President, College Advancement and Chief External Relations Officer at Bow Valley College in Calgary, Alberta. David has a broad professional background, spanning the private, public and education sectors. Yeah, that's all three.

He's a former member of the British Columbia Legislature. He's also served as Deputy Clerk of the Saskatchewan Legislative Assembly. His significant private business sector experience includes executive positions in the resource industries in Western Canada and he's also served as Vice President at three Canadian universities. Those are Simon Fraser, the University of Ottawa and Queens University.

David Mitchell is a governor and fellow of the Royal Canadian Geographical Society and past president of Canada's Public Policy Forum. That's right, this is that David Mitchell. He's served in many board and many volunteer boards, theater parliamentary, science, art.

Go to www.davidjmitchell.ca to learn more. David, welcome to our show.

David M.: Pleasure to be with you David.

David: I want to recollect that David and I met each other about 3 months ago for the first time in decades on a downtown street, near the famous five statues in downtown Calgary at the Olympic Square. We connected 25 years ago in Vancouver and within 5 minutes, I just had this sense of wow, this man is a great energy and we got into a great, deep conversation very quickly. Thank you for that, and thank you for your invitation to be part of your convening, David.

David M.: David, it's been such a delight to reconnect with you all these years later and to compare notes on our respective paths. As it turns out, we've been working and pushing and striving in the same directions for a long time.

David: Yeah, different venues, similar hearts. One of the things that I was delighted to hear on similar hearts and similar offerings to our leadership communities is David Mitchell, I don't know how you found the time, but you recently published a book on convening. What is convening, David?

David M.: I've been doing it. You've been doing it. I bet you our listeners have been doing it for our whole lives. Convening, a smart person asked me recently, isn't it about bringing people together? And her insightful question contains the answer. That's what it is.

The process of convening, in its many forms, brings people together in meetings of various kinds for an exchange of views, typically on a very focused subject. And it's both an art and a science. We do it in our personal lives. We do it in our professional lives.

But to do it thoughtfully, to do it mindfully in the true spirit of collaboration and dialogue requires a bit of effort. I thought I would just write a very basic guide to convening which might be helpful for individuals and organizations to develop their own capacity to convene, David.

David: Yeah. It seems like such a natural thing and yet so often, it's not done well. It's kind of skipped over. It's like bad sex.

David M.: If we don't pay attention, it can become a rote exercise. We all have too many meetings in our lives. Everyone does. They're the bane of our existence.

But with a little bit of preparation, a little bit of thoughtfulness, I think it's possible for all of us to convene meetings, small and large with diverse people who wouldn't normally be sitting around the same table together and we can be doing things like developing and understanding, developing some mutual respect and maybe even some trust and it takes a little bit of effort. But I argue that it's worth that effort.

David: Yes. Practice makes perfect. Perfect practice makes perfect. Attending to the art of convening is so critical and it does take time. Dr. Bob Acton, just before the break, talked about an executive coming on to a call that he was on just lunging right into the doing, without respecting the welcome, the convening, the inclusion; just launched in.

And what I'm hearing you say David, is it takes awareness and respect in inclusion. But tell me maybe one more element of what's in your wisdom, your background and in your book about convening. What's an element that our leaders across the world might take away and ponder?

David M.: David, I think it's, one at the same time so simple that we might overlook the real basics of setting the table or a meaningful conversation, a dialogue, and actual collaboration. Convening is a very important tool in the art and practice of collaboration, which is easier said than done.

There are a few basic items that should be on any convener's checklist. What is the size of the group that I'm bringing together? And can people be participating online through a webcast, via Skype, using technology? And the answer's yes.

But there's nothing that really can substitute for the human moment of in-person contact in a relatively small group. When I say small, the optimum size for a meeting would be anywhere from 10 to 20 people, let's say. It could be a little smaller but it couldn't be much larger if you're going to provide an opportunity for everyone to be an equal participant.

I think creating a safe space for dialogue where people can express themselves as candidly as they're comfortable doing so, no attribution necessary, that's also an important element of very successful convening.

And I'll just mention one final thing, David: the venue. It seems so obvious, but the venue, the physical space where the meeting is taking place is so important that we often overlook it. How do we sit so that everyone can be an equal? The obvious best answer is a circular format where there's no head of the table in a formal sense.

Is there natural light in the room so that that can be conducive to not getting caught in an environment that gets stale and rather tense after a little while?

We shape our houses and they shape us. We shape our meeting spaces and that determines what goes on within them and what kind of a conversation takes place.

There are some very basic elements of successful convening that just need to be briefly reviewed before we launch into it. We need to set the table.

David: What often happens in organizations is they have a rectangular room with a rectangular table and everybody takes the same chair no matter what they're talking about or which process they're in. A lot of successful interior designers now are designing rooms for different purposes, and that's what I'm hearing is the more inclusive, the more natural, the more open, therefore the more, might I say, collaborative and reach to creative.

David M.: So true. And many meeting spaces, whether they'd be in conference centers or in educational institutions or in hotels may not be ideal. But if they have any flexibility, they can probably be reconfigured in a way that provides an opportunity for a spirit of dialogue that is respectful of everyone.

And I'll tell you one thing, not only is the rectangular table sometimes a problem because it's difficult to see who's sitting alongside you 3 or 4 people down, you want to be able to see everyone eye-to-eye, face-to-face.

But also, the traditional classroom style is not so effective. We don't know a lot about learning and education as it turns out. But one thing we do know is that people don't learn by sitting in rows with a person just standing up in front of the room, imparting knowledge.

That's not dialogue, and that's not the spirit of real convening the way you and I are talking, David.

David: Yeah. Our guest, David Mitchell, has been president of the Canadian Forum for Public Policy. When he was at Simon Fraser University, he created a world class convening space, the Center for Dialogue in Downtown Vancouver on West Hastings Street. You told me the story of how that came together. Can you describe your vision and what that is towards convening and inclusion, maybe just give us some background on the Center for Dialogue?

David: I'd be very happy to do so. I was privileged to be part of a small team that helped repurpose an old heritage bank building into an extraordinary conference center that today, here we are 15 going on 20 years later, is extremely well-used for gatherings. The main meeting room, which is the ground level of what used to be a bank, is now called Asia-Pacific Hall. And Asia-Pacific Hall is a large room, very high ceilings, natural light pouring in, beautiful artwork on the walls where there isn't natural light pouring in. The room is configured in four concentric circles.

When people enter this room, which can hold up to 150 people, one of the questions that is often asked first is, where does the chair sit? And it's a terrific question to ask because the answer is, wherever the chair wishes to sit, she or he can sit because the room is circular, and the chairs are all swivel chairs where you can turn in any direction to face whoever is speaking. But people are all working and talking and thinking in a very democratic fashion as equals, either in a large meeting filling the whole hall or using just even one of the concentric circles for about a dozen people.

The spirit of dialogue was part of the plan right from the start. And the notion of dialogue, David, I should tell you, there isn't a large body of literature but there is a little bit of literature on the subject now, about how dialogue fits in with collaboration.

Convening is not an end in itself. It's a means to something, and it's a means toward genuine, authentic collaboration. And that was our vision from the start when we conceived of and renovated this beautiful building and turned it into what's now called the Wosk Center for Dialogue in Downtown Vancouver.

It has had an influence and impact on the groups who use the space because the outcome of the thinking, the partnerships and friendships and relationships that are forged in that environment have endured for a generation almost now.

David: Yeah. So, I would provide a future dream for all of us, our listeners in Russia and China, in British Columbia, in Utah, in Colombia, think about creating that center for dialogue wherever you are so that we can have those concentric circles of equality and inclusion.

David, before we close, I'd like to ask you, what's one thing you would challenge our listeners to do or be or change?

David M.: I would issue the same challenge that I apply to myself regularly. And I'm sometimes embarrassed but I must remind myself of this, but I think we all do David, which is not to make assumptions about other people's perspectives. We all do it, but we all know less than we think we do about other people's points of view.

And to be open, genuinely, a spirit of openness to the conversations, to the dialogue, to the relationships we're forging because there are stereotypes about people from different places that are often very, very inaccurate.

So that's the one wish that I would send out to you David and to all our listeners, to relax our assumptions and realize that we probably don't know as much as we think we do about each other, and be open to learning.

David: Yes, and a fresh perspective. Thank you so much, David Mitchell, for your wisdom. The time has just flown by and I really value your willingness to share some of your expertise today. Thanks David.

David M.: Thank you David, it's been a pleasure.

David: Now today listeners, we've talked about sports. We've talked about vision, leadership, convening and collaboration. We've experienced the leadership of Bob Acton and David Mitchell. And I'll say again, in collaboration, we are looking to break out of normal and Break Through to fresh and exciting insights and possibilities.

One step is, what is possible that you wish to unlock? Two, who are the three people that you have wished to bring into to convene with, to help create your dream? And what will you do to start right now?

Thanks everyone. Talk to you next week. Now let's work together better.

Chapter 2 Collaboration and Sports featuring Tristen Chernove and Martin Parnell

David: Welcome everyone. Today's theme is collaboration in sport. I'm really thrilled that my two very successful athletes, friends, Martin Parnell and Tristen Chernove will be joining us in today's radio show. This is exciting stuff because Martin, you may know him as the man that did 250 marathons in one year for the right to play for children. You may know Tristen as the man who just recently won a gold, silver, and a bronze in the Rio Olympics.

Let's get going. Before we get to Martin and Tristen, I just want to tell you a little bit of stories to give you some background with respect to collaboration in sport. In my book, *Break Through to Yes: Unlocking the Possible within a Culture of Collaboration*, I provide 10 steps to collaboration, and a quote I want to say as often as I can, and I hope you will remember, in collaboration, we are looking to break out of normal. That's right, break out of normal and Break Through to fresh and exciting insights and possibilities. You'll see with both Tristen and Martin, they have taken where they are and created something that is totally fantastic with respect to the challenges that they had, the beliefs they have, the values they have as leaders, collaborators, and amazing sportsmen.

Let's talk about it. Being a rock star in sports can get you rocked. In sports, you can get rocked. Professional sports leagues find market in a few select of their superstar athletes to be a great strategy to engage fans and sell tickets. These athletes will be the first to tell you they depend heavily on their team for success. Think of your favorite team sport. Think about come-from-behind victories, an exceptional display of athleticism. Whether you play or watch basketball, baseball, football, hockey, soccer, lacrosse, whatever it is, understand that winning is a team effort. Very occasionally, one athlete may control the play and take the ball or puck from one end of the court or field to the other and score. But, most often, that athlete will be foiled. Those athletes become the targets of the other team and are the lonely ones in their own dressing rooms, sitting by themselves in the dressing room. "I score all the goals and you guys don't. Ha-ha-ha."

My son, Dan Savage, played all sorts of aggressive team sports in his youth. One of his hockey teammates was an excellent skater and liked to keep the puck for himself. He scored a lot. When summer came, the sport turned to lacrosse. That same teammate tried being "the show" only once. On his very first shift in lacrosse, he was hit so hard by a player on the other team, he flew backward in the air. He learned his lesson from that moment on. He realized that passing, especially in lacrosse, is the best way to win. He and the team, including my son, went on to the provincial championships that year. He learned a great lesson. He was not only a better lacrosse player, but a better hockey player. He played as a team, he played his position. Play as you have practiced and know we win as a team. In your organization, play your position, play as a team, practice, play as you practice and win as a team.

Think about practicing. How often do we practice in business? We have meetings. How often do we practice our strategies, our negotiations, our communications, our leadership? Perfect practice makes perfect. Two things that are necessities of winning teams in sports are slow to become part of the winning formula for corporations. Practice how and how often. Do you and your team practice negotiations, meetings, conflict resolution, operations and simulations?

In the past 20 years, our organizations have practiced safety drills, fire drills, CPR – that's cardiopulmonary resuscitation – and working through emergency simulations. While we practice safety, we rarely practice any other equally important procedures, processes, or skills. The second thing that sport teaches us is that how the value to organizations, yet slow to be adopted, is coaching. Coaching and practicing go together. Coaching helps us see other perspectives, create new visual goals, and allow us to try out different ways of doing the same thing to see how the results may differ, given different people and situations. At every level, from the frontline to the corner office, coaching and practicing greatly enhance our probability of making the best and developing and managing the best relationships. Or, you can choose to be that solitary superstar at the top that repels those that you need to succeed. Think of the context of the lacrosse player being rocked off his feet by the other team by trying to win by himself. In the 21st century, we love the rock stars of music, politics, sports, entertainment. Now, we have another visual of a rock star, the guy flying backwards in the air after getting rocked.

My friend, Rod McKay, was chair of the Heart and Stroke Foundation of Canada, advises leadership is difficult. Leadership that depends heavily on collaboration is more difficult. What is collaboration? We talk about it. This is my 28th podcast on Voice America. Let's go back to that. When you Google "collaboration" you get over 330 million results – that's million results. It seems that there's a lot interest in learning about collaboration. But, what is collaboration represented as? Well, we go back to the old school Merriam-Webster's Dictionary. It defines collaborate as "to work with another person or group in order to achieve or do something". This could be a definition of a median or a football team, but kind of flat. I prefer this definition: collaboration is highly diversified teams working together inside and outside a company with the purpose to create value by improving innovation, customer relationships, and efficiency while leveraging technology for effective interactions in the virtual and physical space. That's the Wikipedia definition. I think that's far more abundant profound full.

Let's make a joint proclamation that we value collaboration as a powerful way of leading and learning. Collaboration isn't an act. It's the way we lead. It's the way we are. To collaborate isn't simply to work together; it's an organizational culture. That's why my book, Break Through to Yes: Unlocking the Possible Within a Culture of Collaboration. That's right, Break Through to Yes: Unlocking the Possible Within a Culture of Collaboration. That's why I developed the world's first collaborative leadership and team development 360 assessment. Let's focus on the team. Let's focus on the "we", how "we" are, how we work together, as opposed to the rock stars.

We'll feature the 360 assessments in next week's show and focus on the team and the way we work together, not on the rock stars. We succeed together better by collaboration. Here we go, here's an idea. Is this right for you? Success in sports always requires collaboration and collaboration over time. That's right, success in sports always requires collaboration. Not sometimes or most often, but always in collaboration over time.

Our guests today, Martin and Tristen will have their experiences on our show. They'll share with us their lives, their commitments, their sports, their successes. Collaboration is a culture, and the way we succeed over time, it's not an event. I'm a former board member of the Heart and Stroke Foundation, and we encourage research, we connect with people, we connect with health providers, we connect with those in need and those in need are unborn babies all the way through to 100-year olds. Their tagline is "Life, we don't want you to miss it."

Check out one of my 2015 podcasts on Voice America on Collaboration in Heart and Stroke. Just recently, I participated in the Heart and Stroke Foundation Ski for Heart at Lake Louise, Alberta in Banff National Park to raise awareness, raise money, and encourage healthy living. I had the great experience of snowshoeing for three hours in the Rockies with Alan Keller. Alan just returned from climbing the highest mountain in Antarctica. This summit was the last of the seven summits that Alan peaked. Climbing the highest peaks on each of the seven continents is a big deal. Very few of us successfully climb Everest. Far fewer, again, climb all seven summits. Alan told me that he needed to put together or join a team for every summit, and that every climb demanded the complete commitment of every team member, not just the ones that make it to the top, but everyone that got you to the top. There are some amazing athletes that get so close to the peak of Everest, but out of their wisdom, their commitment to team, they don't make the final few hundred meters. It's a team success. You don't do it alone, and more important than reaching the summit, is to get back down safely.

There's a culture. In climbing culture, sometimes, and it's getting far better now, but sometimes that climbing culture required us to summit, and then we'd get ourselves into trouble because we had nothing left to get us back down safely. I want to provide a call to your future. Just close your eyes for a moment. Imagine yourself as a champion in 2020. You and your organization are celebrating a huge Break Through. You've broken through the yes. Together, you have accomplished no one had dreamed of possible. You are elated. Hold that feeling.

Now here's a call to action. Here's three steps;

1) What is the possible you dream of unlocking? Write this down. What is the possible you dream of unlocking?
2) Who are three people that have the expertise to help you? What's the possible you dream of unlocking, who are three people that have the expertise to help you achieve that dream, and
3) what will you do right now to start? What will you do right now to start?

There's lots of resources, videos, podcasts, articles, blogs at davidbsavage.com, and including I encourage you to work through, check out, download, and work through my 10 Essential Steps to collaboration. What we'll do now, that's the setup and now the next two segments, we're going to have these delightful opportunities to talk to Tristen and Martin. We'll just take a break now.

David: I am so pleased to introduce my good friend and somebody I deeply admire, Tristen Chernove. Tristen is Airport Manager at Canadian Rockies International Airport and he's done that since December 2009. He's also President and CEO of Elevate Airports Inc. He has this international airport leadership and leadership internationally in sports and much more. In the past, he has worked to strengthen the business at MBJ Jamaica Airport, aerodrome airports in the Dominican Republic, Nassau Airport in the Bahamas, Liverpool, and Doncaster Sheffield Airports in the United Kingdom, and operational readiness and airport transfer at Paphos and Larnaca International Airport in Cyprus. That's enough for a lot of people's career, but from 2006 to 2009, Tristen also represented Canada in paddle sport at the international level, and there's three national paddle sport gold medals between 2007 and 2009 world championships in Sydney, Australia and Prague, the Czech Republic. Tristen has earned two world gold medals: one silver and one bronze medal.

In 2009, things shifted a bit for Tristen, and notice the resilience as we talk to Tristen. But in 2009, Tristen was diagnosed with Charcot-Marie-Tooth disease, which is a degenerative disease of the peripheral nervous system. In his efforts to counteract the disease's impact, Tristen switched from competitive paddling to cycling, where he has become two-times track world champion and won a gold, silver, and bronze medal at 2016 Paralympics in Rio. Tristen is also crowned British Columbia's Business Person of the Year for 2016, and he plans to continue chasing the pinnacle of athletic success in his current sport and passion: cycling.

What I'll add to that is Tristen and I participate, support, and volunteer for the Kootenay Rockies Gran Fondo that my Sunrise Rotary Club hosts. It's a Gran Fondo in the Cranbrook-Kimberley area of British Columbia, and Tristen hosted a cycling race on an international airport. I think it was a couple of years ago now, Tristen. As we explore collaboration in sport today, welcome Tristen and hello.

Tristen: Thank you David. It's great to be here talking with you this late. In person, of course, it's always even better, but great to share some moments with you, and I appreciate that quite descriptive introduction very much. My mind was reeling in memory as you were going through those things. Yeah, it's a pleasure to be here with you and your audience today.

David: I'm, one, just delighted with Voice America. We were actually – last analytics I got from our executive producer, Camille Nash, it showed that we had listeners in 31 countries. With you and Martin today, maybe it'll be 41 countries.

Tristen: That'd be great.

David: One of the things I love you so much for is your holistic approach to leadership, to business, and to sport, and your resilience. You've had some pretty big curves thrown your way, and you just seem to check it out, make some choice, commit, collaborate, and win.

Tristen: Nicely put. Maybe we have time today to talk a little bit more about what that's been like for me.

David: I've got some questions for you, and I want to start out with probably the framework. What role does cycling play in your life today?

Tristen: From the outside looking in, it probably looks like cycling is my entire life because I am all-in at the moment. But, I would narrow that down to say cycling really provides a huge amount of happiness, stress relief. A lot of this comes from the fact that it fulfills my own pursuit of excellence. It's where I'm driving to chase excellence right now, and it's really where I'm able to focus most acutely on creating then best version of myself, which then I hope to then roll over to all the other aspects of my life.

David: Go ahead, Tristen.

Tristen: I certainly have found that I personally always need challenge in my life. In fact, even when I was diagnosed with my disease and started losing the body that I was familiar with, it didn't take long before I looked at that as a gift, thinking, "Wow, the harder the things are for me as far as overcoming challenges, the more elated I am with the result of overcoming." So, now I'm even deeper in challenge, so I'll get even deeper reward, and that has been the truth. I often think one of my favorite quotes is this, people who follow cycling would know the name of Greg LeMond, but something right now, cycling is this constant challenge for me and something that he said that always rings in my ear is the challenge, of course, never fades. It doesn't ever get any easier; you just go faster. I think it's a wonderful quote.

Cycling provides this environment for acute and heightened aspects of myself to be revealed and worked on. Everything comes in the surface of maybe in a more dramatic way in many sport or environments where you're pushed to your limits. For me, it provides an opportunity to learn more about myself.

David: I just want to repeat that again, a bit of what you just "insighted" us with. That is, the greater the challenge, the greater the commitment, and the greater the success. I'm thinking many of us, as we get older and our health is challenge, tend to give up stuff. With you, Tristen, it's the motivator to say, "Okay, got to get going. I got to make some changes," and experience the new you.

Tristen: Yeah, absolutely, and I know I really focus on the fact that the harder it is to do, the greater the reward by the end of the day by doing it. We should really be happy to have these challenges. I think, as I was thinking about the fans, a couple of other things popped into my mind about what it is for me and what those challenges really are about today, because the challenges, of course, change as we meet our goals to that process. I think what you've touched on is a bit of mental toughness aspect, something that's ringing through my head these days. I was just at a training camp recently in California, and Roger Freestone who was working with us in the evenings. He is an amazing mental coach, particularly as he is world-renowned in the aspect of mental training for performance.

I like his description of mental toughness which is the ability to override human nature. When I lose or break something, and then we start to always -- when things are challenging we always go to the negative first. I don't know what part of our survival instincts and background that it was adopted it from, but we seem to always hear the self-doubt and the unhelpful self-talk. What he challenged us with that I'm really trying to do all the time when I'm training or competing is just paying attention closely to the inner dialogue, and as soon as I hear myself saying something, I just must ask -- it's only one question you must remember to ask: "Is this is helpful?" and if you're constantly weighing every internal thought against that measure, "Is this helpful?" What I find is, a lot of times, no it's not, and then, of course, the hard part is how do you change that recording and change it to something that is helpful? I'm still sort of caught in that area. At least, I'm noticing all the time when it's not helpful, I'm trying to replace it with a good recording of something that is.

David: Yeah, it's like mindfulness in Olympic cycling, in a way, to take that pause and notice what's going on, and then make a conscious choice.

Tristen: Yeah, exactly.

David: What's been the biggest challenge in your cycling career, Tristen?

Tristen: This is twofold really. I think the biggest challenge is being someone into cycling later in life. I'm going to be 42 this year. My life is very full of family and work as well as cycling. The biggest challenge is balancing those things and insuring that I'm not neglecting any one area. That's really the biggest overall challenge, and managing the time, which really means ensuring that the time that's spent is the top-quality time in all those areas. Again, it's not so much as a negative challenge. It's a good challenge. You got folks forcing me to make sure that when I am with my family because I do have to be away quite a bit. That's high-quality time, and when I'm working, it's very productive, and when I'm training because my training hours are very limited compared to many of my competitors, it's super high-quality training. That's one area.

I guess, physically, my biggest challenge would have to be this past September at the Rio Paralympics in the road race when I was caught up in a crash very early in the race, only about 7 kilometers in, and ended up with a badly injured shoulder and lots of typical bruises and road rash and stuff. Unfortunately, my front derailleur was broken on the bike. There were many elements at play early in the race, and by the time I was back on the bike the field was out of sight, about a few minutes ahead.

So, physically, this was my biggest challenge because I had to control that self-dialogue and stay positive so that I could have the physiology working right for me to have my best performance and try to work my way back into the field. I played out that that was the one race I couldn't get on the podium, but I am very happy. One reflection of that, a lot of things, post-crash went as long as well as they could, and I moved from last competitor. So 67th up to 15th by the time the race was over, and I learned a ton about my ability to override human nature during that event, for sure.

David: You and I talked about this previously. That's a huge switch, and talking about making the pause and, "Is this helpful." The reptilian brain of me and many would probably say, "Screw it. I'm done. I'm at the end. Everybody is gone. My shoulder is injured. My bike's not ride-able," and yet you got back on and you came in 15th. I can only imagine the faces on all those 55 people, plus or minus, that you passed on your way back into the leadership. That's such an amazing story of the mental focus and commitment that you're not giving up

Tristen: Exactly. In a dream world, would I have to play it out differently and not have the crash, absolutely. But, being given that that was the hand-out on that day, I can walk away feeling like I did the very best that I was capable of with that hand. And like you said, there were five of us on the ground after the crash that couldn't get back in right away. I was the only one that did re-enter the race. There was something different going on with the dialogue with others, I'm sure. That challenge, I'll keep with me, because that's a great gift going forward. I know that even when it seems super-unlikely to get back into the place you want to be, whether it's in a race or anything else, just stick to the process and push through.

David: The theme of today's show is collaboration in sport. Did you do all this by yourself?

Tristen: Absolutely not.

David: Kind of a leading question.

Tristen: Yeah. I mean, I'm surrounded. That's a huge part of everything. All my choices are who I'm surrounding myself with. In fact, David, that reminds me of I was just recently interviewed – not relating to sport at all, but just on the business side of things, and someone asked me about lessons for other entrepreneurs, and I said, "It would be the same for cycling. Surround yourself with the best people who are giving you the most of what you're looking for, and you've got success whether your endeavor turns out the way you want it to, or you go bankrupt. It doesn't matter because you've got the relationships around you and built relationships that are giving you what really matters in life," and it's been the same with cycling.

I think my success has to do with the fact that, right from when I started cycling here in our community with incredibly supportive and positive people to be with, that translates over to incredible and experienced coaching staff, and at anyone of these events, I might have six experts with me looking after everything from helping me through, like I said, mental coaches, nutritionists, physiotherapists, tactical coaching. I'm kind of like the clay that these people are all working on together to try to get the product of the best they can, and I'm onboard as well, but there's a lot of hands working to do that.

David: Thank you, Tristen. Just in our last minute, what's a key message that you'd like to leave our listeners with or challenge our listeners to do?

Tristen: I think, especially for anyone out there that used to setting a lot of goals, what I've learned is that the process is the most important thing. I would challenge people to not set goals that are way out there shiny, big result goals, but to set goals that are very process-focused, that are trackable in small increments, and every time you review how things are going, always start by asking what went well or what is going well before you start to take a part of what needs to be improved. That ties back to the mental toughness piece about don't go to the negative. Ask yourself, "Is this is helpful?" and if it's not, replace it with something positive.

David: Every pedal stroke is a pedal stroke towards that gold medal. Thank you so much, Tristen, I really appreciate it. How can people follow-up and connect with you? Would you prefer to give them an email address or a website that people can follow-up in your amazing story?

Tristen: I've been meaning to put together better forms for being in touch with people. It's not come down to my priority list enough to get its attention yet. So, for now, I think the best way is probably email, which is elevateairports@gmail.com, and I'll share with you, David, if I do end up setting up another easier way for people to track where my competitions are taking me, or what's next, and how to get in touch. I'll do that, but for now, email would be best.

David: Thanks, Tristen Chernove. You're an inspiration, you're a leader, and you continue to inspire me. Thank you.

Tristen: Thank you for the time, David, and thank you for listening, everyone.

David: Our next guest is another great friend, inspiring athlete, sportsman, and leader, Martin Parnell. Martin is the author of Marathon Quest and Running to the Edge, and speaks on having a finish-the-race attitude, overcoming obstacles to achieve your full potential – finish the race. Martin is written for or been covered by CNN, BBC, CBC, The Huffington Post, The Globe and Mail, The National Post, Runner's World, Men's Journal, Canadian Business, and Maclean's Magazine.

He's well-known, respected, he speaks well, and he's accomplished so much. And he's accomplished so much not so much for himself, but for sport, and sportsmen, and children around the globe not just Western Canada, but around the world. In a five-year period from 2010 to 2014, Martin completed 10 extreme endurance quests including – now get this – he ran 250 marathons in one year. That's 250 marathons. Not 5K races, but full marathons in one year, and he raised 1.3 million for the humanitarian organization, Right to Play. You can find out way more about Martin and get him to speak to you, connect with you at MartinParnell.com and see what he can do for you in the long run.

Today we're exploring collaboration in sport. Welcome, Martin.

Martin: Yeah. Thank you, David. It's great to be here.

David: You're a runner and much more. What does running mean to you?

Martin: Well, I came to running pretty late. In 2002, my brother challenged me to a marathon. I was 47 years old and I basically hadn't run before. My relationship with sport's been a little bit love-hate. As a kid I was known as a huggable child. I think the politically correct term is "fat", and so I really wasn't picked for any teams, never really played any team sports at a higher level, but I love sport. Mom and dad played tennis and badminton, and they would always take us out on the weekend doing stuff. Really, never at any level.

As I said, it wasn't until at the age of 47, I started running, and to be honest, running for me, initially, was a way of coping with a very traumatic situation a year earlier in late 2001. My wife, Wendy, died of liver cancer. For me, running was a way of exercise and just sort of trying to cope with a very tough situation.

David: Very tough. What's the biggest challenge you've ever faced?

Martin: It sort of ties in again with a physical situation. In February 2015, I was diagnosed with a clot on the brain. I had traveled to Winnipeg. I was giving a keynote at a conference, and the night before, I was sick. I had terrible headaches, and the organizer took me to a hospital in Winnipeg. They did a CT scan and found a massive clot right across the top of my brain and they put me into induced coma for 24 hours. I've been recovering since then for the last almost two years. Thankfully, I'm through it and I'm back running.

David: Huge challenges there with the death of Wendy and the blood clot. Earlier on this show, I talked about my involvement with the Heart and Stroke, and I'll just take a little bit of a health moment for our listeners is Heart and Stroke has an acronym FAST, and oftentimes people suffering from stroke or heart, and I know it wasn't a stroke, but I just want to grab this opportunity, Martin. People suffering, often, from most diseases or emergencies don't know, or they resist the thought that they might be in real trouble.

FAST is talking about stroke is Face is your face drooping, most often on the left side. Do you have trouble moving your arms over your head? Do you have trouble speaking? FAS, and then the T is time. Getting attention is critical. If you want to run your marathon, you got to respond – read and react immediately, as they would say in football. Read and react, and deal with it. Don't resist, don't sit back. Our friend, Martin, has had some real challenges. Earlier on our podcast, we talked to Tristen about his challenges and turning those into Olympic victories. Martin, let's get back to your key message. Tell us more about your finish-the-race' attitude and what you bring.

Martin: To me, over the last 12, 13 years, ever since I started running, I've been on a bit of a journey. My background is a mining engineer. I work all over Canada for 25 years in BC up in the territories and in Ontario and Sudbury. As I said, my life changed when Wendy died, and I got into running, and I found that running was an outlet, and for me, initially, it was about time. I found I liked it. I finally found something I could do, and I ended up qualifying for Boston, and I've run three Boston marathons. I found it was a way of pushing myself physically, which I never really done before. I ended up getting into triathlon doing three Ironman Triathlons, and then into ultra-running, and this was running races of 100K and up to 100 miles.

So here I am in my late 40's, early 50's really pushing my body and as the finish-the-race' attitude, you're looking at ways of doing things I'd never done before, and that led me to a bike trip across Africa. I spend four months cycling from Cairo to Cape Town. But, the revelation there was, along the way, I did sports with children. I played table tennis, and soccer, and running with the kids, and I saw the power of sport, and that really led me to Right To Play. The children's charity, they helped over a million children around the world through play-based programs and teaching them life skills.

Definitely a journey, David, with the sport, and using sport from my perspective for greater good. For some reason, I'm very good at doing long boring things. I don't know; I can just keep going and going. I've used that for fundraising to help the kids, and also, quite frankly, when I was diagnosed with this clot on the brain, I was released from hospital after two weeks, and as I was leaving, the specialist said, "Martin, you could have died twice." That sort of got my attention. They said the first time was from the clot. If they hadn't have caught it, within five more days, I would have been dead. And that ties into your FAST acronym. The clot was actually a rare form of stroke. They caught it in time. That was a huge, huge thing.

But, he said the second way I could have died is from massive organ failure. But, he said because I was relatively fit from the running, my heart and my kidneys were strong enough that it got me through a very difficult time, and it made me realize that running in fitness is the best life insurance you can have. We talk about a finish-the-race attitude, well obviously, the big race is life. So, whether we're taking on projects, or it's business, or personal, to get it done, to get it finished is really what we're looking to do.

David: Yeah, it's like an old rock song about it's better to burnout than rust, something like that. Those of us in the second 50 years of our life, Martin's message is just critical. We can live far longer if we're fit and healthy and living on purpose, and not living in front of TV.

Martin: Exactly, David, exactly.

David: I want to bring in something that another amazing thing that you did just a few months ago, could you tell our listeners about your trip? And there will be a book and a documentary, I hope, coming from your trip to -- go ahead.

Martin: Yeah, absolutely, David. It's funny how things are linked. Back in October of 2015, I was in recovery from the clot on the brain. I was at home, but I was feeling pretty sorry for myself. I couldn't run much. In fact, I just started walking again. I'd been told to take it easy, not to push it. So, in fact, in October of last year, I kind of just started to do a K here, and I was at the computer, and my wife, Wendy, sent me a link to the Guardian newspaper, and there was a story about the first ever marathon of Afghanistan.

The essence of the story was a group of international runners had gone over to a town called Bamiyan just 180K northwest of Kabul, and they had run with a total of 70 runners. The rest of were Afghan men except for one Afghan woman. Her name was Zainab, and she became the first ever Afghan woman to run a marathon.

But, what struck me about the story was, for runners, the challenge is our hydration, nutrition, pacing, and so on. For her, the challenges were verbal and physical abuse while she's training. People were calling her prostitute, they'd throw stones at her to stop her training. In fact, in the end, she went back into her garden and ran around this walled garden for training.

I'll be honest, I read that story and I said, "Martin, stop feeling sorry for yourself, get your butt in gear," and I signed up for the 2016 Marathon Afghanistan, which was held on November the 4th last year, and I went over to Afghanistan for an amazing trip.

David: And how many women raced?

Martin: In the second one, there were five international runners, but this time, there were five Afghan women. So, the first race in 2015, there was one. But, this year, there was five. But, what really blew me away was there was also a 10K race with the marathon, and there were 150 runners, but over 100 of those runners were girls, girls who ran the 10K, and this is huge in that country. And there's a group called Free To Run. They're a charity, and they encourage, enable girls and women to run and to do these long races in countries like Afghanistan, and Pakistan, and Iran.

My knowledge of Afghanistan was strictly from the news, all the terror bombings, and all the bad news. But, then it's like a lot of things. When you really dig into it, there's a flicker of light over there, and it was, as I say, the trip and running with these women and supporting them was an absolute highlight.

David: Fantastic. Inspiring, and I guess before we go, Martin Parnell, what's one thing that you would challenge our listeners to do, be, change, or be aware of?

Martin: It sort of has come down to this for me. In life, you don't have to do a lot, but you've got to do something. Look at a way to give back, and it just obviously doesn't have to be about sport. From my perspective, obviously, it can be. Maybe run a 5K, do your first 5K, or if it's music or art, but look at a way of doing something positive, of giving back. Let's build a bridge and not walls here.

At the end of last year, I had my 8th annual Run/Walk in Cochrane, and it was in support of a girl's school in Afghanistan to rebuild a volleyball court, and we had 120 runners come out, and some had never run/walked, never been part of something like this, and in total, we raised over $7,000. So, that's all I'm asking. Do something. Make 2017 the year that you make a difference.

David: Thank you so much, Martin Parnell. Finish-the-race attitude, overcoming obstacles to achieve your full potential. Martin, thank you.

Martin: Thank you, David. It was a pleasure.

David: Now, listeners, I want to close this show with something that's just been consistent through the conversations of Martin and Tristen. Martin talks about overcoming obstacles to achieve your full potential. Tristen talked about, basically, overcoming obstacles to achieve your best potential. Tristen also talked about each step in the process. It's a process. It's not, "I want to be a gold medalist." It is, "I got to cycle today. Even though it's cold outside, I'm going to get on my bike." Martin's talked about just do something, take a step, take another step, push that pedal, be out there, save your lives. It saves our lives. For everybody running a marathon, there's many more timers, nutritionists, physiotherapists.

Sport and collaboration has been our theme today. We've had Martin Parnell, and Tristen Chernove, incredible athletes, incredible men, incredible leaders. We've talked about sports, working together, 7 Summits, Heart and Stroke, cycling, marathons, leadership, and collaboration. In collaboration, we're looking to break out of normal and Break Through to fresh and exciting insights and possibilities.

Think about those three questions I gave you earlier; work on them.

1) what's the possible you dream of unlocking?

2) who are the three people that have the expertise to help you out;

3) what will you do right now to start your first step before you run that marathon?

Now, let's work together better. Talk to you next time.

Chapter 3 Collaboration and Organizational Culture featuring Mike Thompson and Stephen Hobbs

David: Welcome friends around the world. Today's theme is collaboration and assessment. Today's guests are Mike Thompson who is CEO of SVI, a talent development company on a mission to create irresistible companies and extraordinary people. I think with Mike he'll show us that those are joined at the hip; they are necessary components. We also, later in the show we will have Dr. Stephen Hobbs who guides entrepreneurs and executives to design and realize extraordinary life and business legacy experiences for the self and with others. So, listeners, what's the feeling within your organization? How do you feel in your organization? I want to get you inside that feeling right away.

Do you feel anticipation, excitement, frustration, anger, delight, abandonment? Are you tired of things happening over and over and over and over and over? Today, together we're going to explore organizational cultures and what makes them great, or not. We talk about the tools that Stephen and I offer to help your organization progress faster. My book isn't called how to pretend to collaborate and call a meeting nor is my book called how to encourage groupthink. It's called *Break Through to Yes: Unlocking the Possible within a Culture of Collaboration.* Yes, a culture of collaboration, collaboration is how we work together, and you are listening because you are looking for ways to work together better. Let's jump right in with the amazing Mike Thompson. He's a collaborator extraordinaire. I've got his most recent book *Forging Grit* right in front of me. It's a beautiful story.

He engages us into leadership and working together better and 360 assessments and team development through wonderful stories. Mike is the CEO of SVI and Mike an SVI partner with complex global organizations. That's right complex global organizations to train, engage, assess and develop their entire workforce is one of the most forward thinkers in leadership. Mike coaches' executives and next generation CEOs at many of the world's largest companies. This is true. We are fortunate to have Mike on the show, the radio show today. Mike's toured the world. He doesn't stick inside of board rooms and conference halls. He's studied leadership in some of the most primitive environments to gain deeper level leadership insights in all types of communities and cultures around the globe.

He's the author of three top selling business and leadership books: *The Organizational Champion: How to Develop Passionate Change Agents at Every Level, The Anywhere Leader: How to Lead and Succeed in Any Business Environment.* And, most recently in 2016, *Forging Grit: A Story of Leadership Perseverance.* Mike holds a master's degree in leadership and ethics from John Brown University and serves as the president of the Dallas Chapter of the Association of Talent Development. Mike is also received numerous recognitions including business of the year finalist and the 40 under 40 award in his home state of Arkansas. Welcome, Mike.

Mike: Hi, David. Thank you very much, it's a pleasure to be here.

David: Where are you today, Mike?

Mike: Well, my home state is Arkansas, but I live – I reside in Dallas, Texas and that's where I am today.

David: Well, welcome Texas. When Camille Nash our executive producer talked to me back in December of 2016 Camille said, "You know your top three listenership audiences are England, Texas and California." So, you must be Texas.

Mike: Yeah, yeah. I've got to say, Texas weather in January is outstanding, mid-70's, beautiful, sunny day.

David: Fantastic and you're not on the road today.

Mike: No, not today. Tomorrow, but today is good.

David: Let's talk. I'd like to start off with some of the questions that are on my mind. Mike, you hear collaboration thrown out often but what can leaders do to maximize the collaboration process?

Mike: It's an interesting question, David, because I believe this term collaboration gets kind of thrown out and people might often think that collaboration is just having a conversation. While I know that's part of it, I think the term collaboration draws much deeper meaning to the table and one of the things that I find really, interesting as we think about collaboration is people oftentimes show up to a meeting or a collaboration session and they really haven't confirmed their own position. They come ready to listen, which is nice. Listening is a powerful thing for leaders. But, I don't think we can come to the collaboration session only ready to listen.

We've got to come ready to contribute as well and so, oftentimes I'll challenge our team and others to say, 'before you show up at this session, you need to spend time in personal reflection.' I like your term group think. If you don't bring your own insights and your own opinions, then you run the risk of falling into group think which might be counter to a valuable solution or counter to your values and beliefs. The biggest thing for me, one of the biggest things for me for collaboration, is showing up ready to contribute and ready to listen. It needs to be a two-way process there. That means that you need to put some investment of personal reflection time prior to a collaborative session.

David: Thank you for that. How many meetings do we go through and it's just like Groundhog Day. It's the Sermon from the Mount, somebody at the end of the rectangular table doing all the talking, a few people responding, most people just listening and not engaged.

Mike: A lot and I think it's happening more and more. You don't see organizations – oftentimes you don't see organizations know how to just dialogue and have that productive meeting. You might see someone owning the conversation and then they realize that they're owning the conversation and they want to kind of retreat a little bit, so they'll throw a question out there to the group with no response. And that, obviously, doesn't create for a productive meeting. So, the contribution side is important.

David: Well, let's just close this meeting since nobody is really prepared. I'm just going to do it myself. How does that work?

Mike: Right.

David: One of the things that I've written in my book and I see it in yours as well, Mike, is the willingness to be courageous, to be the outsider, to challenge what is expected. To say, "I've got a different perspective here. Will you listen to me?"

Mike: Right. Those are my favorite leaders. When I am in a discussion with others around the table and there's pushback, I really, really value that because my idea alone is not nearly as valuable as my idea plus your idea. When that dynamic happens, suddenly, my idea plus your idea kind of brought together creates that wow idea better than it could ever have been if it was just one of us.

David: Thanks for that, Mike. One of the things that we as leaders have difficulty with is getting a sense of how collaborative are we as a leader and how collaborative is our team? We get hints of it but with SVI and you've got a great team that I've experienced in the last eight months, you're really on the money and you've got experience and expertise with some of the largest and most complex corporations. In thinking about the term what gets measured gets done and the thing with your SVI 360 assessments, it gets measured and it's a foundation for evolution. Can you tell us a little bit more about the SVI approach to 360's?

Mike: Certainly. It's a great way to capture data. Not just make it all about emotion or all about opinion or about perception. But, it's a way to collect data from up, down and across within the organization. Sometimes we might be good at leading up and that means being effective with our bosses. Sometimes we might be most effective leading down through the organization, leading our direct reports. And sometimes, we're better leading across the organization where we work effectively with our peers. What the 360 tool does is it captures data from all those groups, from our boss or our supervisor, from our direct reports, from our peers and it delivers that data and says, "You know what? Here's the areas you're extremely competent in."

Maybe extremely competent rated by your direct reports, but your boss or your supervisor might not rate you so high in that competency and, so it gives you the insight so that you can say, "You know what? I'm doing fine with this competency leading down in my organization, but as far as leading up in the organization, not doing so good." It helps people really focus in that critical area and be intentional with closing that gap. But, the 360 is such a valuable tool because it gets that exactly what it says, that 360-degree insight. What I'm most excited about really, David, is just the partnership that we have. We have never identified or even seen a 360-degree assessment that measures a competency model behind collaboration until we ran across you.

So, the opportunity to talk to the expert, you, and have you put your collaboration competencies in the 360-degree tool, now allows anyone at any time to capture those insights and that data around how they're doing from a collaboration competency up through the organization, down through the organization, across through the organization. When all an organizations' leaders commit to capturing those insights and the data, that's really where you can move the needle on this culture of collaboration. So, I think the 360-degree tool is a really, really powerful way to create that culture of collaboration.

David: Thank you for that, Mike, and for our listeners you can go to my website davidbsavage.com and check it out and contact either SVI or I. I'm proud of the world's first collaborative leadership 360-degree assessment that we've co-developed. I know that many of our audience have experienced 360s. Some of them, what I find, is very common leaders will say 'I guess I don't delegate enough. I better delegate.' And then it's kind of flat. It's like budgets and strategic plans in some organizations. You do it and you think about it for a month or two and then you let it go.

What SVI and myself are doing are really creating a platform for continual improvement for constant change, for a strategic advantage of how do we excel as an organization through assessments and then with those assessments, in particular, custom design, well divine too, I guess. Custom design what needs to happen over the next months and years. To build this culture it doesn't happen in a meeting. It happens over time in every interaction. It could be something that organizations look at and I would argue should look at constantly and, as a minimum, every six months, every year. How are we doing? How are we progressing? Where's the gaps now?

Mike: Right.

David: I think the other thing I'll jump in here again, Mike, is one of the things we developed together, we collaborated on, was we talk about the foundations of leadership which is values. What are your values and how do you approach that? How do you bring your values to work? How do you make sure that people are safe, trusted, respected, included, listened to and innovate? Mike, what do you think collaboration, as a competency, is becoming? Why do you think collaboration is becoming more and more necessary in today's business environment?

Mike: Gosh, I see its necessity so much in organizations today, more today than ever. The reason being is just because I believe there's so much uncertainty that exists in the global business environment today. Competition is so much fiercer. The speed of business moves so much faster than it used to. Innovation, disruption, these kinds of things bring about uncertainty. Decades ago it was maybe a little bit easier because we could craft an answer book. That answer book would say: gosh here's our business, here's how we do our business, our business doesn't change that often. If you just do these things, our business will be delivered well.

But, in today's business environment, my gosh you wake up in the morning and you read the top news of the day and you realize that everything you had planned had just been blown up. By the way, there's no where you can go to answer it or identify a solution for it because the answer book just doesn't exist. The magnitude of the change, the disruption is so extreme that nobody predicted that this was going to happen and, yet you've got to make a move. You've got to do something quickly. Your business – and that's where this idea of agility comes in with our businesses today. Our businesses must be very, very agile. They've got to move, they've got to shift and it's because we don't know what we're going to face. That's the uncertainty that we deal with every day.

So, collaboration is key because if I'm going to be able to react, if I'm going to be able to build that nimbleness within my organization, that agility within my organization, I better make sure that we are extremely connected as an organization, that we're not all working in silos within the organization because if we're all working in silos then our solution stops with the only thing we have in our mind. But, if we can reach across the aisle, if we have that collaborative culture, then we can quickly connect with others, combine our insights and ideas and formulate a much quicker and much more effective game plan to face the uncertainty that was just presented to us. That connection, that connected culture is extremely important to battle against the uncertainty of our businesses today.

David: Yeah, I love, I was thinking about the word agility and agile and read and react. I'm also looking at your book *Forging Grit* which is a story around leadership and your experience in the Himalayas and Nepal. I'm thinking it was only a couple of years ago, maybe not even that, where there was many of people in both our communities in the United States and Canada who were trekking in that area at the time of a massive earthquake. So, just using that as a metaphor, if we're walking along the base camp trail and we've got our answer book and suddenly there's an avalanche or rock slide or earthquake, do we just sit down and until somebody helicopters in a new answer book? No, we've got to figure it out and help people and save lives and create some safety. I really like that agility and I think earth quakes are not too harsh a metaphor for what's happening in business and organizations in the world today.

Mike: Not at all.

David: As we close here, Mike, what's one thing you would challenge our listeners to be, do or change?

Mike: Gosh, that's – something I've been thinking, I have two things. Can I give you two, David, is that okay?

David: You bet, that's a bonus.

Mike: One is just I think today's business environment and leadership today just takes more courage. It takes more courage because our cultures demand and collaboration demands that we share more not less. We share early and often. We're transparent, we're more vulnerable as leaders. We've let more people in, we don't lead from a guarded perspective. I think that requires a lot more courage today and I would just ask the listeners to really focus on that. What are some things I can do to be more courageous as a leader, to be more vulnerable, transparent, less guarded? If you can do that, that's going to help create a more collaborative culture.

The other thing I would say is it's one of the hardest things to do, but be fully present with the technology today, the social media, it is really, really difficult to go into a collaborative meeting and not be distracted from one of 100 things. But, I've got to tell you the people that have influenced my life the most, the people that have made the biggest impression on me, are those that in any conversation I have with them, they give me their full and deep attention. They are fully present with every interaction and it makes those interactions so much more productive, the trust so much higher and the outcome so much more valuable. I would probably say those two things.

David: Thank you for being so fully present today with our listeners and with me, Mike. Mike Thompson, thank you very much for joining our show today.

Mike: Yes, thank you, David.

David: Welcome back everyone. Our theme today is collaboration and assessment. We're focusing on organizational culture and remember my book is not called *How to Pretend to Collaborate* or *How to Call a Meeting*. Nor is my book *How to Encourage Group Think*. It's called *Break Through to Yes: Unlocking the Possible within a culture of Collaboration*. Collaboration is how we work together and it's a system, it's not an event. I am so delighted to introduce to you, my friends, Dr. Stephen Hobbs who is also my friend. Stephen is, what he describes as a gray, digital nomad. He's worked on six of the seven continents. By day, Stephen guides entrepreneurs and executives to design and realize extraordinary life, business legacy experiences for self and with others. By night, he co-writes about Hour Rest, a magical forest of awareness where trees are educators. Yeah, trees are educators to children.

We're going to go into that shortly with Stephen. Stephen created the Write to Shade program he funds through philanthropic efforts of his business, WELLth Movement. Stephen's background includes self-publishing 12 books. Yeah, 12. He's a business mentor, life coach and a university professor. We've got some great quotes from Dr. Stephen Hobbs. They include, "Legacy is the organization of extraordinary life experiences." "Leadership legacy is the organization of extraordinary workplace experiences." And, "Collaboration is the organization of workplace culture." And, I think, listeners, I think you can tell exactly why I've asked my friend and mentor and coach, Dr. Stephen Hobbs to join us today. Welcome, Stephen.

Stephen: Thank you, David, it's great to be here with you.

David: It is wonderful to have you on our show. Let's go back a little bit about the magical forest of awareness. Tell our listeners more about that. I've learned a little bit about this, everyone, in the last couple months and it's a brilliant metaphor and I'll let Stephen explain it to you.

Stephen: Well, to share the story of awareness I'd have to go back quite a few years when I was working in Eastern Africa, country Uganda and I noticed there's a lot of schools that don't have trees in the schoolyards. We were working on a program to help them plant trees into the school yards and on the hills. One of the things I started to recognize is wouldn't it be great if the kids had these trees but to have them from a shade perspective, so they could do their reading, writing and arithmetic and so

I've thought about how could I start to support this wonderful opportunity to plant trees. So, it's grown and grown and grown. I created the Write to Shade program to fund that and, obviously, you need some products and services, so I created Awarest, which was this magical forest where the trees are the educators of children and I have created a council of nine trees and we are going through writing books that introduce the trees to the children and to grow it and grow it and grow it from there. No pun intended but it is to grow and to grow and to grow.

David: Yeah, and legacy is an important word in your work.

Stephen: Yes, if I could just share just a little bit about that. Legacy is really about what you gift to others. I'm being very purposeful in the use of the word gift because there are things that you can give to people but there are things that you can gift to people. Awarest and Write to Shade is my gift to the world.

David: So you also have, amongst your gifts to the world, 12 books. Maybe pick one that just comes to mind that you might find helpful for our listeners. What's the name, what's it about and where do people buy it?

Stephen: I'll do it in reverse action. It's on Amazon both in the kindle and the soft cover. The book is called *Help Them Help YOU Manage-Lead*. It's about nine educating approaches that people who manage and lead can use to help their employees and even help their customers to help them to manage and lead because when you know more from your customers and their employees in their words, you can do much better in how you approach your managing and leading. This book was born out of 22 summers of being a white-water rafting guide sitting in the back of the boat thinking, "How do I help my crew have a great experience." Because, I meet them, I don't know them, until they get off the raft a couple hours later, how much we can be friends using these educating approaches. So, I just took that experience, that extraordinary experience and placed it in the workplace and that's what the book is called *Help Them Help YOU Manage-Lead.*

David: It's a wonderful book, listeners. I've got it, I've read it. It is a gift. One of the things even in the title our listeners are probably curious about is okay tell us why you talk about manage and lead as different things. What does that mean?

Stephen: They're not so much different as they are complementary. To have managing you have leading and to have leading you have managing. I know when I see people advertise courses that say, "Come get your leadership and your leading down." Well, if you're going to do that you must understand management and managing. Whenever I present them, I put them together, so manage/lead is always a combination or managers/leaders. I always use them in combination because of their complementarity.

David: Here's a question that I think is a powerful question. Stephen, are extraordinary experiences collaborative?

Stephen: I believe they are if we go back to the notion of what collaboration is about which is that you can be assertive in what you want to present but you're cooperating while you're doing it. That's a sense of collaboration and that comes from years ago, Thomas Kilmann book and they have an assessment that they use. I've always had that stuck with me over the years and if you're going to create extraordinary experiences, which is what I hope your listeners would be doing if they're in the workplace or even in community, is that extraordinary experiences are experiences that have certain characteristics like they're dramatic, they're novel, metaphoric and transferrable, just to name a few because they help people go through transformation.

So, if collaboration is truly working inside an organization within community, then you are creating extraordinary experiences because people are going to go through a transformation with you and that's the connection that I draw.

David: Let's take your wisdom, the next step for our listeners. We've talked about extraordinary experiences. What's the connection between extraordinary experiences and workplace culture?

Stephen: Ah, yes. Well, if my definition of workplace culture is about human interactions and the artifacts that result from those interactions. They're together whether it's community, whether it's workplaces, whether it's charitable organization, when we gather together to work together and use collaboration then there are these interactions that take place and the artifacts that come from them are things like products and services and experiences. What I've sort of noticed over time is that this whole sense of extraordinary experiences is something that you can create in the workplace culture, but more so, if you're really working well in your workplace culture and you're creating it and supporting it, it can become an extraordinary experience. It can become metaphoric and transferrable and novel and dramatic in such a way that it offers people a place to transform their lives whether personally and professionally. So, there is this wonderful link between extraordinary experiences and workplace culture.

David: It is so attractive. It's thrilling when I hear you describe extraordinary experiences in the workplace. We have so much opportunity right there. Now, to take this a little further, is collaboration a fundamental element of workplace culture then, Stephen?

Stephen: Oh yes. I will dance with that one, David, that is true. Collaboration is so important to workplace culture because this collaboration that we're talking about allows the person to certainly share their voice and their position, it also gives them an opportunity to share what they're masterful at, what they can contribute and gives them a chance to share their authority where they're coming from. If everyone is collaborating in a way in which you can share what you're masterful about and your voice and position and your authority and we use the collaborative concepts that you've talked about through shows and other – and through your book David. I know we've had lots of conversations about it, that collaboration is one of the fundamentals to the organizational workplace culture and I would certainly encourage people to learn more about collaboration and how it applies to workplaces.

David: Now, I started the show at the top of the hour with respect to what's the energy or the feeling that our listeners have in their organizations, in their communities, in their families? Is it an extraordinary experience? This is energizing, this is attractive. How do we get more of that? It is very appealing.

Stephen: I agree wholeheartedly on that. The thing is with extraordinary experiences, the experiences determined by the participant. You can set it in motion, like from an educator point of view to a manager, leader, you can set it in motion. But, it's the employee, the customer who gets the opportunity to say where they're going with it being extraordinary or not.

David: Yeah, so there's – it's not extraordinary like more mundane, it's extraordinary.

Stephen: Yes and I like how you said it, "Extra-ordinary."

David: So, I'm thinking what, so our leaders and listeners around the globe can get a sense of an extraordinary experience, can you, would you provide us either an example or a feeling? What is extraordinary like?

Stephen: Well, let's just go back to experience. All learning in life is about experiences. But, the extraordinary is those characteristics I gave you. You might look at the vista, this wonderful mountain range and it be an experience. The extraordinary might be you might take a photograph and use it to write something about the mountains. I'll give you one that's personal to me very quickly. I had an experience in Uganda where a machine gun came through the window of the vehicle and for three minutes I was questioned about where I was going. There was a lot of things that happened during that time, but when I left that experience, it became extraordinary because it was a young soldier and she was about 14 or 15 years of age holding a machine gun pointed at me. I called her my three-minute mentor. To me, that's an extraordinary experience.

David: Extraordinary, I can feel that one, I can feel the adrenaline in my veins. So, before we finish, Stephen, what's one thing that you would challenge our listeners to do, be or change?

Stephen: Well, in the theme of where we're going I think it would be words matter and really listen to the words that someone is sharing with you because they're giving you clues as how you can help them to help you manage/lead. It gives you clues into how you can collaborate with them. It gives you clues about how you can create an extraordinary experience that might be of great value to them. Words matter.

David: Dr. Stephen Hobbs, the gray digital nomad and, as you can tell listeners, he has a wealth of experience that's W-E-L-L-th of experience in his WELLth movement. Stephen, thank you so much for sharing your wisdom with us today.

Stephen: Thank you, David, it was great and best wishes to you and certainly to your listeners.

David: Today, in our radio show we've had the wisdom of Dr. Stephen Hobbs and Mike Thompson. Two amazing men who bring nature, bring challenge, bring mountains into the conversation and extraordinary experiences. Let's move on. Let's go into the final section where we talk about something that Mike raised, the complexity. Today our world is filled with complex challenges. As leaders, when our response to complex challenges is duality, i.e. right versus wrong, right versus left, business versus environment, management versus people and staff, politicians versus media. We all encounter increasing resistance, frustration and failure.

So, how do we Break Through to our yes? Now, think about newly elected President Trump. The American President and his days and days of executive orders. President Trump believes that he is fighting terrorism yet his "Muslim ban" has outraged millions across the globe. Many are questioning whether America is safe for them. Many believe America is great and we need a far better understanding of others. Many believe that President Trump is exactly what is needed now.

Personally, I believe America is a great nation that is becoming increasingly divided and I'm sad to even say those words. My friends and family members that live and work in the United States are finding that they can no longer even talk with their friends and family about American politics. Anger, pride, ego, frustration and more. I am right; therefore, you must be wrong. Brothers and sisters can't talk, they see the world so differently. What if none of us are right or wrong? What is there was no winner or loser? What if there's no certainty? What if together we could find a better insight and strategy to move forward? What might we learn together? What would we learn by engaging a wide diversity of backgrounds, perspectives and expertise?

So, late January, former and last leader of the Soviet Union, Mikhail Gorbachev was quoted in the Washington Post. He listed some problems: the militarization of politics and the new arms races. It's militarization of politics and the new arms races, I thought we were done with that, but we seem to be sliding backwards. Mikhail talks about tanks and weapons in Europe being placed closer together as if to shoot point blank. Think about the Ukraine. Gorbachev is quoted as saying, "It all looks as if the world is preparing for war." Now, whether you love Ronald Reagan or Mikhail Gorbachev, they were the ones that came to the brink and stepped back for the benefit of the world.

You know, do like Mikhail and Ronald do, where cooperation and mutual disarmament may have averted World War III. Around the planet we seem to be growing angrier, angrier and more isolated as leaders, as people. Where is that getting us? Do we want to be pounding our chests, excluding, building walls? To avert World War III and our planet, in your organization and at home, seek diversity of perspectives. Listen deeply and find the collective wisdom that will solve our challenges rather than enlarge them. Listen and respect one another.

In my book, I offer the 10 Essential Steps to Collaboration. Of the ten, number four is Seek Diversity. Number three is Embrace Conflict. Number ten is Make It So.

In my Break Through To Yes, my friend David Milia from the University of Calgary Haskayne School of Business writes, "Can we collaborate when our selfish, polarized views conflict with those we should be collaborating with? In business, we have a name for a group of folks who all get along and have the same opinion on something. It's called group think and it's not good for business. I would put forward," this is David, "I would put forward a true collaboration is a willingness to have a set of people with diverse competencies, world views and experiences with the added ingredient of wanting to pursue a clear and concise objective come together in a safe space to talk about their position and how they hope to add value to reach that objective. Even if it's not in alignment with others." Thank you, David, for that.

if we seriously wish to improve our team's performance, we must work together better. This means inside and outside with all our stakeholders. Success always requires collaboration and collaboration over time.

It's not an event and you can't do it by yourself. Look at the ten essential steps, you can download them for free at davidbsavage.com. How do we figure out what we are doing and what's needed now? Remember what gets measured gets done. When we choose to seriously check where we are, I invite you to work with our collaborative leadership 360 assessment. Check it out on our website. Here are some key questions from that collaborative leadership assessment. We talked about values, we talked about foundations, we talked about agility. We've talked about extraordinary experiences.

Now, are you able to adjust to changes that take place during the collaborative process? These are questions from the assessment. Are your meetings purpose driven and focused on the end results? Do you allow different people to lead at different times and support shared leadership? Are you opening to new ideas or realizations? Do you truly cultivate the capability of others? When conflict arises, do you address it proactively? Do you have an approach, guidelines, agreements in advance? Another question in the 360 assessments, remember this is – 360 means people work for you and that you work for and your peers on either side rate you and we all rate each other and then we assess it, see where the gaps and the strengths are and design the improvement process.

How often do you seek to collaborate with clients and stakeholders in the process of change? So, I really encourage you to go through my collaborative leadership and team development 360 assessment. The intention is to drive better results through better ideas, processes and teamwork. Take any one of the questions on the assessment and discuss it with your people at each weekly meeting. Start now, start today. This needs to be an evolutionary experience. Do it now, start these conversations every week. Where's the 360 assessment and your culture of collaboration, how does it fit? What is the process that I'm encouraging you to do?

Well, in my progressive offering, we do an exploratory analysis in focus. We provide you the collaborative leadership 360 assessment and all its benefits. We look at a new process design, what's the system, the culture that you want to create and build upon? Then, we look at your business development leadership and team development programs and agreements. Yeah, the agreements to set up accountabilities. I offer a collaborative workbook for teams, a learning guide and I also offer webinars, workshops, books, videos and podcasts. So far, there's 27 with 50 guests now. You can go to Voice America, iTunes or my website. Most of this is free. If you really want to do the work, engage me. Of course, one on one coaching. Let's hold this space, it's not an event.

Let's do a combination of assessments, coaching, system redesign and encouragement to develop that agility, trust, innovation and courage. So, now imagine yourself as a champion in your work in 2020. You and your organization are celebrating a huge Break Through. What's the feeling when, together you've accomplished what no one had dreamed possible. You've had that extraordinary experience, you feel elated, you're agile, you've done it. You're seen as one of the very best and you see your team as completely ready to take on the next opportunities. Feel your success, let it resonate within you. What is your success? Feel that, want that, want that extraordinary experience. Develop the agility.

So, here's a way to do it. Here's my three steps that I offer this week. My call to action.

1) how do you assess and evaluate your leadership and team performance? How do you assess and evaluate? Do you stick a wet finger up in the wind and see which way it's blowing or are you going to be serious about this collaborative leadership and culture and innovation in this complex world? Second step, once you've thought about how you assess and evaluate your leadership and team performance.

2) what services make best sense to you to start making this progressive change? Is it a 360 assessment that I offer or SVI offers? Is it online learning? I offer webinars. Is it in person workshops? Is it coaching by me or others that you've talked to, heard from, Stephen, Mike, Bob, David, Tristen, Martin.

How do you really focus, how do you step in to what's possible? Join one of my ongoing leadership circles, it's like a president's club saying, "What's possible and how do we collaborate across organizations?" I offer a lot, there's lots to be understood and gained and capitalized on. Yeah, capitalized, take advantage. Don't be part of the herd, get out there.

3) what will you do right now to start, to move forward? What are you committing to? I guess in this moment, in that spirit of collaboration, I'll make you an offer. Any listener that contacts me by March 1 and refers to this radio show, this podcast I'll give you and your organization 15% off the price of any of the packages that I offer – 15% reduction, you just contact me and say that you heard this offer on this radio show. Let's move forward.

So, look at all of this at davidbsavage.com. Look at all of this at SVI and Mike Thompson, the WELLth Movement and Dr. Stephen Hobbs. There are many people able to help you move forward, many great people, part of my honor is the ability that I must connect people globally. Connecting with you, I'd love to hear your feedback, your challenges, your diverse perspectives.

David@davidbsavage. Send it to me and let's talk about it, let's build this culture of collaboration globally and in our families and organizations. With Dr. Stephen Hobbs and Mike Thompson, we've talked about leadership, legacy, organizational culture, assessments and tools to help organizations perform better together and much more.

Remember, in collaboration, we are looking to break out of normal and Break Through to fresh and exciting insights and possibilities. We're faced with disruption and complexity and challenge and conflict. How agile can we be? How inclusive, how extraordinary can we be, how successful might we be? So, I encourage you assess and evaluate, measure it. Make a choice of what I offer to you, what Stephen offers, Mike offers and many others. I can make recommendations, contact me if you've got a specific issue. If we can't handle it, I'll tell you who I know that I respect and can refer you to. But, do it now. Thank you for listening today, this has been an important conversation. I'm glad you're part of it. Now let's work together better.

Chapter 4 Collaboration, Company Dispute Resolution and Mindfulness featuring Julie Murray

David: Welcome back, everyone. This is David B. Savage. So glad that today we're going to have Julie Murray join us. She will join us later in the show. In her work Julie advocates for slowing down and digging below the surface so that deeper meaning and greater understanding can emerge.

Today we explore the old variety and theme of mindfulness and talk about it in the frame of corporate conflicts and personal awareness. Our theme today is collaboration, company to company dispute resolution plus mindfulness.

It might seem that courtrooms, litigation, lawyers, games, big boardrooms, "C" suites and mindfulness and personal awareness are so different, but they aren't. The strategies to win personally and professionally and in conflict are very similar. So, let's make this about you.

Have you ever had a conflict in your life? Of course, you have. Daily, probably like me. Have you ever felt you could have done better resolving that conflict? Well, I do. I'm learning all the time. That's why I dedicated my career to negotiation, dispute resolution and collaboration, how to work together better. Would you like to explore ways of creating better outcomes? Well, that's what we're going to do today.

As we go through this radio show think about what do you wish to change, and in this moment and every moment what's true for you, what do you wish to change. How can we make it better?

Let's start with I've got a million stories of conflict in my book *Break Through to Yes: Unlocking the Possible within a Culture of Collaboration.* Some of my readers have said, "Hey, David, you've failed an awful lot." Yeah, I have. That's why I wrote the book. That's why I'm a student of negotiation, collaboration and dispute resolution.

This example is just one example, and it happens too often. This is an oil and gas industry example, company to company conflict. "He makes me so mad. Why do they think they can get away from this with this? I don't even want to deal with him anymore. I am so furious, I just can't talk right now." Have you ever felt these emotions? Yeah, the reptilian brain, the amygdala, takes charge. "My company is ten natural gas wells that we own jointly with company X. I'll just call them company X for right now. The production from these wells is good but the price for the natural gas is very poor so we are barely making any money, barely breaking even from our interest in these ten wells. To move the natural gas from the wells to sale we must process it and deliver it by pipeline to the purchaser.

A few years ago, company X and my company agreed to drill and then build the natural gas processing facility and a short pipeline to deliver our gas to market. Since company X owns 75% of the natural gas and we own only 25, it seemed right to let company X operate the production, the wells, the facility and the pipeline.

Seems all reasonable. Except that I just found out that company X is letting another company, let's call them ThirdCo, deliver their natural gas through our facility and pipeline. They are charging ThirdCo less to use the facility and pipeline than what I am being charged. Give me a break. I paid my share. They haven't paid anything and they're coming through for less than I'm paying? This is ridiculous. We own 25%. How can ThirdCo get a better deal than I do? I've invested capital. They're just paying a fee on throughput.

If I was getting the deal ThirdCo has I would probably make money. Instead, I pay for 25% of the system and barely break even. Why didn't company X talk to us rather than giving ThirdCo a separate and sneaky deal? Yeah, I think it's a sneaky deal, but I don't know for sure. I paid $5 million for land, drilling, completion, facilities and pipeline and I'm barely breaking even, let alone repaying any of the cost to buy the land, drill the wells, put them on production.

ThirdCo owns no share of the facility or pipeline and they get a lower cost than me. I am so angry. How could company X do that to us? That's so unfair. They need to be taught a lesson. I've tried to negotiate with my joint venture partner, company X. They keep putting me off. They ignore me. When we finally met their interpretation of our agreement is so different than mine.

Well, that's it. I hired a litigator, a lawyer, to go to court. I want to get company X straightened out. I want the judge to tell them that I'm right. I'm right, they're wrong, let's go to court, I'll show you.

Well, that happened a year ago. Company X and I don't talk anymore. Both of our companies are now paying big time for lawyers and we're losing opportunities to work together on other developments. We no longer trust one another. Because of the litigation ThirdCo has built their own facility and pipeline. They've built their own facility and pipeline. That's really hurt. Without ThirdCo's natural gas going through our facility the cost per unit are getting higher and higher.

Now, neither company X or my company are making any money. What gives? Well, we're losing money, ThirdCo's gone. They're making money I think, I hope. We're probably going to have to shut in our ten natural gas wells rather than continue to lose money. Do I have to wait another year and tens of thousands of dollars to get this resolved? I sure hope not. This is crazy. I just don't understand it. How can this go from bad to worse?"

Now, this is just a pretend example, but I've seen many conflicts like that. I hope you get the feeling of frustration. We've done the right thing and now we're being screwed. In my 42 years in business I've worked with oil companies, renewable energy companies, mining companies, tourism companies, healthcare companies and more. In company to company conflicts, no matter what the industry, our reptilian brains often move us to anger, frustration and then litigation into court.

Here's some of the reasons we get into conflict. Just recently, Lynda McNeil and I did a workshop for the Petroleum Joint Venture Association at the Petroleum Club in Calgary. We titled that workshop *Stay in Control* and I think from the theme of this radio show you'll understand that. Stay in control. Don't lose control to the other party. Don't let the bad guys win. Don't let the court system drain you. Don't let arbitrators, mediators, negotiators drain you. Stay in control.

Here are some of the reasons that we get into conflict. These are things that we've explored in our workshops. Well, obviously the technical merits of a dispute and varying interpretations of the agreements, that's one. Another reason we get into conflict is a lack of interest, or even putting priority by the other part. The other party just doesn't want to get invested in this, it's hurting us, but they figure that they can delay, and we'll just give in. Not a chance. We're not giving in. Not a chance. That's just not the way it's going to happen.

Well, we're also all very busy, busy, busy. It's a crime to be too busy to make money, too busy to do the right thing, too busy to innovate. But if we don't have the time to fully evaluate the probability of success, the associated value or risks, how do we negotiate and resolve the conflict? We're losing control because we're too busy, we're not focused, we're not attending to.

Of course, insufficient or lack of resources to properly develop our position. We don't have legal counsel or other expertise, we don't have a mediator, we don't have – well, our negotiating skills could be better, let me put it that way. Any of those things resonate with you?

What tactics do you typically use if the dispute doesn't get resolved? Think about that. What do you do? When a dispute didn't go the way you wanted, yet you knew you were right, what did you wish you had done differently to change the outcome? What did you wish that you did differently to change the outcome?

It's, I don't know, it's frustrating. I've dedicated a lot of my 42-year career to getting parties to work together better, to resolve their own conflict, not lose control. Back in 2003, I believe it was, a long time ago, we found that companies in the oil and gas industry in Canada were increasingly in conflict. Increasingly wasting their time and resources. And some of the processes and practices in the industry rewarded bad behavior.

I and I think it was about 100 volunteers over a four-year period formed the Company 2 Company Dispute Resolution Council. Guess what? All those professional negotiators, engineers, accountants, MBAs, engineers, litigators, mediators, arbitrators, all those folks we put together a handbook on how to resolve company to company conflict, techniques, processes, skills, abilities. We put in this handbook and guess what we called it? *Let's Talk. Let's Talk.* It can be as simple as that.

If we're too busy to do anything other than text or email how on Earth are we going to negotiate? That's one of the things we can change, is just let's talk. Get outside, go for a half an hour walk with that party, explore it. If you want to find out more about our Company 2 Company Dispute Resolution Council, go to www.c2cadr.com. That's www.c2cadr.com as in Company 2 Company ADR dot com.

So, what is the council? Well, it's an organization that can help you get the tools and resources to manage conflict effectively without losing sight of your bottom line. Are you wondering how to get through a challenging negotiation? Well, contact us, we can help you. Do you need some different strategies to improve your business partnerships? Of course, we all do. C2CADR.com.

Let's look at ways, there's many ways that we look for appropriate dispute resolution. Not alternate, but appropriate. I think going to court is an alternate, but it's not the only way, and I'll talk about this a little bit in a minute. I think my focus is getting you in charge, keeping you cost controlled and maximizing your opportunities.

When we talk about how do you go from a failed negotiation to court you've skipped across all the opportunities. We're going to talk a little bit about a situation assessment meeting, there's also mediation, arbitration, litigation, many opportunities. We need to be more aware and conscious of the choices we're making rather than letting our reptilian brain do that for us.

Let's talk about avoidance. In conflict and negotiation, avoidance is very predominant. All of us want not to be in that conflict. It's stressful. The hair goes up on the back of my neck, I get angry. Often there's a power imbalance. You might have all the tools and money and resources that you can beat me up or take advantage of me of out last me or out litigate me. Failed negotiation happens too often.

In my book *Break Through to Yes,* I say collaboration is not an event, it's a culture. It's how we work together. It's the same for negotiation. Oftentimes business people think of negotiation as a one-time event. That negotiation is part of your brand, your reputation, how people can trust you. In my 41-year career there's only been two individuals where I say I would never negotiate with them again. And there's probably a dozen negotiators where I'd say I trust them completely, I would let them negotiate the deal on their own without me. And then there's a whole mix in between.

We've got growing costs, growing timelines, growing uncertainty. It is personal. Disputes are personal. We'll talk about techniques and practices in a moment, but right now let's talk about some percentages. Let's talk about 50%, 25%, 5% and less than 1%. What does that mean?

Well, in my time in oil and gas in Canada and the United States, for some periods of time I found that the court system and the regulatory processes people like the Alberta Energy Regulator and others, what they were finding is about 50% of the disputes that went in front of their panel for resolution, the principles, the people with the authority to resolve the dispute had never actually met. They spent hundreds of thousands of dollars, sometimes millions of dollars, and they've never met. How do you do that? That's craziness. That's the reptilian brain saying I'm right and I'm going to beat you. That's 50%, that's awful. It must be mandatory that the people with the authority to resolve it must talk, must have that coffee, a walk, a scotch, whatever that is. So that's 50%.

Then there's 25%. I've been told by my litigation peers and friends and network that a rule of thumb, and maybe this is accurate, maybe it's not, but I've been told by a number the rule of thumb is that if you go to court then 25% of the time the judge will get it wrong because the judge judges on a whole bunch of different subjects. They are likely not an expert on your subject matter. So, 25% of the time they'll just blow it. Is that what you want? That's kind of like rolling the dice.

Of all the conflicts that get ramped up and into a process, only about 5% ever make it to court. I think it's less now. So why do our agreements and our processes and our thinking take us from where I'm angry and you're taking advantage of me on that gas plant or pipeline or whatever, wind farm, to I'm going to go to court? That's a big jump. Of the ones that go to court only less than 1% are resolved by a court. Less than 1% of disputes are resolved in the courts. So, we get an upside-down system that loses control. Loses control of processes, opportunities, relationships, money and time.

Why would we want to do that? Let's look a little further now into what is the real continuum in between failed negotiation and court or litigation. There's a continuum. Go to the C2CADR.com and you'll see this continuum right on our front page.

Those things, those processes or events, are company to company consultations. Go to lunch, have a coffee, go to a football game together, whatever it is. When parties have most control over the process they're the least formal and they can be more interest based. And confidentiality is determined by the parties and decisions are made by the parties and it's all voluntary. Company to company negotiations. So, you go from talk, consultation to negotiation.

Then you can have facilitated negotiations. You can have somebody like me, or many others, work with you through the negotiations. Then you can have a situation assessment meeting, that we'll talk about a little later. Mediation, some people know mediation through divorce or family mediation. Many courts now have mandatory mediation. The great thing about that is it's a facilitated, guided process and it's a professional process. It's not just something that I mediated. No, that's a profession, respected as a profession. And it's all voluntary. You don't have to agree to anything, nobody's going to impose anything on you.

Then you go to the processes where you have much less control over the process. They're way more formal. More legal, norm based, more expensive and public. So, your dirty laundry is out there for the public. You're setting precedence. The courtrooms are available, the testimony is available. Do you want that? And more than anything, do you want a third party adjudicating your conflict? These include arbitration, binding and nonbinding. There are things like Alberta Energy Utility Board, National Energy Board of Canada and there's processes around the world like this.

I'm pleased to note that the Alberta energy regulator is working with many other countries on building appropriate dispute resolution and public consultation practices and processes that work well in western Canada and they are being co-developed in other countries.

Litigation, regulatory process, arbitration, they are public, they are expensive. Now, mediation can be expensive, but not as much as the others. But arbitration, regulatory and litigation you have much less control. I'm not saying it's not a good thing. In many cases those are exactly the right things to do. But what I will say is make a choice.

We're going to take a short break now and when we come back we're going to talk about a situation assessment meeting, the cost of conflict and start developing the personal and professional awareness and mindfulness. Then we will have a conversation with the great Julie Murray. We'll be right back.

David: Hi, we're back now. Let's talk about the situation assessment meeting. When we talk about our Company 2 Company Dispute Resolution Council and our Let's Talk handbook and the workshops and coaching that I do, and others do I'm a strong proponent of a situation assessment meeting.

Before the break we talked about the continuum between negotiation, facilitated negotiations, mediation, arbitration, regulatory and litigation. I say that there's a time where we need to just check in. Oftentimes masters like the Harvard Program on Negotiation team of Fisher, Ury, Heen, Stone, Fox, and others say you separate the people from the problem. Well, the situation assessment meeting that we've developed separates you from the problem, so you can go to the balcony, to steal one of their phrases, and look at what is the conflict all about.

Let's start thinking about some of the questions that if I was with your company and helping you and the other company in conflict. These are kind of the things that we've looked at.

In a Situation Assessment Meeting (or SAM), we're not trying to resolve a conflict or negotiate. We're looking at the conflict and saying, okay, where are we? How did we get here? What are the real issues? Describing in a neutral fashion, what's the current, how did we get here? The current situation is the result of various causes, pressures, impacts and outcomes. Within all the companies and personalities – yeah, talk about personalities, too.

Sometimes leaders, negotiators, think they must win, they must beat, they must take away more than they give. And then they end up getting less, both. The sum of the parts becomes less than the whole in conflict oftentimes. It gets into a shouting match and a pissing match. What are the challenges that have hindered resolution so far? What are the strategies? What are the values that we want to agree on? What are the costs?

Now, let's talk about all the costs. Costs of action, or inaction, are direct and indirect. Direct costs include human resources, IE people; financial resources, money; and time. Time, money and people, those are important components. Indirect costs in conflict include the potential impact on relationships, personal and professional.

Thinking about these potential costs and current costs, what are the direct and indirect costs? Do this evaluation. Let's work this through in this conflict that we're in right now. What's the people cost? What's the financial cost? What's the time cost? What's the relationship cost? What are the opportunities that we're missing right now because we're in conflict?

It soon looks like a very expensive conflict. The thing that we're fighting about might be, in fact, just the tip of the iceberg. The rest of the iceberg is all the other costs, the fact that your staff can't attend to their jobs, their work, their purpose. Think about that. Really analyze the costs. Do a situation assessment meeting before you get in too far.

In a recent one that I was called to there was two oil companies in western Canada. They were partners in several fields. Their negotiators, their land men, had a good, strong, trusting relationship with each other. They got off side with practicalities versus terms of agreement, different perspectives on terms of the agreement. They ended up hiring the lawyers, going to the examination for discovery, the statement of claim, all that process.

About a year into it and tens of thousands of dollars into it they called me in because they said, "Well, we're spending a lot of time and money and this isn't really getting us where we want to be. It's distracting us from our objectives, our corporate objectives. So, David, would you do a situation assessment meeting?"

What I did is I worked with them for half a day where we answered those questions. What got us here? What are the costs of this? From an independent, neutral statement what is the underlying issue here? And going through what are the opportunities, what are the costs, what are the challenges? Do we need shared, third party expertise? Do we need guidance from anybody else? What are our accountabilities?

Guess what? We broke at half a day and I said, "Okay, it's time that this is resonating, you're sitting on the same side of the table looking at the problem together. We're making a lot of progress. I think it's a good time to break. The two of you call a friend, go for a walk, talk to whoever you need to talk to in your organization. And then let's come back."

Well, half an hour later we came back, we explored some ideas and they asked for a one-week delay. They said, "Let's get together, David, and next week let's work a little further." Well, sure enough we got together a week later, and they'd resolved their conflict. They came up with an outcome that neither had thought about before, but they realized that they could work this for their mutual gain. They could resolve it.

That's what they did. And what I will tell you is whether it's the regulatory process in the ADR programs that I've helped institute in Alberta or in company to company situation assessment meetings, every one of them that goes through shave off most of the issues, so they can focus on what are the key things that we're fighting about and focus on that. It's much more effective and efficient.

Eighty percent of the time within a few weeks of the parties having their situation assessment meeting they resolve it themselves. Because they've focused, they've attended to it, they've got the accountability and the authority to resolve it, and they do that.

It's just a fantastic thing. There is minimal cost in the whole scheme of things, but it allows people to sit together and resolve their problem and save control, I guess, stay in charge, reduce the drainage from conflict, the waste of conflict.

Now, let's talk about space. This is starting to segue to a little bit of our conversation with Julie Murray in a few minutes. The Harvard Program on Negotiation, some of the masters – Fisher and Ury – *Getting To Yes* fame, *Difficult Conversations* – Stone and Heen, *Winning From Within*, Erica Fox. I've met all these folks, admirable folks. Here's some of the key things.

Separate the people from the problem. Go to the balcony. In other words, don't let your reptilian brain run this conflict. Go to the balcony. See it from a distance. Go from the 30,000-foot level. Whatever metaphor or phrase you want to use, don't get into the trenches because you just can't see how foolish I can get, I'll claim it myself. Be hard on the problem, not on the people. I think these are great teachings from the Harvard Program on Negotiation and their alumni.

For example, Sheila and Doug (Heen and Stone) authors of *Difficult Conversations,* I love this quote, "Often we go through an entire conversation – or indeed an entire relationship – without ever realizing that each of us is paying attention to different things, that our views are based on different information."

My friend Erica Ariel Fox is author of *Winning From Within*. Her teaching is realizing that the most difficult negotiations are within ourselves. Here's another great quote from Erica, "A meal becomes good by starting with quality instructions. It becomes great when you add a quality chef." Can you be the quality chef? Of course, you can.

Stay in control. Face to face, remember that company to company dispute resolution handbook is called *Let's Talk*.

Let's talk in person. Let's build that relationship, build the opportunities, build the innovation, communicate, negotiate and collaborate. Know, too, that in collaboration, like coaching, dispute resolution and most transformative processes, most of the great work is done by individuals in smaller groups outside of the room or online session. The landing, or creating, can be even more powerful than inside the physical or digital gathering. Inside the space may simply be where the seeds are planted. The crop may be harvested elsewhere. Very often I wake up early in the morning with a profound solution to a challenge that I had struggled with in my prior business days.

Here's some call to action. Think about this, write them down.

1) explore and identify the best dispute resolution option for you. Do it purposefully and knowledgeably. It could be litigation, it could be a facilities or negotiation. Could be simply asking great questions.

2) engage in a situation assessment meeting. It's a healthy thing. It's like going to the doctor, like doctor conflict.

3) look beyond the problem to find better outcomes for both parties. That's right, better outcomes. You can do that. Look for the space.

4) pause, look for the space, reflect, meditate, be mindful. Let go of certainty, let go of judgment. Let go of being right.

5) Use these tools;

    a. Explore options.

b. Situation assessment meeting.

c. Look beyond the problem.

d. Let go, pause.

Imagine yourself as a champion in your work in 2020. You and your organization are celebrating a huge Break Through. Together you have accomplished what no one had dreamed possible. You are elated. You are one of the very best and you see your team as completely ready to take on the next opportunity. Let this resonate within you. Feel your success.

What changes did you make in the last few years in your personal and professional life to get you to such great success? Did you allow your reptilian brain to rule or did it allow time for your prefrontal cortex to engage? Did you create space for yourself?

One of my favorite books ever is Viktor Frankl's *Man's Search for Meaning*. Don't have time today, but search it, read it, listen to it. This is an amazing man, amazing wisdom. Here's just a few quotes from Viktor Frankl, a survivor of several concentration camps in Germany during the Nazi regime.

Viktor Frankl, "When we are no longer able to change a situation we are challenged to change ourselves." In conflict we get frustrated, angry – this is me talking now – righteous and ready to fight. If you're being chased by a tiger sometimes that response is best. In today's business world that is most often a poor reaction. The reptilian brain, sometimes it serves leaders but most often it destroys opportunity.

If there's one quote that you'll hear me talk about in my coaching, my workshops and my negotiation circles and leadership circles, here's Viktor Frankl again. "There's a space between stimulus and response. How we use that space determines the quality of our life." Yeah. "There is a space between stimulus and response. How we use that space determines the quality of our life."

Our greatest freedom is the freedom to choose our attitude. Now, as another link to greatness my friend Johanne Lavoie, she did a recent TED Talk, Montreal Women. Noted the greatest challenge for leaders today is ADT, attention deficit trait. In other words, we're too scattered, too busy, we're not focused, we need to pause.

Let's pause now and when we come back we will introduce you to my friend, Julie Murray.

David: Welcome back. Welcome for our listeners around the planet. I'm really delighted today to introduce you to Julie Murray. Julie's a professional coach, facilitator and educator with over 20 years of experience working with the education sector. She is a big picture thinker who is passionate about leadership, creativity and amplifying human potential. Doesn't that sound fabulous?

In her work Julie advocates for slowing down, so I will slow down right now. Digging below the surface, remember we talked about that iceberg, digging below the surface so that deeper meaning and greater understanding can emerge. Julie is recognized for her ability to listen deeply, integrate learning, forge strong relationships and communicate effectively. Julie is also a writer, an artist and a student of integral theory and mindfulness meditation. Julie, welcome.

Julie: Thank you so much, David. I'm really honored to have this opportunity to connect with you and all your listeners.

David: Let's start with your work as an integral coach helping individuals to slow down so that they can become more aware and more intentional, and I'll stress intentional, about their lives. How did you become attracted to this work, Julie?

Julie: Well, as you said in my intro, I started out as an educator. In fact, I still very much consider myself to be one. But I spent almost two decades working in private schools, independent schools across Canada. It's interesting because probably for the decade, ten years, before I finished my teaching career I found myself in a situation where I was pushing harder and harder and harder. I had less and less and less energy. I spent a lot of time beating myself up and thinking that it was my fault that I couldn't just push harder.

When I finally did leave teaching because I wanted to explore and grow and look for new challenges as an educator, what I discovered by accident, I really couldn't see it at the time, and you mentioned even earlier in your segment about how sometimes we can't see our own behaviors. After going to a number of practitioners for a sore shoulder and neck I found out that I was burnt out. I had adrenal fatigue, which if your listeners aren't sure what that means it's basically your fight or flight response has been going on overdrive.

For me, for about ten years my fight or flight response was going at a high level. What that meant was my body no longer could handle it. So here I was, someone who prided myself as a very passionate educator and someone who cared about how I showed up for other people, and I literally had to stop. I had to slow down to the point where I spent a lot of time in my house. I had to face a lot of the thinking patterns within myself that were questioning who am I if I'm not moving quickly in this world.

It was an interesting time and an interesting lesson for me to learn, but it was also a huge gift because I learned about some of the benefits, or a lot of the benefits, of slowing down and the benefits of really connecting with yourself.

During that time and that journey I went through a series of experiences where I realized that coaching, working one-on-one with people was really part of that essence of what I loved most about my time as an educator. I stumbled upon integral coaching when I was looking for coaching schools and knew right away, 100%, that it was the perspective I wanted to take in my work with individuals one-on-one. It takes a very holistic perspective and it also encourages people to take that time to slow down and to increase their own awareness of themselves.

Often, we aren't aware of our thinking patterns. For me, for ten years I didn't know what I was doing to myself. And even the detriment that might have been to the students in the room. Maybe I wasn't showing up as well as I could. Integral coaching really offers an opportunity for clients to see. If you can imagine that we all have glasses that we wear day to day that are our perspectives and our conditional beliefs, integral coaching offers an individual an opportunity to see those glasses, to see what their perspectives are and how that colors how they enter the world, how they enter their discussions and their relationships with others.

Then through the process we're offered another set of glasses that maybe gives us a different perspective. That's, I would say, how I became attracted. It just fit so well with me and my own journey and the things that I needed and the things that I see a lot of value in.

David: I trust our audience can understand the direct linkage between going to the balcony and changing your glasses. This is really an awareness to say there is no right, there's just me. So, who am I and how do I want to be in this relationship, how do I want to be in this conflict?

Julie: Absolutely. When you create that space of awareness, if you slow down a little bit so you have more control over how you respond, then you're absolutely right, there's a choice that's available to you that otherwise it might not be. If you jump right into something you might not have the choice of what your behavior is.

Often, it's in those situations that afterwards we're like, "I can't believe I said that," or, "I should have done this." Right? It's that looking backwards at our behaviors. Absolutely the idea of going to the balcony or just taking a moment or working – you also mentioned meditation in the last segment as well, working on just becoming more comfortable with who you are and what are those things about yourself that show up when you're in those discussions with other people.

David: Julie, why does this matter in the world today?

Julie: Oh my goodness. Well, I mean just even looking at the work that you do, David, with collaboration. And really there's so much overlap. I think that's part of why we have so many great conversations when we get together. There's so much overlap in the work that I do and the great work that you're bringing out into the world.

We are in a society now, a time now, where we are moving into increasing complexity in our world. The landscape is shifting. There've been shifts in Europe and in North America. And there is increasing divisiveness. There's a feeling of polarization that's happening in the world today that at least for me feels more visceral than it's felt in the past. I think this work of each of us taking responsibility of how we show up and making sure that who we're bringing into the world when we enter conversations and discussions and in the work that we do is coming from a place of awareness and coming from a place where we're not just reacting from our habits, that we're thinking about how we're showing up.

David: There's also the literal wall building and rejection and separation happening in our world today where we tend to separate ourselves from others rather than seeking them out because they can teach me.

Julie: Exactly. Yeah, in these moments I think, exactly, I think the natural response is to join in on the polarization, to join in on the that's them and this is us. But I think what's needed, and I think it's your step seven that you offer in your book, is that listening deeply. It's leaning in and listening and trying to understand that other perspective, trying to tap into what that dialogue is from a place of listening to understand versus listening to just share your opinion.

David: Yeah, certainly I've been guilty of that about thinking about my next questions as opposed to listening to the wisdom being offered to me right now. That agility, it's an intimate connection, this communication done well.

Julie: Yeah, absolutely. And, how that conversation can change when you enter it in a place where you're listening fully. It's fascinating to see how the people that you're in that conversation with have some of their patterns shift or change because you're showing up differently.

Often, we point fingers and say they always do this or they always do that, but often we have a responsibility in that. When we recognize that how we show ourselves and how we show up, that has an impact. Those conversations, and I think you talk about that as well in your book, but those conversations can go very differently if we show up differently.

David: Yeah, everyone, one of the things that Julie reminds me of is when I get an emotion, explore that emotion. What's really going on for me? As opposed to judging or letting my reptilian brain take charge. I'm feeling frustrated, what's that all about, what's frustration for me, what am I doing, what am I contributing to this, how do I become more mindful. Julie, tell us more about the work you do and how our listeners can find out more about you.

Julie: Sure. Well, I work as an integral coach out of Calgary, Alberta, but I do have clients via Skype in different parts of the world. I'm always happy even just to have a conversation. It doesn't have to necessarily be a coaching relationship. But if there's anyone who has this feeling like life is moving quickly and they're feeling caught up in the whirlwind and they want to be more intentional about how they're moving forward, that's a conversation I would love to have. Just from my own life experience it's a passion that I have, and I would love to connect with people who have that experience going on.

They say that stress is the epidemic of the 21st century. Underneath that stress is an opportunity for us to learn more about ourselves and how we can really add value in the world.

David: I must be valuable because I'm very busy. That is not a causal relationship at all. It's probably the inverse.

Julie: No, it's like a badge of honor in our society. I always think of it as the stone, and I've offered you this image before, David. It's the stone skipping across the lake. I used to love skipping stones when I was a kid living in Ontario in Canada on an amazing bay. Most of us are like that. We're these stones that are just skipping, skimming over the surface of the water. It's not until we stop our busyness and we allow that stone to sink that we really get to know ourselves. That can be sometimes scary, but if we can move through that there's a lot of learning that can add to how we interact with those around us, how we know ourselves and how we contribute to the world.

David: What is your website? Let's not miss that opportunity for people to look you up.

Julie: My website is www.JulieMurray.ca. I also have a bi-weekly blog that they can subscribe to on my website. And another kind of exciting opportunity that I am doing with a gentleman named Ken Wylie, who is a professional mountain guide, lives in BC in Canada, is we also put together a retreat that's a leadership development retreat. It's a corporate retreat in the Canadian Rockies where we're calling it The Listening Leader. I think it fits so well with this concept of collaboration.

It's basically an opportunity, we have three and six-day programs, an opportunity for leaders who are looking to deepen their ability to listen. It's to themselves, to others and the environment around them. It's going to be a fascinating workshop or retreat because it offers individuals an opportunity to be in an unbelievable location. It's a helicopter access lodge that's very remote. Incredible food and accommodation. But then also there will be time in the mountains. So, kind of working on leadership development through experience.

The whole theme is going to be around listening and how do we work better as a team, specifically around how do we tackle this increasing complexity in our world today in a shifting landscape. We're really excited about that, this offering. It is up on my website as well if there's anyone that's interested in learning more.

David: That's JulieMurray.ca. Julie, in this moment before we close this segment what's one thing that you would challenge our audience to be and do or change?

Julie: I would challenge them to let their stone drop. So, make some time and some space in your life to slow down, and take some time for yourself free of distraction. Go for a walk, sit quietly, get to know what it feels like in your body, dance in a room by yourself. But just remove yourself from all the busyness and really start to connect to yourself and start to tap into what truly matters to you right now. It's a huge gift that you can give to yourself and it's a challenge that I offer to you.

David: Thank you, Julie.

Julie: Thank you, David.

David: Today we've had the opportunity to explore with Julie the mindfulness, pausing, integral theory, coaching, skipping stones, dancing by ourselves and company to company dispute resolution, situation assessment, separating the people from the problem and building the relationship and the opportunity, knowing ourselves. Between stimulus and response there is a space. How we use that space determines the quality of our life. So, pause, reflect, let go of certainty, let go of judgment, let go of being right and win, win, win like our theme song from Chuck Rose. Now, let's work together better everyone.

Chapter 5 Collaboration and Critical Thinking in This Age of Lies featuring Doreen Liberto and Chuck Rose

David: Wow, this is going to be a great show. What we're finding is so many conversations about facts, truths, alternate truth, lies, deception, manipulation, reptilian brains – we've got to get around this. We got to save our future. We're going in the wrong direction and it's not just President Trump, not just the Republican Party, it's all of us. It's how we seem to have been captured sort of point in time that our attention spans are now considered less than goldfish. That's scary. Today's theme is Collaboration and Critical Thinking in this Age of Lies. This Age of Lies; not the first one, but it's a dangerous time. Our guest today in the second section will be Doreen Liberto of California, my partner in the Collaborative Global Initiative, and Chuck Rose from Alberta, the friend and colleague who wrote and performed Win, Win, Win or Walk Away, which we'll play the whole thing at the end of this first second, and We Are One, which we'll close the show with today.

I'm very proud to have them both on our show, and this is a live show so just as a reminder, anything that you want to say, go on Twitter, add David B. Savage, tell me what you're critically thinking or send me an email david@davidbsavage.com and engage with us. Let's go. We got so much to cover. We've had so many people say why don't you do a show on this Age of Lies? So that's what we're doing. Alternate facts, goldfish, can't discern the news, advertising, social media, fear, anger, standing rock, nuclear energy, you know barriers to communication. We're going to try to cover so much of this today. We explore and delve deeper into these issues. Why is it more difficult to collaborate or even dialog these days? Why does it seem increasingly difficult to get disparate groups of people to work together?

Whether politically, economically, environmentally or socially, the conversations are increasingly acrimonious, accusatory and less truthful, yeah, less truthful. What is truth and how do we talk to one another in these polarized conversations? What are the techniques and skills needed most today? How can successful collaborations be designed? So, if you're tired of the normal conversation, that coffee/cooler conversation, the Starbucks conversation or that angry conversation as your cross-country skiing; whatever it is, let's change this conversation to create a better future together. What can help us today? Do we really have a shorter attention span than goldfish? What is the difference between social media, advertising, campaigns, news and journalism? Some of our leaders hate the media. Wonder why? Why might you care? What is critical thinking and what resources that available to us?

Join our talk. We're going to talk about some of this and there's so much to be talked about in these times of division, separation, racism, misogyny, and ignorance.

I've talked about goldfish twice now. Let's talk about neuroscience. In *Time Health Magazine*, May 14, 2015, an article by Kevin McSpadden says you now have a shorter attention span than a goldfish, and I'm reading Kevin's article. The average attention span for the notoriously ill-focused goldfish is 9 seconds. But according to a new study from Microsoft, people now generally lose concentration after 8 seconds, not section, seconds. This is unbelievable. Highlighting the effects of an increasingly digitalized lifestyle on the brain, researchers in Canada surveyed 2,000 participants and studied the brain activity of 112 others using EEGs. Microsoft found that since the year 2000, or about when the mobile revolution began, cell phones, Smart phones, iPhones, the average attention span dropped from 12 seconds to 8 seconds. Lately we cannot focus, how do we drive, how do we read a book, how do we have an intelligent conversation, how do we listen? The article continues, heavy multi-screeners find it difficult to filter irrelevant stimuli and they're easily distracted by multiple streams of media. Wow, so I like this 8 seconds or now. It's two years later after this study. Maybe we're down to 7 seconds. We can't tell the difference.

Here is the Stanford study that finds most students failed to distinguish between real news and fake news. I'm reading the article now. The rise of fake new is a topic that is getting a lot of attention lately thanks to the role that Facebook, and other social platforms play in news consumption for a growing number of users. There are other problems as well a recent Stanford study found. According to researchers, most students, more than 80% of them in fact, could not distinguish between a piece of sponsored content or native advertising and a real news article. Really? They also had difficulty determining whether a news story shared on social media was credible, and based on their decision on odd or even irrelevant factors. This is really scary. We can't tell the difference between advertising, self-interested promotion, social media outrage and truth? Now media's come under a lot of pressure, a lot of condemnation. We need more investigative journalists. It doesn't mean we all agree on the same thing. But let's focus more than 8 seconds.

Let's read articles, let's read books, let's listen and engage, have dialog. When we can't tell the difference between lies, alternate facts, fake news and social media and great journalism, we not only have a shorter attention span than a goldfish, but we are easy prey for the ignorant. We evolved with a prefrontal cortex to handle the complex thinking and decision making, so why do we choose to be run by emotions and belief unfiltered, unthought, simple, simpleton? We're not that way. But are the costs? Well, a couple of months ago, Mikhail Gorbachev, former head of the Soviet Union in Ronald Reagan's time said it looks we are preparing for war. I think there is a link between our ignorance, our distraction, our judgments of others, our nationalism or racism, our hatred, our exclusion, our judgments and heading to war. These are great techniques that are used by corrupt and destructive leaders throughout history and it hurts me to say that.

Now I'm known as a collaboration expert. To many I'm an environmentalist. To many I support both renewal energy and nuclear energy and I have spent much of my career in the Canadian oil industry, so there's a judgment. My judgment may not be clear and balanced. I am potentially in conflict. I was told by an angry Californian a year ago David, you're a Canadian, therefore you are the reason our children will die. You are going to promote the tar sands. No. I facilitate intelligent inclusive and collaborative conversations. Probably for the last two years, my most common public talk, keynote workshop, is creating shared value. That's the business strategy that says number one, we protect the environment. Number two, we take our directions from the community and those of us entrepreneurs who do it in that order, environment first, community informs and then we take our strategy and provide services and products that way, we'll succeed. We have an advantage.

Now, that is difficult, creating shared value. What's that? We need to sit down and talk about it. One of my favorite online newspaper, news media is e-Know. Friends of mine in the East Kootenai's have e-Know.ca. About a week ago I saw and article "Oil companies need to pay" on e-know. Big oil British Columbians. We're the Northern California. More than 80 community groups from across British Columbia have signed an open letter arguing that the fossil fuel industry must pay for climate change. The letter was delivered to190 municipalities and regional districts in BC and 50 signed. Fighting climate change only works when everyone does their fair share. The fossil fuel industry expects communities to pay the cost to adapt and rebuild yada, yada, yada. I consider myself an environmentalist, but I take exception to this. If we're always blaming the other, if we're always focusing on the other, it's just not going to work.

Do you know the oil industry in Canada has paid in 2013 alone $18 billion in taxes and employed 550,000 Canadians? In the next 20 years, the oil industry will generate $1.5 trillion in taxes to federal, provincial and local governments. So, let's stop raising prices and raising taxes. I want to talk about – we could go on for hours. I have so much to say with respect to Hollywood stars and environmental groups distracting those intelligent people from the real energy conversation.

What's the conversation we want to have? What's the conversation we need to have? Where do we want to be 10 years from now? Is it renewables, is it nuclear, is it fossil fuels? Is it something completely different? My hope is its conservation. In my book and in my teachings, my workshops, I talk about the collaborative learning game.

So rather than being triggered and having a short attention span, not knowing the difference between intelligence and social media, try this. Instead of arguing or agreeing with each other, allow yourself to engage in a simple game that can take five minutes or 50 minutes. Here's the rules of my learning game. With others, select a hot topic. Make it a hot topic. Seek agreement to know how each of you will play the game. Have at least three debaters each taking different positions. Debate fairly and passionately. Yeah, do this. Debate fairly and passionately, identify what you don't know, where are the gaps, what's the resources that you need, who are the people you need to ask? Then identifying who will find out those gaps in your knowledge, establish a plan, come back once you've all finished your fact finding and celebrate your collaborative learning together.

What is critical thinking? Go to criticalthinking.org. It's one of the great sites. It is really asking the question instead of being engaged or enraged, ask what are all the perspectives around this? I'm reading here. Well cultivated critical thinkers raise vital questions and problems, formulates them clearly and precisely then gathers and assesses relevant information using abstract ideas to interpret it effectively. This brings the critical thinker to well-reasoned conclusions and solutions testing them against relevant criteria and standards. Thinks open-mindedly. Yeah, we need to do this. It sounds boring but are we really goldfish? Are we really that simple? I don't think so. We are complex humans with great prefrontal cortexes with an ability to figure things out together. Here's the Socratic principle, 2,000 years ago, 2500 years ago, "The unexamined life is not worth living" because Socrates realized that many unexamined lives together result in an uncritical, unjust and dangerous world. That's from the critical thinking website.

A great initiative for critical thinking is to get us together and learn together. Play my Collaborative Learning Game.

Another great advance is News Literacy Project – look it up online. It's a non-partisan national education not for profit that works with educators and journalists to teach middle school and high school students how to sort fact from fiction in the digital age. Yeah, isn't that brilliant?

How do you get to the better conversation? It's not by yelling or telling or debating, it's with curiosity. When faced with a heated debate, difficult conversation, attention angry, judgments, don't escalate. Be curious. Ask a lot of questions. Invite them to think critically and express why they believe what they believe. A curious and learning conversation opens dialog and opens the possibility that we both may be wrong. That is where the new wisdom is available and the innovation.

Right now, I've got my good friend of Doreen Liberto. She's in California. Now Doreen's experience includes the collaboration of program management, land use, environmental, transportation, climate change, resource management, sustainability and communication strategies, stakeholder facilitation and team and organizational capacity building. She specializes in complex situations, complex stakeholder engagement. She does it in a collaborative fashion. She works on sustainable land use planning, resource management, environmental analysis, alternative transportation system, greenhouse gas reduction, water management issues, permit processing. Doreen received her graduate degree from Pepperdine School of Law in Dispute Resolution. She's a member of mediators beyond borders, climate change team, working with the United Nations on international climate change agreements and was in Paris December 2015 for the COP 21 meetings. Doreen and I have been friends for about two and a half years now. We are partners in the Collaborative Global Initiative.

Doreen Liberto, thank you so much for joining us. Anything that you'd like to start off with before I start in my questions?

Doreen: Thank you, David, for having me on today. I want to say that this is certainly an interesting time which we live and there are many challenges, and collaboration and encouraging people to collaborate is probably becoming one of the bigger challenges that we have. I look forward to doing more work with you David. I know you'll be in California in April and we're talking about doing some work together then and doing some work on a book, and I'm looking forward to that.

David: Yes, I'm well into my portion at writing and so is Doreen with respect to this very topic. How do you turn ignorance, anger, separation, judgment into collaborative successful learning conversations? We haven't finalized a title, but that's the theme. I think the other thing that I want to share with everyone is Doreen and I will be starting a webinar.

Doreen and I have talked in the last few weeks about the article on the December 19 edition of *Time Magazine*. Joel Stein wrote a wonderful column regarding 2016 being the year of the lie. Oxford dictionaries chose post-truth as the – I guess I can't lie before I start to choke up. Oxford dictionaries chose post-truth as the 2016 word of the year. Doreen take it from here. Like there is so much here. Especially with your background; you've done so much with respect to land use planning, collaborative conversations, transportation, climate change, medical marijuana. We've also hosted some conversations about nuclear energy. I want to open it up for Doreen to share her perspective with respect to collaboration, critical thinking and this age of lies.

Doreen: Well thank you, David. I'm going to start out and reiterate that it has become more difficult to get groups and individuals to collaborate, much less compromise. It appears that over time our values have shifted, and our views have shifted to a point where we've become sporting teams and one side wins, the other side loses. Of course, what we advocate in collaboration is finding common group and then finding a win-win for everybody. Unfortunately, it seems that we're getting further away from that. We look at fake news that people are willing to believe fake news. We have people, and I love this term, uncompromising differences and that is based on my value, based on my principle, I am not going to talk to you. I am not going to change.

When I first started out working in this field many years ago, we would agree to disagree and say we'll agree to disagree but let's come up with some mutually agreeable evidence that we can present and then maybe we can compromise. Then what I found was that people on the other side would come in with their attorneys and we ended up, it became a legal issue and you found that you were no longer agreeing to disagree and then try and find solution on your own, now enter attorneys. The attorneys would then threaten to sue if you don't do the following and you would try to compromise and sometimes you compromise too much, or you'd end up in court and you wouldn't like the outcome of what the courts did, one side or the other. People got a feeling that I won, while the other side felt they lost and it seems like we've drifted further apart from that legal system to a point where it's now become personally.

We are now dehumanizing the other side. By dehumanizing, what I'm saying, is a psychological process where the opponent's view views the other side as being so different, being viewed as being non-human and not deserving any type of respect. Not deserving any type of empathy. I think unfortunately we're coming to that point where it's difficult to get groups to sit down and talk because they're dehumanizing each other. All we must do is just look at the political, the presidential campaign in America that just past and listen to some of the things that were said advocating violence, dehumanizing other people, making fun of people. That's certainly not something that is going to encourage either side to want to compromise, much less collaborate.

I was reading this article the Reason for War and there are two things, and this is an article by Jackson and Morelli. Two things in the article that they mentioned that when you know that you're heading to war – and I bring this up, David, because you mentioned earlier in the program about the former Soviet Union president talking about heading to war. There are two reasons for it. Number one, one side must expect a greater gain for going to war or conflict, and it's going to outweigh the costs involved. The second one is failure in bargaining, inability to reach mutually advantageous and enforceable agreements. When I look at this I feel like we're halfway there in sense that we have a failure to communicate with each other. We're having a failure to compromise, much less collaborate. Not only that, but we tend to believe lies.

I call them accepted lies. That's there's fake news and part of that I think is on social media.

We now can really focus in on opinions and websites and podcasts that agree with our point of view. It's almost like an echo chamber. We hear what we believe. We don't want to hear anything else because we've dehumanized the other side. They're not worthy of being listened to. I will tell you that that really does concern me, and it does make it much more difficult. I do work with environmentalists and as David mentioned earlier, he does work in oil and gas. I've talked with some of the environmental groups about sitting down with people in oil and gas. They're response has been no, they're evil. They'll just trick us again. Absolutely little desire to sit down; it's wanting to fight.

David, I've had this conversation before about how do you do it? At this point David, I've concluded that we really need to change maybe the way we view what's going on. I don't think just talking about is going to help. I don't think just acknowledging the other fake news, yes there are accepted lies. I think we need to start looking at it much more globally and possibly look at setting up dialog groups.

David: Let me just jump in there for a moment, Doreen. Listeners, some of the conversation that Doreen's referring to is about nine months ago Doreen and others invited me down to San Luis Obispo. Two directors of the organizations said wow; David's Canadian, he's had a career in oil and gas, so he's going to bring his salesmanship for tar sands and he's going to be the reason we're all going to die. Of course, the critical thinking part of that was uh - interesting. I've never been involved in the oil sands. I'm a proud Canadian. I believe in responsible energy sustainability. I believe Canadian energy has higher environmental standards and better regulation than any other nations including America.

I asked to talk to the organizers. I reviewed my role as a convener, a critical thinker and a challenger. After about 20 minutes on the phone, I grew frustrated. I told them that if they only every wanted to talk with the people that agree with them, then I had no interest in working with them.

Do you know that while the tar sands are blamed for the death of the world and our future, there are six California oil fields that emit more CO2 emissions then what the Canadian oil sands do? While President Obama blocked the Keystone XL for political, environmental and emissions reasons, America proceeded to build more than 10 equivalent Keystone XLs within their own boundaries. So, we need some critical thinking. Shut out Canadian energy so you can sell more of your own. That's not about Climate change, that's simple business. And business monopoly.

I was again invited to San Luis Obispo. When we did our workshop and had those conversations, we realized that we could dream a common future based on common values and aspirations, that we could collaborate with diverse groups with different perspectives and that I could positively connect the anti-nuclear groups, the Pacifica Gas and Electric interests, the community, the renewable business, the academics. Together, we set an intention for a true collaboration to explore and develop what their energy future might look like. We can Create Shared Value.

In 2017, there is so much animosity. Such much hatred. So much blame. So much misunderstanding. Limited dialogue.

The Trump administration got there, in part, due to the venom they spewed on the Obama administration. The Trump Administration now seems only intent on tearing apart anything that Obama's government did. Where is their dream conservative for America?

We can blame the Tea Party and some Republicans for a lot of this hostility and negativity. We can blame the environmentalists. We can blame the sun.

Now, in 2017, we're seeing in Republican town hall meetings, the hostility and negativity is turned on the Republicans now that they're the government. They can't control what they've started. An estimated 30% of Americans like Trump. One thing I like about this mess is we now have an activated political, social and environmental generation that are stepping up to create our shared future. The git of Trump's ways is to motivate change. And it will not be the change he has been pushing. I don't believe it is Democratic either. Neither America party seems to understand that a big shift is happening, and they are not seen as the leaders or the visionaries.

With our Collaborative Global Initiative, we said let's stop talking about who's to blame and start talking about where we want to go and how do we get there together.

Doreen: I think that's an important point. I think it's also important to point out a couple of other issues and that is where are we heading? As I mentioned, since I became involved in this field many years ago, it has gotten progressively worse. While there have been some bright spots of collaboration, I would say globally, we seem to be heading down this road where it's going to be zero sum gains. That is one side is going to win; the other side is going to lose, and I think at some point we must stand up and say how do collaborators, mediators, facilitators, community activists, decision makers step in and say it's time for a dialog. Time out; we need to bring the opposing sides together and we need to start doing that now.

I want to cite something that Stanford University did several years ago. This was in Ireland over the Protestant/Catholic differences. They brought in groups; some Protestants and some Catholics brought them in to teach them how to collaborate, how to listen, how to reframe the discussion. These were people that were adamantly opposed to one another. After they were taught that, they sat one Catholic and one Protestant across from one another and asked them, how do you feel about each other? One was say I hate that person because he's Protestant. And I hate that person because they're Catholic. Why? Protestants killed my brother. The Catholics killed my sister. And then the facilitator, mediator sat there said wait a minute; let's talk about what the common ground is. You have this anger. You have something in common, don't you, and you both feel the hurt that happened by losing a loved one – you both have that in common, that feeling. It was allowing them to be empathic to the other person even though they were on opposite sides.

What they did from there was basically bring these groups together, the Protestants and the Catholics, train them, sent them back to Ireland to work together in communities in community groups. I would like to see something like that happen in dialog groups where groups of people, both sides are willing to come together, sit down, train on listening, train on other issues to form a dialog, go back into communities and start talking. I think we must do it from the bottom up because I don't think it's necessarily coming from our leaders, this type of dialog.

David: Yeah, I think that is so critical, and we started our Collaborative Global Initiative. The first things we thought about is that there is an estimated 4.5 billion people connected to the internet. When we want a dialogue, and get diverse critical thinking, we could have a Skype meeting, a Zoom meeting, a virtual meeting any time, any place. We just need to know who those people are and create the networks to have these critical dialogs and learning conversations.

Doreen: Right. I think the other thing that we all need to do, and I'm part of this, is we all need to stop dehumanizing other people and understanding that they have a point of view that we may not agree with. But try and find out; as you said earlier, listen to the other side. I love the type of example that you provided with the exercise you provided. And that is sit down, and we'll get three people, both sides of an issue and then talk about it. I would like to see that extending into dialog, and that is which I think where you're talking about is basically give me your position, give me your position. And then trying to be beyond dehumanizing the other person as being bad or evil, and try and understand what the other person is saying and empathize with them, and understand where they're coming from. I think we at this point must take it to that level.

David: Yeah, so, so critical. I'm the oldest guy on the air and I know that I don't know very much. If I've got the right dialog, the right connections, the right people to challenge me and inform me, I'm better off.

Doreen, before we close this segment, maybe if you could talk a little bit about the webinar that we're going to start March 9.

Doreen: I'm excited about this webinar because I, and David I know you are too. We've talked about it – have become very passionate about how do we collaborate in an era of lies, alternate facts and fake news? How do we get people who will not sit down with the other side? How do we bring people together, so we don't end up going down this path of a war? How do we bring the two teams together to collaborate? What we're going to do as part of the webinar series is first we want to dialog. That means I don't have all the answers. I think we need to dialog about what really the issues are, what's happening. We really need to take a very serious look at what's going on in our societies and in ourselves too. Then start talking about where do we want this to lead? Do we want it to get worse? If we want to improve it, how do we improve this? What do we do to bring people together to collaborate? It doesn't mean that we're going to win, and I think it's not even looking at it as a win-lose anymore. We're in it altogether and I think that's how we need to look at it, that we need to start working together better and stop looking at the other side as the enemy.

David: Thank you so much Doreen Liberto.

Doreen: Thank you David. Talk with you soon. Bye-bye everyone.

David: If you're listened to the song Win, Win, Win or Walk Away, you're about to listen to Chuck Rose, who wrote and performed that song. He's allowed me to use it for our Voice America podcasts. At the end of this segment, the end of this live show, we will hear We Are One by Chuck Rose. It's what Doreen was talking about before the break is how dare we think we are separate? How dare we think that we can segregate and be hostile to each other? One of my friend Chuck Rose's favorite leadership comments and greetings is lead from love, not from hate.

Chuck, I'm going to give you a little bit of an introduction and then help our listeners reacquaint themselves with you because you were on my very first podcast in September 2015. So, thank you again for that.

Chuck Rose: Wow, yeah. Seems like it was just yesterday.

David: Before I introduce you formally, it's cool Chuck because Camille Nash, our executive producer on this show, informed me that when we had a bit of a pause for several months in the show, our listenership went up. I hope that now we're back active and we're doing another series through 2017, that I don't drive that listenership down. I think this series and the advice and speakers like you are really going to attract people. Our biggest listenership areas are Sweden, England, Texas, California, China. While you and I spend a lot of our time Calgary, Alberta, Canada, it's not our friends that are populating the big growing base of this Break Through to Yes.

So, Chuck is a professional speaker, entertainer and musician, and he is an expert on customer service and team building. Like me, he's got over 40 years in his business. His business is hospitality entertainment. On February 1, 2017, Chuck retired as managing partner of one of Calgary's most successful pubs; the Hose and Hound Neighborhood Pub. It was a converted firehall, heritage firehall. Chuck does so much. He was successful because of his management and leadership skills. He speaks with business owners on improving staff relations, staff retention, customer satisfaction, and inspires managers to be leaders. Chuck believes in abundance. There is enough for everyone. Just like his words say, there is enough for everyone if we can just choose love over fear. Our Break Through to Yes with Collaboration theme song, Win, Win or Walk Away and We Are One can be listened to at chuckrose.ca. That's chuckrose.ca. Chuck, before I start asking you some questions, anything that you'd like to say to our listeners?

Chuck: Yeah, listening to the little bit that I heard of the previous guest, this whole thing of connection that we are already one, it comes back to me time and time again that the golden rule is not optional. What we do to other people, we're doing to ourselves. The whole dichotomy between love and fear, the people in the world who are trying to take advantage of other people, trying to get more than their share, trying to take a disproportionate amount of the benefit of being here, those people are just hurting themselves. They're hurting other people, but they're hurting themselves as well. When we come to that realization, so many of these problems that we're having in the world right now are just going to fall way. They're going to melt away when people realize that you can't win if you don't make sure that everybody else wins at the same time.

David: Yeah. It's more than walking away. It is creating that new dialog, that global dialog. This is bigger than Trump, bigger than Trudeau, bigger than anyone, Angle or Merkel. This is us. If I might, there is an example in the *New York Times*. When people want to destroy and blame and shame and be, I don't know, racists, nationalists, fascists, sooner or later it will come back, and your karma will get you. I don't know if you saw there was a *New York Times* article just yesterday Chuck on the February 22 *New York Times*. Some of us watch Bill Maher. he's a little bit too out there for me sometimes but I find his guests so interesting. On the weekend, he interviewed Milo – I don't even know how to spell it, Yiannopoulos. And Yiannopoulos is an expressed anti-Muslim, anti-Jew, anti-transgender, anti-everything. He's talked about sex with boys. He's just a nasty piece of work. He's senior editor for Breitbart; a nasty piece of business, a nasty man. I consider him one of those people that I would like to blame, but rather in this show we've been talking about opening dialog and critical thinking and shining light on things. When Bill Maher interviewed Milo, he was condemned for why are you interviewing an extreme right-wing guy like that. Guess what happened? Once that was aired, Milo lost his Simon & Shuster book deal. He lost his speaking spot even at the current political action conference, conservative political action conference. Even the right-wingers of the conservative political action conference, well he's not one of us. He's said to have resigned from Breitbart.

So, sunshine heals wounds I'll say. You put it out there, it will come back and bite you. If you serve the world, if you serve dialog and learning and inclusion, that's the only way you and I and Doreen and billions of others can live. Chuck, we've talked on this show about the age of lies and fake news. Is fake news anything new?

Chuck: Anybody who studies history sees that propaganda goes back forever. In the 20th Century, in the 19th Century, Mark Twain quoted – I think he thought he was quoting the British Prime Minister, but it was one of those sayings that was ubiquitous. There are lies, there are damned lies and there are statistics. The bottom line was that everybody was lying.

Then in the 20th Century, the Nazi's came along, and Hitler was the proponent of the big lie. The more outrageous the lie was, the more likely people were to believe it. His right-hand man, Joseph Goebbels said if you repeat a lie often enough, it becomes the truth.

And now, and I'm not equating him to the Nazi's, although there's certain similarities, and we've got Trump saying, and I quote, "I play to people's fantasies". You know it's one of those things where you tell people what they want to believe, you appeal to their fear, you appeal to their prejudice and they'll accept what you say as true and they'll act on it. It's all this separation between love and fear. The bottom line on it is right now Trump is talking about fake news. He's talking about lying newspapers. He's talking about the news media as being dishonest. The place where they're most dishonest according to him is whenever they point out how dishonest he is. Free press is so essential. That doesn't mean that a free press that agrees with you. That doesn't mean a free press that spouts the party line, that just repeats what the president says. It means a free press that's allowed to question. It also means a free press that has a point of view. That doesn't mean that they're going to tell the truth all the time. They might selectively tell. You really must look past one news source. You can't just trust one news source. You must look past that.

David: Yeah, I'm thinking about Eli Pariser's talk on Ted talks on filter bubbles. It's not just that President Trump gets his briefing from Fox News as opposed to the American Intelligence Agencies, it's all of us. We can't trust the Canadian Broadcasting Corporation. It's wise for us to also read and listen to the *New York Times*, the CBC, news in China, news in Japan, news from England, news from Cuba. Once we embrace that diversity of wisdom and perspectives, then we can find our own truth.

Chuck: It's essential that we understand what other people's beliefs are and the only way to understand that is to listen to their news source. If you want to understand ISIS or radial Islam or the Arab world, you've got to listen to Al-Jazeera.

David: Yeah.

Chuck: Sometimes you're going to hear the same news story from a totally different angle and you're going to realize that to the people in ISIS, they're heroes. They can consider themselves to be heroes, and they're the ones who are on the side of the good of God.

David: They equate themselves to the early Americans fighting the British. They are nation builders.

Chuck: Yep.

David: We've only got about a half a minute left Chuck. This has gone way too fast. I just want to ask you one more key question. Is democracy broken? What are your thoughts on how do we fix it?

Chuck: Oh, I have half a minute to talk about that? Yes, democracy is broken and the biggest symptom of that right now is that all we can do is kick the bums out. No elections in the last little while have been elected so that we can elect somebody because we're for them. It's always been a case of we're rebelling against somebody we want out. That's a sad situation.

David: Yeah, we've seen in America, we've seen in Canada, we've seen it in England.

Chuck: Yep, and here in Alberta, which is I know a lot of your listeners are going to think that's very far away, we've had the same situation where we kicked out a group of corrupt politicians and to kick to them out, we got somebody who is just scaring the daylights out us in a lot of cases.

David: Yeah.

Chuck: The same thing. In Washington, they said we don't want the status quo. We'll give anything to get something different and they've got Trump.

David: Yeah, we got change. Chuck, we're going to have to get together next time when back in Calgary because this is an ongoing conversation. Thank you so much. Before we close We are One, I want to close the show to say thank you everyone for listening, for thinking about critical thinking, the news literacy project, creating global dialog, getting beyond all of this. Practice my learning game. If you want a copy of the rules, email me. Thanks Chuck. Thanks Doreen.

Now we go to what we believe is our salvation is We Are One.

Chapter 6 Collaboration, Europe and Rotary International featuring Elisabeth Delaygue Bevan and Florian Wackermann

David: Welcome [*and welcome in French, German, Swedish, and Spanish*]. We have listeners in 32 countries. I'm delighted to have Elisabeth Delaygue Bevan of France and Florian Wackermann of Germany today. Our theme is Collaboration, Europe and Rotary International. This is such an important podcast radio show for all of us around the globe because every day we hear about politicians, communities and people being fearful of others. We hear about the rise of the extreme right wing. We hear about the rise of a new generation of activists. We talk about closing our borders to immigrants and to trade.

We hear fear. We seek something better for ourselves and for our grandchildren and children and our grandchildren's children. We are better together. Through collaboration and Rotary International, I believe we will breakdown misunderstandings, create friendships and create goodwill. My questions as we start today:

1. Listener, are you concerned about our global future?

2. Does the current state of politics and social debate create some fear for you and your family?

3. Do you believe that your children and grandchildren's future is being jeopardized?

4. Ask yourself, why is it important to connect and serve internationally? Why is it important for you and for all of us to connect and serve internationally?

5. Of course, the theme of the entire radio show series that's gone from 2015 through 2017 so far, why collaborate?

I want to start off with my story about the Rotary Friendship Exchange. I joined the Cranbrook Sunrise Rotary Club about six years ago hoping to be a significant part of the business community, the social community in Cranbrook, British Columbia, Canada. What I realized is this is such a global movement, a global movement that I witnessed, and my wife witnessed when we participated and led a Rotary Friendship Exchange. In this time of wall builders, isolationists, narrow perspectives and fear of people from other nations, the Rotary Friendship Exchange's purpose is to bring people together across the globe for reciprocal visits, education and ongoing connection. We've got that.

The Four Way Test of Rotary International is;

1) is it the truth?
2) Is it fair to all concerned?
3) Will it build goodwill and better relationships?
4) will it be beneficial to all concerned?

Those four questions of the Four Way Test are, I think, about 100 years old or more. What better way to think about how we collaborate, how we negotiate, how we relate, how we connect The Rotary Four Way Test, look it up. In April and May 2016, Rotarians from British Columbia, Idaho and Washington State were hosted by Rotary clubs in the south of France including Toulouse, Montpellier, Revel, Carcassonne and more. There were so many great places. We were treated royally.

We made great new friends in the Languedoc area of the south of France and from our district in Spokane, Washington, Kennewick, Washington, Coeur d'Alene, Idaho and Grand Forks British Columbia. We were delighted that some of those Rotarians from the Languedoc-Roussillon area, Midi-Pyrénées region in the south of France visited British Columbia, Idaho and Washington in August. Specifically, the Toulouse and Balma Rotary Clubs came to the east Kootenay's as part of a 16-day exchange tour of Grand Forks, Cranbrook, Sandpoint, Kennewick and Spokane. It was wonderful and a wonderful show of Kootenay friendship, Rotary friendship, volunteerism and generosity.

The Rotary clubs of Creston, Kimberley, Fernie, Cranbrook and Cranbrook Sunrise collaborated to give our guests a special introduction to the many features and the great lifestyle of the east Kootenai's on the west side of the Rocky Mountains. Some of the highlights include the Creston Valley, Tenaha Museum and Guide, St. Eugene Mission, the Cranbrook Railway Museum, history museum. Fort Steele, Wild Horse Creek, a barbecue in Rotary Park in downtown Cranbrook where we danced and laughed and had fun. Marysville Falls, Kimberly, the North Star Rail Trails, the Cranbrook Farmers Market, the old-growth forest trail at Island Lake. Some of those trees are 800-year-old cedars. And, a tour of downtown Fernie. Special thanks to the five Rotary clubs and dozens of member volunteers and their presidents and leaders including Riley Wilcox, Sandy Zeznuck, Gwen Twelling, Randall McNair, Patrick Barkley, Carla Nelson, Bud Abbott and friends, Marlena McFarland, Jim Caputio, Ron Popoff, Heidi Romich, Don McCormick and so many more for their hard work and open hearts. We enjoyed great meals with all five clubs.

Why is a Rotary Friendship Exchange, RFE, important? Well, here's some of the benefits. A, increase friendship, education awareness and collaboration across the world. Our guests, Elisabeth and Flo will talk about their initiatives and how we can work together and collaborate to help others. It also circumvents the prejudice, ignorance, isolation and helplessness that is too prevalent in media, social media, politics and communities today, it seems like it's more than ever or at least more than the last 50 years. It provides an opportunity to learn language, culture, history and perspectives.

It creates collaboration and influence and power to volunteer projects bringing our own communities together so people that live in the same city, same town, village, area collaborate. And, it engages our guests as ambassadors for Canada, British Columbia, Washington and Idaho. Equally important it invokes the potential of economic alliances, entrepreneurship and leadership for our region. Airbus and the Kootenay's Rocky Mountain International Airport, College of the Rockies, golf and ski resorts, housing, center of excellence, shelter box, end polio, these things can benefit because we work together better, and we can collaborate with our combined strengths and resources.

Rotary Friendship Exchange is a great way to travel the world and show off our communities and see others. Our guests and families plan to return for longer periods of time. My wife and I plan to visit our hosts and new friends in France again this year. We're hoping that some of our French guests will come back here and spend time and we're hoping that we will spend up to two and a half months in the south of France. We think people like Maryann and Ron Jenkins, Judy Wivchar and Roger and Magella Brown for hosting. And our guests were Michele,

Marie- Josie, Benita, George, Cathy, Lawrence and Michelle. They were all good friends that we will open our homes and hearts to at any time now. We would hope our families will build on that connection.

In addition to Rotary Friendship Exchanges another way to cross these boundaries, break down these walls of ignorance and create learning and opportunity is the Rotary International Youth Exchanges. High school age students from around the world go on exchanges for up to a year. They have the opportunity to learn new cultures, ideas and languages. Today, our Cranbrook, British Columbia, Canada club is loving Klara Fernlof, an exchange student from Sweden. She teaches us about Sweden and her world and experiences ours. She teaches us about what it is to be a 17-year-old in Sweden. In the past couple of years our Cranbrook Sunrise Rotary Club has hosted youth leaders from Switzerland, Italy, New Zealand, Australia and many more great nations.

I am hoping our grandchildren will live in another land for a year as part of their Rotary experience. That could be my greatest gift to my grandchildren is helping them get the opportunity to be on a Rotary International Youth Exchange. So, here's my idea. It's actually – I like to put out an idea each week in our broadcast. This one is not a new idea; this idea is the object of Rotary. This is published by Rotary. The object of Rotary is to encourage and foster the ideal of service as a basis of worthy enterprise and to encourage and foster first the development of acquaintance as an opportunity for service. Second, high ethical standards in business and professions, the worthiness of all useful occupations and the dignifying of each Rotarians occupation as an opportunity to serve society. Third, the application of the idealist service in each Rotarians personal, business and community life and fourth, the advancement of international understanding, goodwill and peace through a world fellowship. That's right, international understanding, goodwill, peach through a world fellowship and it truly is a fellowship, of business and professional persons united in the ideal of service.

This morning at my Rotary Club I was honored and delighted to introduce Peter Hisch, a professional forester as the newest Rotary member in the world. Peter is a professional, a perfectionist, a good friend and a man that puts service above self. I'll give you a glimpse of just one more local member of my club. This is an interview taken on Dennis Parsons, who is a 15-year member in my Cranbrook Sunrise Rotary Club. So, here's what Dennis had told us, "Rotary has a motto that states service above self. The fact that Rotary works in the local community as well as the international community appeals to me," this is Dennis. "Within Cranbrook Sunrise Rotary, I was the director of international service for a couple of terms and was able to work with other Rotary Clubs in establishing microcredit loan programs in the Philippines. Designed to help impoverished women bring their families out of poverty. I was also the Cranbrook Sunrise Rotary liaison for the Honduras market children program which helped children afford to go to schools, so they could get themselves out of poverty by getting a better education. I had the pleasure of being the Sunrise Club president 2006-2007. Rotary International has a program in place to train and motivate the incoming presidents for their year in office. This program is called PETS- Presidents Elect Training Seminars and it benefits a Rotarian even well after their term of service in office. I've been involved in several volunteer ventures some of which include the

Friends of the Library book sale, Rotary Club sells books and helps funding for the library. There is so much to do, so I respect Klara Fernlof of Sweden, Dennis Parsons of Cranbrook, Peter Hisch of Cranbrook and many more.

The fourth objective of Rotary is the advancement of international understanding, goodwill and peace through a world fellowship of business and professional persons united in the ideal of service.

My call to you, listener and fellow friend, whether you're a Rotarian or any other service club or doing this on your own. My request, call to action is in the next ten days, contact three people in different nations and talk about how we may collaborate and advance international understanding.

We live in a time of the internet. We are more connected than ever there is an estimated, I think it's four billion people connected on the internet. We have Facebook, LinkedIn. We have friends, for those of you that have friends internationally, make a call, make a Skype call a Zoom call a telephone call, whatever it is. I challenge each one of you and invite you to reach out to three people in the next ten days who you do not know and who live in different lands. Let's create that fellowship.

Now, after the break we will be joined by Elisabeth Delaygue Bevan and Florian Wackermann and we're going to talk about their experience. They are both leaders in Rotary in Europe. Let's take a break and we'll be right back.

David: Welcome back everyone. I want to give a special thanks to Marie-Josie Caire. She is the leader of the Rotary Friendship Exchange in the Languedoc-Roussillon area of the south of France that cared for us so greatly and introduce us to Elisabeth and Flo. So, thank you Marie-Josie. I would have loved to have you here, but I know that your other commitments kept you away. Let's turn to Elisabeth Delaygue Bevan of France. I met Elisabeth in Montpellier and Elisabeth is a true international leader. She is someone that represents Rotary and international global leadership and service. She is a mother of five children, two of whom are Rotarians and one is in Rotaract. She's a doctor, a specialist in nutrition with her own clinic. She joined Rotary in 2004 in Rotary Club Pézenas. I'm sure I'm not pronouncing that right Elisabeth. But, you can – district 1700 she was the club president 2009-2010, assistant governor in 2012-13 and 2013-2014, district governor 2015-2016 and has participated in seven international conventions. Part of the organizing committee of the Rotary Institute in Montpellier in October of this year, 2017 and Elisabeth, welcome. Anything that you want to say before I ask you some questions to get us started?

Elisabeth: I'm fine, thank you. I'm very happy and honored to be part of this conversation and interviewed for this with special listeners. It's very interesting for me.

David: Let's start, Elisabeth. You are a leader, international leader, in Rotary. What is Rotary?

Elisabeth: For me, Rotary is a worldwide organization of professionals. You've been talking about it already quite well, but I think you want to make it special by saying that we meet regularly to help our community and to create lasting change globally as well. I think our big strength is that we have different intellectual diversity, I would say, and we share different views concerning one same problem, so it's a strength and it helps us to get over some difficult problems. Our goal is really to serve above self and we engage ourselves with a wide diversity of backgrounds, perspectives and expertise.

David: Thank you so much for that. A couple of things that are very important. The diversity of perspectives, that balance, that international perspective and you also highlighted too that it is – while we're focusing on this show, the global opportunity for Rotary and fellowship and understanding and service at its foundation it is a local organization that serves locally very powerfully. Elisabeth, what are the principal projects of Rotary?

Elisabeth: Now, I think we have quite a few projects. One of them is to fight illiteracy and poverty and we want to promote clean water and sanitation and we take part in the fight of different diseases. For example, 30 years ago polio was endemic in 125 countries and now only three countries are endemic. This is because Rotary joined efforts with UNICEF and big organizations and this was possible because of Rotary starting it. We try and help to buy equipment for medical researchers, we organize blood drives, we help young people and provide scholarship to students around the world, free scholarship. You said it before, we provide Rotary Youth Exchange in different countries for the young people and the Rotary members, they prepare the young people to their first job interview and that is very important for them. In France, we have lots of refugees now and we try to help them integrate and find jobs and by doing that we hope to break the cycle of poverty in these poor communities. I think that's really what is very important for me.

David: Thank you so much. Now, on the international level, what are the main occasions for meeting other Rotarians from other countries? How do we do that as Rotarians?

Elisabeth: Well, you were talking about the Rotary Friendship Exchange, but we have the annual international conventions every year and this year it will be in Atlanta because our Rotary Foundation was started there 100 years ago. We have presidential conferences in different countries with themes which are based on our main programs and we have institutes in each area of the globe. This years, Europe and French speaking Africa will be meeting in Montpellier, France in October. The theme is very important because it will be Rotary acts with young professionals. I think it will be very passionate. These meetings are important because they allow us to build friendship and to understand different cultures and to make important decisions, really.

David: I will come back to the Atlanta conference, the world conference in Atlanta this year. I understand that Bill Gates, a long time Rotarian, will be a key note speaker speaking about Rotary and his involvement and passion. I also hope that my wife and I will participate, be in the district conference that you're organizing in Montpellier for October.

Elisabeth: We're looking forward to seeing you.

David: You have some asks there, let's talk about that because big conferences with significant objectives like this, what help do you need?

Elisabeth: We need money, I'm afraid. We need some sponsoring. We would like to have some participating a person who can help us to organize it. Yes, it would be very interesting.

David: We will talk more about the conference and more about your involvement and your districts involvement shortly. Before we turn our attention to Florian Wackermann of Germany I always ask my guests a final question. What's one thing that you'd invite our listeners to change, to be aware of or to do?

Elisabeth: I think it would be possible to challenge some of your listeners to sponsor the institute in Montpellier.

David: Wonderful. How do they get a hold of you or is there a website we can send them to, Elisabeth?

Elisabeth: There's a website on Rotary Institute Montpellier 2ol7.com. They will be able to participate in any possible way it would be lovely.

David: Great, thank you for that challenge and it is a service and an opportunity to build fellowship and connection. Now, from Germany, from Bavaria, we have our next guest, Florian Wackermann. Now, Florian has lived, worked and graduated from universities in France, the United States and Germany. He holds a PhD in economics and has worked in managing positions in the food and tire industry. Besides, he's a motivational speaker with – well I'm not even going to try this, Florian.

Florian: It's a rhetoric's class and it's giving speeches on how to give speeches to motivate people when they need to get up in front of other people that they can really get a connection with their audience and make a lasting impact. We're teaching people how to give great speeches.

David: Would this be like Toastmasters?

Florian: In a way. It's more focused on the individual and really getting people ready to speak at whatever occasion they need to speak.

David: Thank you, that is such good work. I'm a director of the Canadian Association of Professional Speakers Calgary Chapter and the studies show that people would rather just about do anything other than stand in front of others and speak.

Florian: Exactly.

David: When we speak our hearts it is so easy and so inspirational. Thank you for that work.

Florian: Thanks.

David: Let's get back to a little more about your background for our listeners. Flo volunteers and is very involved with his community throughout his life in soccer, politics, in the family of Rotary and with Rotarian activities being the biggest part of the last years. He belongs to the Rotary Club of Germering, in the suburb of Munich, Germany. Besides taking responsibilities at the club and district level, he served in Rotaract as co-chair of the global Rotaract and Interact community. Let's talk about that a little further. Let's there is so much about Rotaract, Interact, well Interact committee and let's help me understand a little bit more before we go any further, about Rotaract. Flo, can you explain what Rotaract and Interact do for Rotary within Rotary?

Florian: So, Rotaract is the youth organization of Rotary for all those people aged between 18 and 30. So, it's really meant to give young adults the opportunity of serving, of learning and widening their horizons and of making friends who share similar interests. It's very similar to Rotary, organized in pretty much the same way and it's tailored and focused to what young people between 18 and 30 need and care for. Similarly, with Interact it's for people between 12 and 18. Same thing around the world, much more connected with some adults who advise these youngsters even though their projects are tremendous even in Interact. It's really a similar thing to Rotary yet it's for young people between the ages of 12 and 30.

David: Listener, I hope you understand this. Where ever you are, if you're in Sweden, London, California, Columbia, in western Canada, at least, Rotary used to be seen as a bunch of older white guys doing volunteer work. That's changed so quickly. I know our club is very young, very female and increasingly diverse. What Rotary, what Rotaract and Interact that Flo has just explained to us, it's so important to get them supported as young leaders and Rotarians who serve our planet. Thank you both, Elisabeth and Flo, for that. Flo, what's so special about doing volunteer work in an organization like Rotary?

Florian: It's always surprising that people are willing to spend their Saturdays in conference rooms while you could just go out to the park or go to ski. The impressive thing in the family of Rotary is that you can really make a difference, which is, like the examples that you are mentioning, there are tons of situations where people come up to you and say, "Oh we should do this" or, "shouldn't we do that?" Or, "Couldn't we?" In the family of Rotary, there's always someone stepping up and saying, "Let's do it." So, you really make a difference in an engaging and dynamic atmosphere. And, while this is true of many non-governmental organizations, I guess the thing that separates Rotary from many others is that you really learn new perspectives every day with this diversity that is meant to be there.

So, you should have in every club people from different backgrounds besides when you meet internationally you meet people who have completely different everyday routines from yourself. The third thing is that you make wonderful friends. It's whatever you're willing to roll up your sleeves and pitch in and help then you're more than welcome to join. So, that's the inspiring, engaging atmosphere of Rotary where it's really you can make a difference, you can learn new perspectives and then you make friends with it. From my perspective, that's what's so special about doing volunteer work in Rotary.

David: Can you think of one example, one person before we go to break, that exemplifies this Rotaract, Interact and the work that's being done?

Florian: Like Elisabeth mentioned, work with immigrants, we had a project in my club where we went with kids of refugees on four weekends in the summer. We went to the zoo with them. Once we were in this house of giraffes, they suddenly – it was a protected area and they suddenly became children again from these very cool teenagers, they were very interested in what a giraffe would do, how the digestion works. It's really you can feel how you make a difference for those kids and you suddenly become friends with people who share a completely different background from yourself.

David: So real and so important. We're going to take a quick break here and then we will be back with Flo and Elisabeth and we will speak, together, about breaking down the barriers and activating hearts.

David: We're back with Rotary district leaders from Germany and from France. We are with Elisabeth and Florian. I will finish with the one-on-one with Florian now and then we'll have a group discussion on Rotary and fellowship and the importance of service. In Rotary, Flo, leadership positions are only held for one year and then they rotate to different leaders. What barriers does this create and what are the positive impacts of this way of collaborating?

Florian: Yeah, it's true it seems sometimes strange or surprising to people not familiar with Rotary. To me, it seems like there are more positive impacts than barriers. While it's true that some projects or initiatives will be stopped after one year because the successor just isn't that much interested in it or that a new person will in the beginning always need time to get used to the new position. So, all those who have held the position before need to be very calm and give them this time to learn and that sometimes we are very sad that someone is leaving a position. You say, "He was such a wonderful president." Or, "He was so good in charge of setting up our program. That's sad for him to leave that position." But, on the other hand, there is so much that we can learn from this rotation.

For example, new ideas can always be tried out because everyone who is holding a position has this one year to really make it happen. So, we're not going to see this attitude of, "Well that's what we've always been doing." I've seen many cases where, like five years ago we discussed something and we're trying to implement a project and it just didn't work. Then, five years later there are young people or new ones coming into the position or just into the club and they have the same idea, they attack it in a different way and they just make it happen. So, this keeps us very, very innovative and always on the edge of what is thinkable or dream-able or doable. Then, you always have this pressure to get your project done within your term. So, if you want to make a difference while you're serving as president or district representative, you really must get your project to a finish line in this year.

This pressure that is inside of the structure will make you achieve things which is wonderful to look back at. Then, you have the last positive impact that I'm seeing is that you can try out yourself in different roles. It's really – some people feel very well being secretary or being in the second row. Once they're in the first row they experience how wonderful it is or vice versa, those who always want to be the leading person and then once they serve as president they feel like, "Well, I felt better at being vice president or being just in charge of the program." It gives us the opportunity to find our best leadership role while really achieving projects and making an impact. That's why I'm very happy about this rotation of leadership positions.

David: I think that also speaks to we are a team. There are no heroes, there's nobody that gets elected for four years. We do this together and we rotate the responsibilities.

Florian: Absolutely.

David: The theme of my radio show, my work and my book is collaboration. The theme of today is Europe and Rotary International. Flo, from collaboration and Rotary, what lessons can you take to the professional world?

Florian: I guess one thing is you should always talk about goals and the vision because if the people you work with see the objective or the point that you're going to, then they will be very happy to join in and join forces or join hands. To me, it's really communicating with clear goals and then it's a trust in the ones you work with because whenever you're collaborating, there are people who are doing things differently than you would and what you learn in Rotary is that a different way can be equally be successful. So, if you really trust the other person on whatever chore he is assigned to, then most likely you will have the result that will benefit all of us.

David: Yes, thank you for that.

Florian: the one thing I would put highest is to acknowledge other peoples' effort because in volunteer work, if you don't acknowledge or you don't praise or celebrate whatever successes you have then people very easily lose the eagerness or the fun of it. So, if you take this to the professional world, then acknowledging the effort and the contribution is really something that keeps people motivated.

David: Yes, engaged, diversity, innovative and service. What's one thing, Flo, that you would challenge our listeners to do, be or change?

Florian: Yeah and it links kind of to what you said before. Because I thought if people can call or write to someone that you meant to thank for their effort and just tell them thank you and let them know how appreciative you are of whatever this person has done that impacted you. I guess this is something where you can then create positive energy at the other person and will make sure that this person is going to be very eager to work with you again.

David: Elisabeth, please join us. Elisabeth, we talk a lot at the foundations of Rotary about values and ethics and who we are as Rotarians and how we are in the world. Why is Rotary important to you? What value or ethics does it speak about you?

Elisabeth: I think it's the – Flo was very clear about it. It's the personal development that you gain when you are part of Rotary being a treasurer one year, being a secretary another year and being the president. You learn such a lot from these different positions. I think it's a real gift as Rotary and it's a gift that you want to share with other people being part of this organization and to be able to not change the world but add a little piece to the whole scheme of life. You feel so happy to be able to add – we say in French, add a little stone to the whole building. I don't know how you say it in English. You feel like part of the big scheme. Is that clear for you?

David: Yes, that makes perfect sense. You are – we are each placing our stone and building that foundation, building that structure for fellowship, for security, for safety.

Elisabeth: Peach and fighting disease and all these projects, all these programs. None one is better than the other. It's always fabulous, interesting to have the ideas of the others and to work all together. It really is very exciting.

David: Flo, you the same?

Florian: Yeah, totally. What is so inspiring to me is that you meet with people who take their own responsibility first. It's not always asking what someone else must do but it's this question of what can I do? And then, you have tons of ideas and that's why you have this diversity of projects and so it's this leadership development within ourselves based on values that are really of taking responsibility for the world we live in and that is tremendously dynamic or inspiring for everyone who participates.

David: Flo, you've got a PhD in Economics. My degree, my bachelor's degree is in economics. I always felt economics was my way of understanding the world and history. Along that, is there an economics frame for Rotary for you?

Florian: Totally. On two levels. One is the maximization of benefits for our lives and in life, it's not always the monetary profit that we take from something, but it's being with friends, being in an aspiring group. The second thing is there is some way that young people need to develop leadership skills. You can do this within an environment of schooling which may be as far away from the real world. Or, you can do it by being active in non-governmental organizations like Rotary. So, there is a dual benefit of being active in a volunteer organization that it's fun with it and that you're getting happiness out of it is really making it even more worthwhile. So, I guess even from an economics viewpoint it would make sense to sacrifice time for Rotary.

David: Elisabeth, you are a very highly respected leader in the Languedoc- Roussillon district in Montpellier. You're hosting this amazing conference in October. Also, one of the wishes that I have for my grandchildren is that they will go on Rotary Youth Exchanges and ultimately, I will be able to host more Rotary Friendship Exchanges and go on more on my own. We noted in your introduction, Elisabeth, that three of your five children are – well two are Rotarians and one is in Rotaract. Why did they choose that, Elisabeth? What's important to them about their involvement in Rotary?

Elisabeth: I think it happened because being a mother of five children I took them where ever I went on a project. I took them with me and they were very happy to be part of this whole atmosphere. I remember my little – the younger one, Victoria. She went to picking up – you stand at the end of the supermarket and you ask people to give part of their trollies for people who need them. I don't know what you call it. It's a sort of collecting goods for the other people. One old man came to my daughter and he gave her a box of chocolates and she wanted to put it into the whole collection. He said, "No, no this is for you." And my daughter was very moved by this and she said, "No, no." He said, "Yes, I want to thank you for being helpful and participating in the collection." Since then, they've all wanted to be – you get more when you receive more when you give. You know what I mean?

David: Yes.

Elisabeth: So, they became Rotaractors and then Rotarians because they could see the importance, the gift it was to give. When you give your time, you give yourself, you get much more back.

David: Before we close this show, I'd like each one of you starting with Flo, to just give us a final thought. In this era, age of lives, separation, fear, ignorance, immigration, what's one final message that you want to give to our listeners in the 32 countries on behalf of you and Rotary? Flo, if you could start?

Florian: I guess in every country you have some person in history that stands out as an idol, as someone positive. There's nothing holding each of us back of being a role model for the people around us. That's what Rotary asks us to do with service above self. It's something that's extremely fulfilling if people look up to you as a guidance and as a helping hand or a hand reached out across nations, across countries and across all these prejudices that are brought forward in such a crazy and surprisingly harsh way. It's really step up and be the role model that you can be.

David: And Elisabeth?

Elisabeth: I think probably because I'm a doctor I think very important is to listen to people and when you listen to them, it's already a gift because so many people are in such a rush all day long, nobody listens to them and they feel left out. As soon as you listen to them they feel understood and they feel better. I think Rotary is a community of people listening to other people and it's important, I think it's the joy of it really.

David: Thank you so much, Elisabeth and Flo. I couldn't have said it better. This is exactly the message that we want to share with the world to build understanding for the three of us and millions of others, we found Rotary as a perfect venue to do that. Again, our call to action is listeners, in the next ten days, contact three people in three different nations and talk about how you may collaborate and advance international understanding. Think about what you might do internationally in a not for profit, in a service club, in Rotary if you wish and consider a Rotary Friendship Exchange. Everyone, thank you for listening, this has been an honor to interview Elisabeth and Flo. They are people I dearly respect for their work and their leadership. Let's work together better.

Chapter 7 Collaboration and Human Sexual Trafficking featuring Lance Kadatz and Cliff Wiebe

David: Greetings everyone. Thanks for coming back and listening to *Break Through to Yes*. This is David B. Savage. This is a critically important podcast and show today. I've got two experts: Cliff Wiebe and Lance Kadatz, that I've come to know in the last few months. Our topic today is critically important. It's sad, it's horrifying, and you can be part of the change and fixing this or at least minimizing it. Our theme today is collaboration against human sexual trafficking. This is a horrific experience. This is about people who do not have a choice. This is not something that I think our values would allow me and probably you to go unnoticed and to a large extent it has gone unnoticed.

Today I'll be asking Lance Kadatz for his wisdom and advice and how he's collaborating to collaborate against human sexual trafficking. Lance has been the executive producer for the last two years for a feature film called *She Has a Name*. You've got to see it. I saw it in Calgary a few weeks ago, it is excellent. It was released in December 2016 and it is hoped that it will raise awareness of human trafficking. Also with us today is Cliff Wiebe. Cliff is the strategy officer for Next Step Ministries in Calgary. Next Step Ministries helps women exit sexual exploitation in Calgary and in Alberta. We know there are initiatives like this growing around the world. Of course, there's the police agencies, Interpol, there's the United Nations.

Here's two men that are taking a stand with their groups and collaborating with others for something that is so important. Just to try to land it a little bit, today we're going to explore the global reality and the local reality of human trafficking and explore ways we may collaborate to fight this horror. Start asking yourself some questions and these are some of the answers that we'll get in the next hour. Why does human sexual trafficking exist? What's the importance of choice? Does it exist in your home area? What's being done and how can I reach out and collaborate to reach women and girls, men and boys? There are huge costs of not stepping up and reducing this.

How I got involved was a good friend of mine, Donna Hastings, who is the leader of the Heart and Stroke Foundation of Alberta, the North-West Territories and Nunavut. Donna is, also, on the board of Next Step Ministries. When she told me about this problem and the local impact in the city of Calgary, I was horrified. How can this be? How can we just turn our eyes away from these girls, these women? What about choice? It's a gray area when we talk about human trafficking. The gray area might come in, well, what about women that make a choice and sell pornography or whatever? There's a whole values and ethics piece around that. I really want to differentiate todays conversation with Lance and Cliff about choice.

This is trafficking. This is inhuman. This is not a woman or a man making choices on how to make a bunch of money. This is crossing our ethical and well, just so many boundaries it's hard to believe and it's very real. What are we talking about? It's not what you might think it is. It's much bigger. For some reference, go to the United Nations online documentation look at any number of sites. Watch the film *She Has a Name*. Go to talks with people like Next Step Ministries in your area. It happens, and it happens throughout cultures. According to the Federal Bureau of Investigation, in America human trafficking is involuntary servitude, involuntary servitude.

They're not business people, they're strippers. These are people that are slaves.

"Human trafficking," now I'm quoting from the FBI, "human trafficking is believed to be the third largest criminal activity in the world." Third largest criminal activity in the world. That's horrific. It's a form of human slavery that must be addressed at the interagency level. Human trafficking includes forced labor, domestic servitude and commercial sex trafficking. It involves American citizens, Canadian citizens, Swedish citizens, Malaysian citizens, everybody. There are no demographic restrictions. They talk about smuggling, modern day slavery, beatings, starving, drug addiction, lack of identity. Women and girls being basically enslaved.

So, a little bit of definition to start us off, from the FBI, "Domestic sex trafficking of adults is when persons are compelled to engage in commercial sex acts through means of force, fraud or coercion. Sex trafficking of international adults and children is when foreign nationals both adult and juvenile are compelled to engage in commercial sex acts with a nexus to United States, Canada, Columbia, through force, fraud and coercion." This is just horrific. They are our daughters, they are our sisters. We've got to step up. What I'm going to do now is I'd really like my new friend and mentor on this subject, Lance Kadatz, to step in.

Lance has been the executive producer for the last two years, as I've said, of the great film, *She Has a Name*. It's not a documentary but it tells a great story. It tells a story that needs to be heard to activate and mobilize. Lance hopes that the film will raise awareness of trafficking through partnerships with agencies around the world. He expects to fund freedom by sharing revenue with their existing partners and new local partners to save thousands of people currently in bondage. In January 2017, Mr. Kadatz retired as the chief financial officer of Rifco National Auto Finance, a publicly traded company on the Toronto Stock Exchange venture. Lance co-founded Rifco in 2002 which lent over $750 million during its time.

Lance was a finalist for the Ernst & Young Entrepreneur of the Year Award for Western Canada. Lance Kadatz has been and will remain on the board of directors of Rifco. Prior to founding Rifco, he had a corporate career in corporate banking with the Royal Bank, etc. He has five children, nine grandchildren and a lovely wife, he tells me. I haven't met Maureen yet but I'm sure. And yes, there is a focus especially when we see people being trafficked as our sisters, brothers, daughters, sons, granddaughters.

Lance, welcome and I've got a few questions to ask but any preliminary comments you want to share with our audience?

Lance: Thanks David, for inviting me for sure and for attending the screening in Calgary. It was great to have you there and the introductions that you've made since that time are going to be fruitful, I'm quite confident in that. I think it's just great to be here and I'm anxious to try and shed some light on how we are trying to impact this huge, huge problem of human trafficking.

David: Yeah, Lance, since that screening in Calgary we've heard of a similar project to what Cliff will be sharing with us in a few minutes in Houston, Texas. I'm sure there are projects around the world. But, it's a necessary conversation. What I'll say since my attendance and meeting you in Calgary at the Plaza Theatre, I've had this conversation and everybody I talk about the film, *She Has a Name*, says, "Wow, how do I get involved?" So, let's start with how did *She Has a Name* come to be, Lance?

Lance: The film started as a labor of love, for Andrew Kooman who is the writer of it. He was working in Malaysia in the late 2008 or '09 area there and became aware of the human trafficking problem and he, the statistics were that he was faced with were just overwhelming to him. UN estimates that 2 million children are exploited every year in the global commercial sex trade and less than 1% are ever rescued.

David: Lance, I want to say that again because when I heard that statistic it blew me away and I thought, "That can't be true." But, can you say it again about the 2 million and the 1%? That's incredible.

Lance: Yep. The United Nations estimates 2 million children are exploited every year in the global commercial sex trade and less than 1% are ever rescued and that includes young girls that are forced to sell their bodies as much as 15 times a day and the average age of children forced into prostitution is 12 years old. That was for Andrew, that was a daunting and overwhelming statistic that moved him to his core and as a writer, he wanted to do something so what he did is he wrote a play called *She Has a Name*. And the play was premiered in 2011, was critically acclaimed play, toured across Canada, has toured across the United States since then.

It finished – in January it finished a stint in off Broadway. The play is very impactful and was critically acclaimed where ever it played to sold out crowds and many of the reviews said, "This is such a powerful story that needs to be shared. It really should be a movie." So, the production team started on the project to make it into a movie back in about 2013 and obviously a movie can unpackage a story much bigger than the play can. So, I became involved in the project – there's five producing team members: Andrew Kooman, the writer; Daniel and Matthew Kooman who are the directors and producers and there's two other producers: Shari Aspinall and Donna Abraham. So, that is the production team and so that project came to me – as you said in my introduction, film production is not where I've been, where I come from.

I'm a financial executive of a publicly traded company that I've since retired from a couple of years ago. But, this project came across me, I was looking at it as an investment and got to know the team, fell in love with what they were trying to do, had seen the play, was impacted by the play and to be honest, I wasn't sure whether this group of young people, very talented young people, was going to be able to get this done. So, I decided that I would try to help in raising the money for getting this film made and as it turned out I was able to achieve that. That's how the film came to be. For me, the chance to – you know, human trafficking – I think human trafficking has – it's such a big problem. Human trafficking is one of the most prevalent, violent, destructive crimes committed globally.

The only crimes greater are the illegal drug trade. Human trafficking enterprise is $40 billion a year. We're all faced with how can we make a difference and I believe that by lending my talents to try and help this film get made, that there would be a chance that maybe I could make an impact and that maybe tens of thousands of lives could be saved, and we could turn the tide on that awesome statistic that only 1% are ever rescued.

David: Let me ask the question, I think it's important for our listeners to know why did you call it *She has a Name*?

Lance: That's a great question. I think it's because you know, I don't know the answer to it. I'm sure Andrew – I've never actually had the question posed to me before. But, I think part of the reason is the girl in the film is referred to by her room number, 18. You only know her by her room number and I think that the people in these situations have lost their identity. They are nameless, they are disposable. One of the statistics that I've recently become aware of that's put out through Exodus Cry in the US, which is a great organization, is that human trafficking probably is worse now than it's ever been, and part of the reason is that slavery has been around a long time but 100 years ago, the financial investment for a slave was material.

Equivalently to today's dollars it would be like $40,000. But, they put a price on a trafficked human being now at $90. That is basically a disposable person. And that is such – that's why I think it's called *She Has a Name* because all these people don't have names, they don't even have identities. They're just ... abused.

David: I know when we come back from our break we'll be continuing to talk with Lance and we'll also introduce you to Cliff. There is incredible work to be done here. She has a name, she's not number 18. She's just not a commodity, a thing to be used and abused. This is horrific. This is a place where people are coming together and collaborating and while we've got so much more to say, let's take a break now. We'll be back with Lance and then Cliff and listeners, Tweet @DavidBSavage or email me david@davidbsavage.com. To ask more questions and you can be directly connected with Lance, Cliff and I and others who are trying to make this big change. So, we'll take a break now.

David: Welcome back everyone. We're talking about how do we collaborate against human sexual trafficking estimated to be one of the leading global crimes, horrific story. Lance, before the break we were talking about *She Has a Name*. Why did you do it? What are you trying to accomplish through *She Has a Name*?

Lance: The film's made to create awareness for human trafficking in a dramatic story based on a true event. The event is a container truck that ran out of gas traveling into Malaysia from another country that broke down and by the time anybody got to it there was half the people in the container had died. So, the story is about two 15-year-old girls that come out of that container truck and it's the dramatical story of them. One escapes, and one becomes 18 and becomes trafficked into a brothel. So, we wanted to tell a story. In this story, you get a chance to see the despair of 18 and the hope that comes from the recovery system and aftercare.

It's a story that tugs at your heart and it raises the awareness, but it also mobilizes you to make a difference. We're trying to create a movie that can be used by the agencies around the world that are on the front line fighting human trafficking so that they could partner with us in the distribution of the film and share in the revenue that comes from the film through accessing their distribution networks and doing screenings and pushing the DVDs and soundtrack and those types of things. They can all share in the revenue. This was our way of mobilizing or trying to collaborate with all the agencies around the world that are fighting this battle. We currently partner with International Justice Mission Canada, Iris Cambodia, Global Act in Switzerland. It's a worldwide – we're trying to go worldwide with this for sure.

So, we believe that if we can put the face of a young 15-year-old girl on a problem as big as this, it's difficult for anyone to ignore it or want to ignore it. It becomes more real and once it becomes real you want to make a difference. That's where we're going with the film. The film is getting rave revues all around the world. It premiered in London and members of The Royal Family was there. It was in Cape Town and Belfast and it's screening in worldwide centers all over the world. That's our goal is to raise awareness and partner with the agencies so that through spreading the word of the film and that they can generate revenue that can enhance their ability to get people back off the streets.

David: So, how do people connect with you, find out more? Tell us a little bit about the website or any suggestions of how people can reach out and bring your film and create a discussion group, create an active group.

Lance: Our website is shehasanamefilm.com and you can arrange screenings there, you can buy licensing for home screening kits, you can purchase DVDs and Blu-ray and soundtracks, and you can stream the movie through redemption codes onto your computer and you can even, if you have a business, you can have counter stands where the DVDs and soundtracks could be sold. We have these kits that you can purchase and help that way. Everything is driven from our website. You can also see, I think there's three trailers. You can really access us through that. In the US, you can arrange screenings on up to 300 different screens through Gathr (G-A-T-H-R). You can log on there and start to bring this film to a community near you. There's lots of different ways in which you can help fund – we call it funding freedom by just watching the movie and participating you can fund freedom.

David: Wonderful, now I'm going to transition over to Cliff because I know that *She Has a Name* and the global impact and awareness that you're having might allow people to think, "Yeah, it's happening in Cambodia and Malaysia" or where ever. No, it's happening within blocks of your home. In Calgary when Cliff and I met a couple months ago, I asked him the question, "Well, in this area, in the Crescent Heights area of Calgary, is there an impact? Is it here?" Cliff proceeded to tell me how prevalent it is in every neighborhood in every city in every culture. Future shows we might have an opportunity to talk to police, to social workers, to groups trying to intervene on behalf of Aboriginal women who are being sexually trafficked. So, as I transition to Cliff Wiebe, I just want you, the listener, to know that wherever in the world you are, it's there and these humans need us.

Thanks, Lance, we'll get back to you a little later. I want to introduce my friend, Cliff. Donna Hastings introduced me to Cliff several months ago and suggested that I'm an expert in collaboration and maybe Cliff might need some help because he's got a lot of people activated. HE's got a great plan, great initiative. So, I just want to collaborate with Cliff and Next Step Ministries and serve the word that this is not only global but it's local. So, a little background on Cliff, he's worked on international and domestic setting addressing poverty issues for the last 20 years. After obtaining his undergraduate degree, both he and his wife spent three years living and working in Indonesia. Upon returning to Canada, he received a graduate degree in nonprofit leadership from Trinity Western University. From there, he went to work for organizations like Compassion Canada and Samaritan's Purse.

Through volunteering with Inn from the Cold in Calgary in 2007, Cliff saw that there was poverty right in his own city of Calgary and made the shift from working internationally to working domestically. He realized that although poverty might look different in various parts of the world, the root causes are the same everywhere which are broken relationships at many different levels, the need for collaboration. Since working domestically, Cliff has worked for great organizations like The Mustard Seed and Next Step Ministries where he's currently a strategy officer. Next Step Ministries helps women exit sexual exploitation in Calgary and in Alberta. Cliff, thank you for joining us. Any opening remarks you'd like to make, Cliff?

Cliff: Well, David, thank you for having me and Next Step Ministries on your show today. You know, you and I met just a few months ago last fall at a Catholic Diocese fundraising event and we sat next to each other. We were talking about this issue and you were saying, "I didn't know about or I don't really want to know about it." But, one thing that you've done which is just amazing and is that you've taken this knowledge about what's going on here and around the world around the issue of sexual exploitation and sex trafficking and you're doing something about it so quickly. I just want to thank you for picking up the mantle, really, and bringing awareness to this issue on your platform, so thank you so much.

David: Well, thank you, Cliff. This is huge work, huge life work that you and others in Next Step have been doing. I just can't imagine the third largest criminal activity globally and if I recall correctly, I believe you told me that even in the city of Calgary, there's an estimated 3,500 women and girls being sold.

Cliff: Yeah. Calgary is just an average city in North America. We have about 1.3 million people here and the city of Calgary itself about four years ago did a study and this is just from what they found that there are about 3,000, about 3,500 women in sexual exploitation or sex trafficking here in Calgary.

David: The issue of sexual exploitation has been around since the beginning of time, unfortunately. Why is it becoming such a large issue now with so much awareness being given to it? What's happened? What's changing Cliff?

Cliff: I think a couple of things are impacting this in today's world. We know that prostitution and people using one another for their own gain has been going on since the beginning of time. But, our world has changed over time and we've become more global, traveling more, the ease of transportation and travel has increased and just recently, in the last 15 to 20 years the one thing that has just exploded this issue is the internet and online access to all kinds of information and images. When something is going on and I'll just say pornography – it's interesting you said it earlier, this is in everyone's backyard, I'm going to say it's in many people's homes. Anyone downloading pornography into their home is probably aiding the industry of sexual exploitation and human trafficking.

Even when it comes down to very much under age children that are being filmed in all parts of the world, there are no borders stopping that from coming in, right in to our homes and our cities here in North America. This is really increased peoples' I guess access to it and then also what it's doing and I'm just going to speak for men here for a little bit and what it really does to men is impacts especially young boys or whatever are exposed to pornography at an earlier age, it impacts their minds, how their minds are developing and how the social norms are being recreated in terms of how to treat people and especially women. And then, it goes from the visual to acting it out and that's why it's just exploding globally.

David: This is far more than objectification and passive viewing. This is a massive industry. These are our daughters, our granddaughters, our sisters, our sons our grandsons. I guess I want to say everything has an impact, there is that butterfly effect that whatever I do in my home in Cranbrook has an impact globally. Everything that happens in the world today, has an impact locally to me. It shows up in my energy, in my life, my values, my words, my boundaries and I just look at it and say it's not only available online, but I guess the gift of our digital connection, our 4.5 billion people that are now connected to the internet is we can change.

We have access to information, we have access to people like Cliff and Lance and thousands of others that are doing the good work. So, the awareness – since my conversation with Donna and Cliff and others at Next Step, I've had conversations with my children who have children just to bring them up to speed, what to look for, be aware of. Let me go back, Cliff, it's such an issue that you're really leading the charge on and it's not only in Calgary, Sweden, Columbia, Malaysia, Cambodia, China, but how do people – how does a community get organized and collaborate around an issue like this? How do we work together to address this problem? It's one thing to be outraged and horrified, but help us move to action.

Cliff: Well, we're still learning about this issue and how to get people together. A few of us just over a year ago here in Calgary were talking about this and said, "Who are some of the players in our community who would want to come together around this issue?" I was speaking with a couple of pastors of some very large churches here and out of that conversation started a collaborative effort called The Church Agency Collective About Sexual Exploitation. We decided just to meet with a couple of things just to say who's out there – first to learn about who is doing what already. Let's not start something new that somebody's doing.

And so, we brought all kinds of agencies and church representatives and everyone together and we meet every other month and the meetings are really about who is doing what, let's learn about how to do it well, let's make some connections within the group and then leading that to change. We didn't know what was going to happen because of meeting together but as of now we have over 130 people on the list representing 60 churches and agencies and government agencies. The government is interested in this as well. In Alberta, here we have Status of Women ministry and they send people to this meeting too. The ball seems to be – it's just growing. You know, when you get a group of people who are passionate about an issue like this starting to talk, to learn, to engage, to go for a lunch afterwards to say, "How can we take this beyond just the meeting" things start to happen.

Just for example, here in Calgary we have an event called the Stampede. It's called the greatest outdoor show on earth and people from around the world come to be a part of this big event every summer. It's a fantastic event but like so many of these sporting events it also attracts the predators and also the need for people's outlets when they're at these events and part of that is sexual. So, women are trafficked into Calgary every year to provide services for the people who are coming to this event. This year, at a city and at a high level, board level with the Stampede and the right people sitting there out of The Collective, feeding people information they say 2017 Stampede they want to be the safest Stampede ever and make it much more family friendly and they want to really attack this issue.

David: That's a very real example of the change we can make. It's time for us to take a break, Cliff. We're going to be right back with Cliff and Lance and we're going to continue to talk about collaborating against human sexual trafficking.

See you in a minute.

David: Welcome back. We're talking about collaboration against human sexual trafficking. I want to continue in this last segment. We're going to have an open discussion with both Lance and Cliff. I've got at least one more question. This one hour we have together is just an invitation, everyone. There's so much to be done, so much for you to do and get involved in. To segue into that, Cliff, what's currently being done in North America and where are the current gaps that need to be filled?

Cliff: Yes, well one of the things that I wanted to talk about too is there's two kinds of approaches. One is awareness which Lance and their film is really bringing a lot of awareness to it. Then there's the other side of it and that's the agencies getting in there and working with women exiting sexual exploitation, working with local police forces who have exploitation teams and when women want to get out, where do they go. Most cities and Calgary included, are setting up agencies to help women exit sexual exploitation. What's needed to make that happen is working with other agencies and organizations in the community but also most of these women are homeless. It's not only internationally where they have nowhere to go.

It's right here in our home city where they're homeless if they leave that work or leave that trade. So, we need to provide housing for them. We need to provide life skills for them, training and a lot of psychological and even spiritual work around post-traumatic stress. And, Lance said it and you said it earlier and that's their identity. They're not just something or an object to be sold but they have value and worth and can be a part of the community and society and really integrating them and working with them to enter back into society. I'd just encourage everyone to look in your own community what's going on and globally and go to the films that are coming out, the documentaries, *She Has a Name*. Go see it, go learn and then go and look at what's happening in the communities that you're living in and really get involved.

Maybe it's just funding it or volunteering or helping in any way they need. Just some current gaps definitely are quick access housing and supports around that. It's expensive to run and it's really needed. Lots of volunteers to just walk and do life with the women as they're moving through kind of the exit process. It takes a lot of grace and it takes a lot of long term walking with somebody to help them get out. So, there's lots to do and there's always more, for sure.

David: Now, Cliff, if this was a Hollywood movie and sometimes Hollywood doesn't show reality, but if this was a Hollywood movie we'd probably have guns a blazing and police crashing down doors rescuing these girls. From my understanding of the walk and next step and the work that you're doing with respect to housing, what would that look like? How are you encouraging the girls and women to get out of their trafficked situation, their slavery? What's that experience for them?

Cliff: Right, this could happen in a couple of ways. One is working with your local law enforcement. The police will sometimes do stings and go online and set up a false name and talk with the women who come to meet them at the hotel and say, "If you want to get out, here's how you can get out." So, you must have law enforcement involved with that part of it. Or, have a phone number – it's interesting next step ministries has an exit phone number that the women who have gone through our program spread all around to that community out there and they call. So, really, it's coming out, it's exiting, it's coming into a house and a home that's staffed where they can find stability, get healthy and start the process.

So, that's where like a safe house – also a safe house that must be anonymous, and it must be protected because a lot of these women have been involved in gang activity and they're leaving that world to get out.

David: Thank you so much. Now I'm going to invite both Lance and Cliff to discuss whatever you think is important. I'll ask some questions and just bring in your own wisdom as you wish in our conversation about how do we collaborate to minimize or reduce I'm not sure that we can ever eliminate it. But, let's just have a wide-open discussion, Cliff and Lance, jump in where you'd like. Why is this important to you?

Cliff: This is important to me and it's interesting because a couple of years ago when I first started working in this field of working with agencies, especially Next Step Ministries who are helping women exit sexual exploitation and think, what's a guy doing involved with this and speaking about it. But, you know what? This is a human issue, it's not just a female issue. My big thing on this especially the clear majority, statistics show, it is men using women. I say, "You know what? If guys are part of this problem, we need to be part of the solution." As much as we need both men and women involved in this issue, we need guys to step up and hold each other accountable and get the word out to say, "This is what's happening. This is help for you guys too to get out of maybe an addiction that you have to sex and using women in this way."

So, I just felt this is a breakdown – causing a breakdown of the family, it's using people as objects rather than viewing them and treating people as valued and worth. I felt I've just got to get involved with this. So, I did and I'm not a frontline worker but I'm an organizer, administrator, fundraiser, those types of things and I guess I can say God has used me to help in that area.

David: Lance, why is it important to you?

Lance: I want to sort of echo a little bit about what Cliff had just said. There's two sides to – our film is designed and we're working with agencies that are trying to steal girls back and get them out by partnering with Next Step Ministries. But, I know that in some of the screenings we've had especially at the premier we had talk backs. One of the question that came to one of the actors was, what was it like walking down the road in Pattaya, Thailand and seeing this? It was filmed right in the heart of that area. She said, "You looked around and you saw people that looked like your father, like your brother, like your uncle and it all looked normal. You had fathers with sons and fathers selling their sons, 'You can pick any one you want, son.'"

I agree with Cliff that we're failing – our society is failing and we, as men, are failing. We need to be better. Part of it is taking them back but part of it is finding ways to reduce the demand. If we reduce the demand, we will reduce human trafficking, it will just happen. So, I think we must work with our governments to strengthen laws and I think prostitution is – everyone needs to know that prostitution is not a job. Nobody grows up and says, "I want to be a prostitute." Somehow through drugs or coercion or whatever, they end up in there in prostitution. So, prostitution isn't a job. Prostitution is violence against women and that's a crime and I think we must view it that way and we must legislate it that way and we must enforce it that way. I think we would really like to see it stop from both sides of the saving the girls on the one side but also reducing demand on the other.

Cliff: Absolutely.

David: Yeah, this is not normal. Let's not allow this normalization. This is awful, this is human trafficking, this is slavery. This is addictions, it's abuse. Let's be part of the change. I want to ask both of you, I'll start with Lance. Before we close today, what's one thing that you'd really like our audience to do or to think about or become aware of or change?

Lance: Well, I can tell you the biggest obstacle that we have in the distribution of the film is the topic. The topic of human trafficking is a disturbing one and people, while they understand it, or they recognize that it's there, sometimes they don't want to know any more about it because they know they'll say, "I'm not sure I want to watch the movie because it might disturb me." But, what I want to tell people is that watching this film – the film was made to be part of the solution, not part of the problem. So, when you see, while the film was filmed in Thailand in real live brothels and real jails were used, but there isn't anything – they will look, and they will see dancers, or they'll be the most overdressed dancers that you'll see. That part of it's not real.

The movie in no way is pornographic. It tells a real story and it engages you, but it will not leave you with a visual that will scar you. It is finely crafted to be part of the solution and not part of the problem, so it engages. At the same time, you will see the hope, but you will also see the despair. So, for us, the film needs to be more than a film. It needs to be a movement in a battle against human trafficking. So, what I would ask people to do is watch the film, if they like it tell two friends. Make them watch the film and tell two friends. And so on and so forth. If that was to work, we could fund freedom in a monumental way and save thousands and thousands of lives. That's what I would challenge people to do.

David: Wonderful. Cliff, what's one thing in this moment that you would challenge our audience to do around the world?

Cliff: Yes, I think the one thing would be to not let this become the norm and David, you mentioned this earlier, it is fast tracking to become the normal way of treating others in our society. If you have a family, raise your kids to treat each other with respect and dignity and not as objects and that's not okay. If you're out with a group of guys or women and this topic comes up or belittling of other people comes up, change the conversation. Take a stand for the right way to talk about others and treat other people. And then, I would say take that one step further and work with your local government and even your federal government and bring people together to look at the laws and you can impact laws in Canada, bill C36 came in about two years ago. It's a Nordic model that says this isn't right.

Everyone around the person who's being victimized will be prosecuted but not that person. The US actually a group of people just stood up and said – I won't say the name of it- but an online hook up agency was shut down. Citizens can make a difference. In your own family, in your own community, speak up for how to treat people with dignity and at a government level work to make a change to shut things down that aren't right and enhance laws that give people hope and dignity.

David: Thank you and I guess I would add my advice, my challenge to our listeners is young girls, women with low self-esteem, lonely, whatever mentor them. It takes one person that believes in me to help me see my success, my brilliance. Some of the costs of human sexual trafficking is the loss of opportunity and the loss of possibility for these young girls and women. Let's help them become positive contributors to all our planet. They are a human resource, they're not a thing to be used and abused. Before we close, Cliff and Lance, just quick what's one last thing and I'll start with you again Cliff, what's one last comment that you'd like to share with our audience today?

Cliff: First, thanks for listening through the program. It's one of those things again, like we said earlier, it's easier to look the other way. But, if you stuck with this whole program and you've listened to it you're not. You're engaging. And so, find out what you can do. Find a local agency, go online, find a local agency working on this issue and give them a call, pay them a visit, learn more. Use education and use the people around you, become a part of the solution and get out there and help an organization. Even if it's funding monthly, organizations like us, and many non-profits can't do this without community support. Get behind it, get behind *She Has a Name* film. Go see it and bring other people. So, really get involved, act, use your voice, use your wallet and this thing can be turned around.

David: Lance, in the few seconds we have left. What's your last comment or encouragement?

Lance: Well, I think sometimes when we say we have a film and part of the proceeds are going to help fight human trafficking that people will automatically think that the film is substandard and it's not of the quality that will stand on its own merit. That is not the case with *She Has a Name*. You have seen it, it does not look like a Canadian film. It has the wow factor and it is Hollywood style as Calgary Herald reviewed, "A riveting, fast paced political thriller." It is, when you watch it you will be amazed that this is a high quality Canadian film.

David: We are out of time now. Thank you so much Lance and Cliff. This has been collaboration against human sexual trafficking. We'll talk to you again, thanks everyone.

Chapter 8 Collaboration, Human Resources and Global Networks featuring Amy Schabacker Dufrane and Japman Bajaj

David: Hey everyone. This is another important radio show broadcast. We're talking about global networks, human resources, collaboration and I think I want to subtitle this one as Zombies or Zippers. We'll get to zombie or zippers, just use your imagination as to why I'm talking about zombies or zippers when we talk about global networks, collaboration and human resources.

I'm very proud today. We will have Amy Schabacker -Dufrane of the Human Resources Certification Institute. Their main office is in the Washington D.C. area; and, just delighted to have Japman Bajaj, an executive at TELUS in Alberta. These are two world leaders, as you will hear. Amy will be in our second segment. Japman will be in our third.

I just want to set it up first for you and thank you for listening, thank you for being here to talk about Zombies or Zippers: Collaboration, Human Resources and Global Networks. The overriding theme today is human resources skills, capacity, innovation and collaboration.

Oftentimes, we think we don't matter or we have organizations that allow us to think we don't matter. We hear more and more about robots and autonomous stuff. We'll do a little pushback on that.

In my work in oil and gas, in renewable energy, in healthcare, in aboriginal economic development and otherwise, people always matter. Think about this for a moment. From your perspective, do people matter? Do they matter to your effectiveness, to your efficiency, to your sales, to your collaborations, to your bottom line? Do people matter? And I ask those very different questions, but they're very much the same.

Can we have one kingpin at the top of running organizations by remote, having robots create? Sometimes, some places, some industries, yeah, increasingly so. But we can't replace the intelligence and the agility and the innovation and adaptability of humans. So, if you say, do people matter, I ask, and why? Why do they matter? Why do they matter to you? Are robots cheaper, more dependable, faster?

So, when we're asking questions about robots or zombies – here's a third label, messengers – too often in organizations that I work with, I coach, I help develop their value and their capacity of their people. I'll use a disclaimer: I don't work on robots, but I do with some zombies and some messengers. People that just show up at work, go through the motions and just can't wait until they're out of there because they don't feel part of our organization. They don't have a role. They are just messengers for the folks at the top.

I don't think any of us wants to be in that position. I've heard some friends of mine say, I hate my job, but I've only got 10 more years to retirement. Wow, that's voluntary slavery.

So why are human resource professionals useful? Oftentimes, we cut and slash, and refocus and we try to dumb down. But why are human resource professionals useful? What do they do for us? What is being done today to build better organizations, more creativity, cost reductions and business success?

We're going to answer some of these questions and I'm hoping that you're going to answer some of them for yourself. What are you doing today and in the next months to build a better organization, more creativity, reduced costs and greater business success?

I am a collaborator. I am a connector. I've got connections around the world. I'm grateful to have a connection with you. The connections that I'm grateful to especially for this show are people that brought Amy and Japman to me.

I met Japman in Calgary just a couple of months ago, a brilliant new leader and thanks to David Mitchell of Bow Valley College in Calgary for that introduction. I met Amy and Julie Rosenthal firstly through connecting with Holly Burkett. She's the author of Learning for the Long Run, great leadership development skills, great book. Holly then connected me to Barry Lawrence, so thank you Holly, thank you Barry, thank you Julie and I'm really looking forward to introducing you in this hour to Amy and Japman.

Just a few days ago, I had two of my grandkids, Quinn and Sarah and we needed to buy some time. We love to do stuff together but on this occasion, I hate to admit it, but we went to McDonalds so that they could get a snack, be diverted and I could just spend a little bit of time with him while their mom, my daughter Alissa, was doing some duties, some running around time.

They brought up the story of the movie, Back to the Future. You're probably aware that Back to the Future went to, I think it was 2015. That's what Quinn and Sarah told me. And they were talking about hoverboards and flying cars.

It's not 2015 now. It's 2017 and there are significant advances in robotization and mechanization, autonomous trucks, autonomous drivers, all that stuff; autonomous things that will vacuum your floor. But what is the cost of robots? Where are the robots in your organization?

Back to the Future might have forecast that we're going to be all just going fishing, going skiing, sitting on the beach reading books in 2017. That hasn't happened yet, and I don't think it'll ever happen.

What I want to encourage you to consider, how do you develop your bottom line through your best resources, your human resources? So that's why I use the question, do you want zombies or zippers?

Zombies, messengers or robots are those staff members, consultants, leaders who just sleepwalk through their job. They do what they're told and nothing more. They are effective machines, but they're not human. They're not agile. They're not innovative.

I think we need to support zippers, those that bring people together. They collaborate. They work well in teams. They reach globally for resources and ideas and innovation, just like Amy and Japman are going to tell us about.

Let's be zippers. Just think of sewing in a zipper into your organization to bring it all together to make it fit right.

Many of you have probably seen the 2016 film Arrival, made by a Canadian producer, talking about extraterrestrials that come to us. And it's a great film. I recommend it. What they find is to finally communicate with the extraterrestrials, they not only have to learn the language together, learn how to understand each other, but at the end the survival of the human race lands on collaboration, working together at 12 different sites. 12

different sites must work together to meet the challenge, the interests, the invitation of those extraterrestrial beings that are so far more developed than we are. It's all about collaboration.

My long-term listeners will know that I'm all about negotiation, developing human capacities and skills, and teamwork. A couple of months ago, we talked about my collaborative leadership 360 assessment. I refer to that. People matter and robots or messengers, zombies, can't do much of these. These are some of the questions in my Collaborative Leadership 360 assessment that I work with organizations on identifying how well they work together. What are their strengths? What are the gaps? What are the capacities that need to be built on?

So, think about it. Are you a zombie or a zipper? When your 360 assessment is questioned, includes questions of you and those that work around you, above, beside and below you on the org chart, do you consistently deliver a positive and valuable collaboration experience? Do you hold meetings that are purpose-driven and focused on the end results?

This isn't yes or no. It's on a scale, Likert scale, but just think about these questions and see how you would rate yourself, how others might rate you and what you might change, with some training that Amy will talk about through the Human Resources Certification Institute, that Japman will talk about, about reaching out with organizations like TELUS and Soshal.

Are you able to adjust to changes that take place during the process? Robots don't do that very well. They're getting more and more intelligent. They're more and more able to think on their feet and evolve their thinking, but not yet.

Do you consistently deliver on agreed upon codes of practice, requirements, accountabilities? How agile are you in your ability to adjust to organizational changes?

In today's challenging business times, not-for profit times, just having messengers, robots, zombies in your organization will drive you right over the cliff. We need agility. We need innovation. We need the intelligence to go through. So, is your messenger, robot, zombie open to new ideas or realizations, or not really? Are you? Are you open to looking at diverse perspectives? Are you open to looking at diverse skills?

A sales perspective on organizations is very different from the operations perspective. The leadership perspective is very different from the perspective of the folks in the front lines, those of your customers, the families of your customers, the communities of your customers. Do you commit to your role and the impact you have on others? What is your intention?

Mostly, how do you cultivate the capabilities of others? Are they better when you leave? I should hope so. If they're better when you leave in the short term, then that's not a good sign. But our role as leaders is to make the system, the process, the paradigm, the people, the groups, the teams and the bottom line work better.

So, the call-to-action at this point is, think about where your zombies are. Think about how you sew into your cultural fabric, more zippers. Use that metaphor. Where are our zippers? Where can they bring us together globally, skill-wise, perspective-wise, innovation-wise, leadership-wise? How do we serve our future better? What's possible with that?

Imagine yourself as a champion in your work in 2020. You and your organization are celebrating a huge Break Through. Together you have accomplished what no one had dreamed possible. You are elated, and so are your shareholders or your stakeholders. Feel your success.

What changes did you make in your personal and professional life to get you to such great heights? What certifications have you earned? How are you as a human being and who is needed on your team? These are critical reflections, meditations. Be mindful of this. You might ask yourself when you wake up every day or when you shutter down every night: is my organization better today because I was here? Are the people here better today because of my influence and my vision, my collaboration and how I've supported their capacity-building and their network building?

Big questions, big challenge and that's what makes you above the rest. That's what makes you a zipper and not a zombie.

We'll take a quick break and we'll be back with Amy.

David: Welcome back everyone. This is a segment that is very, very important to me. Sometimes we try to take shortcuts in our organizations and what I'd say is human resources, human resource capacity building is not a shortcut that will benefit you. I'm delighted today that we've got Amy Schabacker- Dufrane.

Amy is the CEO of the HR Certification Institute, Human Resources Certification Institute, where Amy focuses on developing collaborative, long term partnerships in individuals and organizations to looking to create and deliver change around human resources. Before joining HRCI, she spent more than 25 years in leading human resources functions with organizations including the Municipal Securities Rulemaking Board, the Optical Society, Marymount University and Bloomingdale's.

Amy has been an adjunct faculty member at Marymount University School of Business Administration in Arlington, Virginia since 1998. So, she knows her stuff. She also serves on the advisory board of Columbia Lighthouse for the Blind and as a commissioner for the National Commission for Certified Agencies, that's NCCA. She is the recipient of the Leadership Nonprofit Award from the HR Leadership Awards of Greater Washington.

Amy holds the HR Certification Institute designation of senior professional in human resources. That's a pretty high honor, a high level of commitment to teams in working together.

She has an MBA and Masters of Arts in Human Resources from Marymount and a BA in Management from Hood College and Amy and I were just talking off the air about our long term, mutual interest in how do we get people to collaborate. So, Amy, welcome.

Amy: Thank you. glad to be here.

David: Let's start about this role that the HR Certification Institute and you and July, talked about Barry and the others who are working so hard to help our world and help our leaders. What do you think about the notion that with all this automation, i.e. robots – and I've talked about zombies – are taking over, replacing people and that there won't be a role for HR?

So, what do you think? Are we just going to go fishing, Amy? What's this all about? What's your perspective?

Amy: I think that HR, as we have known it has evolved significantly over the decades, the least that I've been in the profession. And it will not stop evolving. We know that based on reports in Harvard Business Review and reports from the different bureaus of labor statistics, at least here in the U.S., that HR is going to grow significantly over the next 10 to 12 years.

And it's because our people and our organizations are changing at such a rapid pace. And what an exciting time to be in HR because we are challenged to retool people because of this idea of robotics and artificial intelligence that's happening out there, and we are challenged by this. We're challenged because we must retool people because robotics won't replace us. They're going to amplify the needs that we have in our workforce, not only today but tomorrow. And there was a report that was just published within the past couple of weeks by Josh Bersin on this notion of automation, and that in fact people have said that robots are going to take over our jobs and we're going to, as you say, go out fishing.

But that's not going to be the case. We've got to retool ourselves, not only in HR but every worker would have to retool ourselves to rise to this challenge of being able to use our brains and really differentiate ourselves in the workforce. So, it's a challenge.

David: Yeah, it's bringing to my mind, Amy, that it's not only us versus them, robots versus humans, but robots need controllers. They need people to design them, plan them, program them. We must be agile and be in control of the robots. This isn't something that's just happening in an Orson Wellian scenario.

The speed of change, the challenges, the global challenges, we're seeing faster and faster, which creates opportunities and without the right people in the right places at the right time with the right skills, my company's going to miss out.

Amy: That's right. Yeah and economists are spending a lot of time kind of talking about this very notion as well, and they're saying and challenging CEOs to think about how do they differentiate themselves. And the biggest differentiator is their people. So, it's huge.

David: Yeah. When I used to run small oil and gas companies in North America with a few others, when we talk to investors, the response was always, you can do all the intelligent science, spreadsheets, all that data you want. But we only invest in people. So that's a strong reflection to say no matter how complex it gets, people matter.

Amy: That's right. They matter in everything we do.

David: In a 21st century HR organization, what does it look like? What are the other skills apart from being a subject matter expert do HR professionals need if they want to be successful? We've talked about the analytics, the business intelligence, digital. What does an HR professional need to be ready for and with?

Amy: I think that's a great question. I get asked that a lot and HR professionals need to understand the organization it is that they're working for. They've got to understand the business. How do they make money? What are their customers saying? What are the financial metrics that signify if something is a success or it's a failure, or an opportunity to get better?

So, having that strong understanding of the business, a strong understanding of the culture, the culture that the organization currently has, and are there elements of that culture that need to shift and change? So being that chief culture person who is making sure that that culture is morphing as the business is changing.

They've got to have strong financial acumen. So, this idea of analytics is important, understanding those key metrics, but it's having a strong understanding of the PNLs and what are those things that are growing or detracting from the business.

I think that that strong understanding of the customer is important. So, HR, having an opportunity to do an internship within your company so that you're working in different facets of the business, but what better way to understand what your sales team is up against, what your business development folks face every day, what are the financial challenges that are happening, that are occurring on your finance team? What are those marketing opportunities that we need to better understand and what people might we need to help us with those challenges?

I think those are all important skills that set an HR person apart from an HR person who's sort of the rules and tools HR person. So, you really need somebody that understands and you, as the HR person, must understand those metrics that differentiate your organization.

David: Yeah. I liked that rules and tools. The HR professional is in an increasingly challenging spot where they are, to use my metaphor for this show, they are the zippers. They're the ones that bring it all together. And not only bring it all together for what is in the reports from the past, but it's important for the HR professional to be able to foresee what's needed next in the 21st century. It's a challenging role and we've got to be ready.

Amy: We really do. And you can't bring people to your organization if you don't understand what those challenges are. What are you really searching for in the people that are going to move the needle for your organization? And you've got to understand those challenges to make those changes happen for your business.

I'll go back, and you'll hear about a lot of the articles that are out there in the press, really give HR a black eye. Although the articles are challenging to the function of HR, HR takes a lot of black eyes because HR is experimenting all the time, good people are because you need to see what will work within your organization. You need to do a lot of experimentation.

So, some experiments work and some work, and you learn a lot from those and you change, and you reposition, and you try again. So, I think that it's such an exciting time to be in HR and as I talked about before, it's really an opportunistic time for somebody who's looking for a career change, to jump into HR, because HR has a lot to offer.

David: I think it would be very appropriate to say before somebody can go into the C-suite, they must have HR capacities, capabilities to be able to do be that zipper in the organization. When you talk about a black eye in some cases, we're all about agility, performance, achieving the corporate or not-for-profit objectives. That can only be done with an agile, capable team.

We often are seduced into flat organizations where there's one person at the top and everybody else is equal. In my experience and in my consulting and leading for 41 years, if you're looking for short term results, that can be great. But if you're looking for agility, innovation, creativity and to fill spots for your organization that you didn't think possible, one person at the top can't do that. You need human resources aligned and ready. So, I've got…

Amy: I think to build on that a little bit, Mary Barra from GM, she is a person who started in HR and now she is running one of the largest, if not the largest carmaker on this planet. Has she faced challenges? Absolutely. Is she criticized publicly for what she does, but she also receives a lot of accolades for what she does. But she understands the importance of HR and the importance of having the right people to support you. So, I think she's a great example of somebody who is in the C-suite, leading a large organization who's really moving the needle in HR.

David: Yeah, and really moving the needle as General Motors is. They're a whole different company than they were in 2008.

Amy: I was just thinking about the mistrust that was happening in General Motors and how she really had to use her organizational design and development skills and organizational behavior skills to move the needle.

David: Yeah. Thank you for that. I think that's a great example, a real example for our listeners around the world. What would you say to a CEO about the importance of the HR function in their company?

Amy: So HR is the most important function of your organization. As I mentioned just very briefly before, the most important differentiator for you according to any article that you pick up, any economist that you talk to, is your people. And thinking about ways to grow your business, that is the single most important differentiator for growth.

I think that HR has got to be integrated across your organization in order to be effective. It can't be siloed. It can't be, as I said before, rules and tools. It needs to be a place that's full of creativity and opportunity to meet the challenges of the future.

And we know that this contingent workforce is growing. Right now, if you look at our entire workforce, 20% of those people are not employees of a "company". They're sort of an independent person. And if an organization isn't paying attention to the culture and they're not paying attention to people that make up their organization, they're going to lose that intellectual capital to this sort of independence and organizations will lose what it has grown and coveted for since the existence of that particular organization.

A CEO has got to be paying attention to this because you've got to have people that are committed to your cause, whatever your cause is, whether it'd be producing cars or reducing world hunger, whatever that cause is, you've got to make sure that you've got people who are very committed to what it is that you're doing, and you've got to cultivate that culture. And HR is the epicenter of making sure that your organization is moving forward and making sure that the people are engaged and are understanding where the organization is moving towards.

David: We've heard from Amy Schabacker Dufrane and what I've heard is as CEO of the Human Resources Certification Institute and in her life and in the people, she surrounds herself with, this is a no-zombie zone. Thanks Amy.

Amy: You're welcome.

David: Welcome back. Zombies or zippers, global networks, human resources and collaboration is the theme of our show today. I am very honored by a current and future global leader, Japman Bajaj. Japman is an innovation specialist and entrepreneur that has successfully built several initiatives, businesses and organizations over his career. He's an award-winning entrepreneur.

He is the co-founder of Soshal, one of Canada's top digital agencies, employing over 40 people and dominating Canada's higher education market. He is currently an executive at TELUS, one of Canada's largest companies and supports TELUS Health, Canada's largest health technology firm.

In addition, Japman is the founder of the Calgary Hub of the Global Shapers. You have the Global Shapers, a community of the World Economic Forum. Yeah, that's right, the World Economic Forum and lead that hub to attain global influence in just one year.

He was the co-chair of Shape Conference in Alberta, which is tracked as an international audience for the first time and wrote and compiled the innovative bid that not only beats out major cities like New York, Chicago and Boston, leading strategic partnerships, sponsorship and fundraising.

Japman is the co-founder of Gen Y Ottawa, actively involved in mentorship of young leaders and Japman is a sought-after speaker. He has spoken from a variety of stages around the world. Welcome, Japman.

Japman: Thank you so much, David. It's still humbling to hear that biography sometimes and it feels kind of obnoxious, so I apologize.

David: I guess people like you, I would affirm your success through your global network and just getting fellow visionaries together to make a difference.

Japman: Yeah. It's been interesting, just kind of briefly on the Global Shapers community in the World Economic Forum, we've spending a lot of time over the last couple of years here talking about what we term the 4th Industrial Revolution, which kind of talks a lot to what you've been talking about today around artificial intelligence and automation, and that profound question of, do people matter and then are we building societies in which people actually matter to us at a societal level, let alone a business level.

Some of these experiences have been eye-opening because they have, in fact, opened my eyes to conversations that I don't think I was having otherwise. So, I think the timing of kind of where I come from and where I am at today with this podcast, with this broadcast is interesting because now that I've taken a bit of a career shift in the middle of a big large organization, that we grapple with some of these topics but in a very different way and it's from a different perspective.

I'm really excited about our conversation today. I think there'll be a lot of cool insight that I'll gain and hopefully that I'll be able to share with your listeners.

David: Thank you for that Japman. And I think by hiring you, as I said to you a couple of months ago, TELUS shows that they are very innovative and smart, future-focused organization. I think simply, you are the connector. You are the zipper. You're the one that can bring people from around the world to innovate.

Let's start off with some questions. When people think about human resources, they tend to primarily think about getting hired. Has collaboration allowed you to access new opportunities for employment or business in your career?

Japman: Yeah. And it's interesting because there's a couple of ways to look at this. From the individual standpoint, HR really does primarily feel about all about recruitment, especially when you don't have a job and then hopefully you get one and it kind of evolves to compensation because once you get a job, you really want to focus on how you're going to be paid.

Having been on both the individual side and the organizational side of that HR function, the role of collaboration, it has the potential to be profound. I use that word kind of carefully because both individuals and organizations need to access and employ that potential for it to be of any value.

We often hear phrases, 95% of the jobs they're in the hidden job market or it's all about who you know. I think as much as we want to claim that we want to live in a pure meritocracy, I think the fact is that we don't. Political opinions aside, not to turn this into one of those, but I think you don't need to look too far from certain government offices to know that meritocracy isn't exactly what our systems are based upon anymore.

But that said, I think competency is still never been more important. You've been talking today about automation and AI, and we heard from Amy that kind of HR, as a function is growing. I think the truth is somewhere in the middle to be honest. I think the world is ill-prepared for this robotics revolution that's imminent.

I think as a result, HR is never more important than it is today because I do kind of think we'll have fewer and fewer people working in these traditional jobs that we've defined, so competency becomes super important. Collaboration becomes super important, especially if you believe yourself to be particularly competent because the availability of those traditional jobs and placements, I think at the very least, it's safe to say those traditional jobs are at risk.

To that effect, I think as you and Amy spoke about, culture becomes very important. I think it's important when we think about recruitment and collaboration, and a recruitment model to keep in mind the culture of the organization we want to work in. Coca-Cola's most innovative employee might look very differently from Tesla's or from NASA's.

Culture, maybe it's about who has more foosball tables for you as a jobseeker. But for some other people, it might be far more profound than that. So, culture is going to be a big driver.

David: Yeah. I think that the connections, because there's so much choice out there, yes, we could buy a program and have 10,000 resumes on our computer. But at the end of the day, it's about relationship. It's about belief. It's about trust and vision.

Japman: Yeah.

David: And you don't get that from robots. I think the other thing that comes up for me, Japman, is let's realize that the automation of our workplace is not the service industry. It is litigation firms. It is some of the top paid jobs available right now. Some of those people on the million-dollar club are at risk. They better know it and they better get ahead of this parade.

Japman: Yeah.

David: They do. It's through their network.

Japman: In some of my mentorship, one of the things that I try to talk about a lot is there might not be any greater skill any more than adaptability because Amy alluded to, the world that's moving so quickly, organizations are transforming so quickly that if you're unable to adapt, that might be your biggest downfall as a professional, as an individual. So, I agree with you 100%.

David: Yeah. So, one of the things that's most greatly impacting office and work cultures around the world is the telecommuting and teleworking. Many people have commented that such work style has greatly reduced the synergistic effects of face-to-face collaboration. What do you think about that, Japman?

Japman: Yeah, that's interesting, stemming right from this whole when we see automation and we think about how much we used to travel on a plane or a car or train to a bus to go from city to city to have these meetings and now, so much of it happens over video conferencing and teleconferencing.

I primarily work remotely myself. I work from home quite a bit or I work from remote offices quite a bit.

I mean I'd buy the argument that face-to-face collaboration is unbeatable. In my last life, when I was running Soshal, technology company, we were working with institutions that right down to social media, web and mobile technology development, even in the middle of that life, I remind people that the online component of your brand or your function or your organization or whatever operative word you want to use there, it's kind of like that 90% of the iceberg that's below the water. There's weight, context and substance there. It's important. There's value to what you don't see under the water. But that face-to-face contact really represents the thing that people can touch, see and feel and it has a ton of value.

But I mean, that said, I work in a global company with 50,000 people around the world. And oftentimes, I'm sitting on these video conferences and phone calls that try to traverse time zones, countries. It is mind-blowing how far we've come to close the gap, to try to make it as real and human as possible because if we're going to talk about human resources, it's not just at the individual level. It is the collaboration of teams within these types of companies.

I will always, I consider myself quite the old school millennial. I'm 30 years old today, but I often call myself the 80-year-old millennial. I think there's an element of the old school, that old face-to-face touch mentality that you just cannot replicate. I think there's an effect. I think we see the effect on true productivity when we don't get that type of touch.

It'll be interesting to see how it kind of continues to evolve and how far we get. Maybe there's a virtual reality component. Maybe one day, David, you and I will, the virtual reality headsets, we'll be wearing our headsets and we'll be sitting in the same room in our virtual reality headset world. But for now, I guess we continue to do things over the phone and do video conference.

David: Yeah. It works for me and it's greener, more sustainable. I love the face-to-face when it's important, but I love the fact that I can talk to my clients in Australia, my friends in France, is real.

Japman: Yeah. And that's an important point. Maybe I'm taking this as a small opportunity for a plug here, but my company now is very proud of its carbon footprint measurement or limiting and restricting how much we impact the world through that lens of environmental friendliness and that green lens.

So yeah, that's a big driver. That's a big motivator. It keeps our electricity bills down. It keeps our travel bills down, but it's also a big contributor to our environment around us.

David: Yes. It allows us to connect and understand from each other like never in human history. And at the same time, we can stay where we are, where we want to live with our families.

So Japman, we've only got a couple of minutes left but this is an important question. You are an entrepreneur. You've been in all sorts of for-profit, not-for-profit organizations of all sizes. And now you're a leader in one of the world's most advanced telecommunications companies, that's TELUS. Does collaboration impact small companies in the same way it impacts large companies?

Japman: Yeah. It looks very different. In my experience as a small company, a small startup, as a young 20-something was interesting because people around you, they seem to almost be bending over backwards to help you and to help you grow, and to help you become more viable.

It's an amazing – I mean, startups, in this day and age especially from a startup perspective, if you're not collaborating, you're dying. It's not even a measure of how much will you succeed. In many, many cases, it's just a measure of will you even survive.

I think when we think about that specifically at the HR function, we used to work with other small companies and keep an eye until letting go from their worlds and their companies, because the fight for talent is always so...we've talked about it today. Talent is the most important thing and companies talk about how people are their most important asset. And then in many instances, it's very, very true.

From a small company perspective, I find myself with my entrepreneurial hat on is, collaboration you seek it out and it's quite readily available; until it's not actually. I've had one friend of mine. She told me, people will always be out there to help you until you turn around 40. After you hit about 40 years old, you become everybody's competition. But until then, everybody is there to help.

On a big company lens, it's an interesting position of societal power, if you will, because a lot of smaller organizations come to you looking for you to be their commercial client, that big company first client. If you're a startup or a community organization, you're coming to TELUS because you want some funding or some sort of mentorship opportunity.

So, collaboration looks differently. It just ends up – it just looks different. It ends up looking more like a, we are the wielder of significant amount of power, whether it's through funds or sheer human resource and being able to, whether it's to people or leverage a volunteer initiative or whatever that is.

From a big company perspective, we end up collaborating a lot in our community giving or we end up collaborating a lot when we do things in maybe more rural and remote parts of a country because smaller operators can derive greater economic impact than we can, and we can help develop those parts of our country that way.

Collaboration just ends up looking very differently from those, going back to that kind of theme earlier, who leverage its potential. That is ultimately kind of a big characteristic that defines whether you're successful with your collaboration or not. The potential is there. You need to really feed that potential, otherwise it's just superficial and it's like a green card. It feels good once a year but that's about it.

David: We've had two amazing guests today and we're out of time. And again, we can go on for many, many more podcasts just on this very subject.

Japman Bajaj of TELUS, thank you so much. Today we've had Amy Schabacker Dufrane of the Human Resources Certification Institute.

And the issue is and Amy and Japman talked about, they're fighting for talent. They're fighting for the right talent. So, are today's times in the 21st century business a threat or are you the one being fought for? Are you a zombie or are you a zipper?

Thanks everyone. I hope you enjoyed today's show.

Chapter 9 Collaboration, The Secret Marathon and Going the Extra Mile featuring Kate McKenzie, Shawn Anderson, and Martin Parnell

David: Collaboration, The Secret Marathon, and Going the Extra Mile. That's what we're going to talk about today. We've got Shawn Anderson, Martin Parnell and Kate McKenzie, three people I'm very proud to know and support, and encourage you to know and support. They're doing some incredible stuff, and as Kate and I were just talking about before we went on the air, we are better together. We can achieve bigger dreams by collaborating.

My book, Break Through to Yes: Unlocking the Possible within a Culture of Collaboration aligns with going the distance together. No one gets left behind. Remember the African proverb, "If you want to go fast, go alone. If you want to go far, go together." The Secret Marathon inspired by a story of courage, a young woman and her legendary marathon mentor trained in secret for the marathon of Afghanistan only to uncover that, for the runners, this marathon is much more than just a race.

We have legendary marathoner, and you'll hear more about my friend, Martin Parnell, and those that are regular listeners will know that Martin was just on our show a few weeks ago. He's the guy that did 250 marathons within one year for Right to Play and others. Filmmaker, Kate McKenzie, is talking about this amazing story and the film that they're creating now and how you can support them. We've also got the inspiring Shawn Anderson. In 2017, Shawn, while finishing his seventh book, walked across England and Ireland to take his "go the extra mile" message on a speaking tour in Central America. It's pretty cool.

Now, I love mountains, I love activity, I love getting into the adrenaline, the pheromones, whatever it is through being active in the mountains. In our backyard, we have the Great Divide Trail. The Great Divide Trail is like the American Continental Divide Trail, but it's a Great Divide Trail that goes up to Canadian Rockies. If you wanted to go from start to finish, it starts at the Montana - Waterton Lakes National Park, Alberta border, and goes up to Kakwa, and some people are now extending it up into the Yukon. There have been several people. There's maybe three to six people per summer that take up to a month to complete this Great Divide and the Great Trail in the Canadian Rockies.

Explorer Magazine, just last month, published an article and called it The Greatest Loneliest Long Trail in North America. You are not going to have the Pacific Crust or the Appalachian traffic jams on the Great Divide. You'll be able to go for days without seeing anybody else. My wife and I have been taking pieces of the Great Divide Trail each summer for the last few summers, and it takes preparation, experience, collaboration, and each summer, we try to do this three to six-day backpack.

Now, in the summer of 2015, we decided we would ask a friend. It's not only the more the merrier, but when you're in grizzly territory and when you're on trails that are not marked, you must use GPS, at best, it's better to hike with four to six people - a little tougher to do it with two. Mountain springs were very dry in the summer of 2015 and there's no real trail from Waterton to Castle Mountain wilderness area; just GPS.

So, day 1, get your head into this, day 1 starts with a 17-kilometer or 12-mile hike, and a 2,800 meter, one-mile elevation gain. That's just on the first day. By day three, there was little water. It was dry. None of the springs were running, and we'd seen no one else in two days. Our friend was in trouble. She was very fit, but had no long-distance hiking, or running, or walking, or backpacking experience. She was in trouble. She had her head down and she was chanting in grizzly territory. She kept separating herself due to the pain she was in.

Later, on day 3, we had one chance to hike down a mountain creek drainage for about 11 kilometers, or 6 1/2 miles to get to a road and hitchhike back to our vehicle, or continue for at least two more days. When we expressed our concerns to our friend about the wilderness, the lack of trail, the lack of water, my wife and I just said, "You know, we better not. You're really struggling, you got your head down, you're missing the whole trip. I think we need to come back another time." We had to overrule her. And she was determined and angry. She was going to continue to go for days more. She couldn't see the predicament she was in.

Five hours later, when we got down to that road where we could hitchhike back to our vehicle, she could barely move, and yet she was determined. She kept laying down. Yet, five hours earlier, she was determined to go that extra mile, go the extra two to three days in the wilderness without water. It's not about an event or a short-term goal. It's about being healthy together, keeping each other safe and healthy, and because we realized we could not trust our friend in the wilderness to keep herself safe and healthy, and therefore, keep us safe and healthy, we won't be taking her on another backpacking trip, or at least not without others or without a lot more pre-discussion.

The reason I talk about this is it's important. When we talk to Kate, and Martin, and Shawn, you'll be inspired.

You'll want to get out there and do it, but be safe. There's a lot of mountain climbers that have died because they think the objective is to get to the peak. The objective is to get back to base camp after you've done the peak, just like negotiations. Oftentimes, we think negotiation is a one-off deal. No, negotiation is a relationship. It is the way we are, the trust we build, the way we can collaborate, the way we can create shared value, and that's when I do my negotiation mastery circles. I do it over four semesters of four months each. It's a monthly routine with coaching, instructing, journaling, reading. It takes time to change our habits, change the way we are, and really build those positive progressive relationships where we can all win and be better off, and it takes a group. Nobody negotiates by themselves. It's a system.

Now, if you are tired of very short-term results, if you're tired and frustrated by others' failure to engage meaningfully, when you have an objective, your negotiations fail, or your dreams fail, what do you do? You need commitment, you need time, you need focus, you need to go through those hills and valleys. In some ways, you're going to need to fail so often, whether it's a long-distance run, or a business deal, or helping women, helping all humans be freer and the ability to dream their dreams.

Now, let's invite Kate McKenzie and Martin Parnell into the conversation. Let me introduce them first. These two are just amazing people I'm so proud of. Kate McKenzie is a professional communicator whose passion is to help people with great ideas, creatively and effectively, communicate their ideas to the world. She is the founder of Positive News Platform World Views Project, co-director and Executive Producer of the Secret Marathon film, and author of Passport Project, an interactive book to help you explore and find adventures. She's currently completing her Master's Degree in Digital Media, and some of you already know my good friend, Martin Parnell. He's the author of Marathon Quest and Running to the Edge, and speaks on having a finish-the-race attitude, overcoming obstacles to achieve your full potential. Martin has written for and been covered by CNN, BBC, CBC, The Huffington Post, The Globe and Mail, The National Post, Runner's World, Men's Journal, Canadian Business, and Maclean's. In a five-year period from 2010 to 2014, Martin completed 10 extreme endurance quests, including running 250 marathons in one year, and raising 1.3 million for Right To Play. Kate and Martin, welcome, and let us know, tell us both your secret marathon and why is it so important to you?

Martin: Thanks, David. It's been an amazing journey, and you talk about collaboration, and I must say, working with Kate and together with Kate and the journey we took to Afghanistan. We'll only allow this story to come out really in a worldwide situation. It started somewhat instantly back in October 2015. My wife, Sue, gave me an article from the Guardian Newspaper that talked about the very first marathon of Afghanistan. What struck me was, in the mountain, there was one Afghan woman. Her name was Zainab, and she was the very first woman to complete a marathon.

As a runner, the challenges in training are hydration, nutrition, but for Zainab, it was abuse - verbal and physical abuse. People called her prostitute, they yelled at her, they threw stones at her, but she just persevered. She trained in her garden and she ran the first marathon. I was sick at the time, I was recovering from a clot on the brain, and she inspired me to say to Sue, "If I get better I am going to go and run the 2016 marathon of Afghanistan," and that was the path I was on during 2016 to get ready for that, and then I met Kate.

David: So, Kate, why is this so important to you and what's it all about?

Kate: Well, you know, when Martin first told me about this story I just thought, "Oh my gosh, what an amazing story," because, I think, for me, as a Canadian, I sometimes take it for granted that I can put on a pair of runners and head out the door, and I'm free to run, I'm safe. And here I was hearing about these other women, and women that are just like me, women that are attending the university and they're the same age as I am, and yet they aren't able to be free to go and run outside, and I thought, "Wow, what could we do? How can we help?" Because, I know what it feels like to feel scared when you're outside, and I waited too long to go for my run at night, and it's dark outside, and you don't really feel safe, and I couldn't imagine doing that way every single day. This idea that we could maybe do something, but by running with them, running alongside, that that would help everyone to be a little bit freer, and that just struck me as an amazing thing to do, and so I couldn't turn down the opportunity. So, when Martin told me about this, I said, "Can I join you? Can I come?" because I want to be part of this. I want to support what these women are doing.

David: It's such a fantastic thing when I think of somebody, 10K runs and things I've done tough, moderate, etcetera. There's always crowds of people and lots of motivation, lots of advertising, lots of people cheering you on, but this was a secret marathon. Even getting there had to be a secret. Tell us a little more about that.

Martin: Well, maybe I should also add in that Kate is very modest. Kate not only wanted to come along, but she wanted to run a marathon, and Kate, up to that point, was a 10K runner, and she said, "If I'm going to be part of this, then I want to run a marathon." I was honored to develop a training program, and Kate is a phenomenal student, and she stuck to a 20-week program, 800 kilometers. Together, there was a lot of planning involved in getting to this start line. One of which was, for Kate, multifaceted training for a marathon, and on top of that, we had the whole security situation over in Afghanistan, and that was a big hurdle to get over, to get our head around. We had warnings from the Canadian government on a travel advisory obviously talking to people. The single story of Afghanistan is bombings, the Taliban, and so on and so forth. So, we had to do a lot do a lot of due diligence, and as well, Kate wanted to bring a film crew, and Kate, there was lots of challenges there, I would say.

Kate: Yeah, I think one of the hardest thing was that, for a traditional film, you're usually talking about the film a lot before you even are able to capture any of it, and you're getting all sorts of people on-board, and yet here we knew there was this amazing story that we wanted to be able to bring to the world, and really to share this story of courage with others. But, yet, we couldn't really talk to anyone about it. We had to keep it a secret because there was concern that if we talked about it too much that it could bring added pressure to the race that it could become a threat for terrorist attack.

We were only two months out from when we going to be going over to do this marathon, and we still didn't know if we would get all the funding we needed to go over and do this film, and it was at that point that, really, I think was one of our biggest collaborations, because we had a local company called Biz. It's a telecommunications company, and they said, "You know what? We believe in what you're doing. We want to have this world where everyone is free to run, and we're going to give you the seed funding you need to go over and do this," because we understand you can't talk to a lot of people about this right now, but we believe this is too important to not share this story.

David: 99% of us will just sit by our TV set, or listen to Voice America Podcast, or iTunes. Why are you guys so crazy?

Martin: I'm from England, David. I'm from England.

Kate: I think it's not so much -- yeah, there's a huge risk, and when you look into your family's eyes and you can see that they're scared for you, and you're asking yourself, "Okay really, why am I doing this?" For me, it just came down to the idea that if there was inequality anywhere in the world, then there's inequality everywhere, and I want to be the kind of person that stands up for equality. I think, in our world right now, there's a lot of people that are putting out messages of fear, and misogyny, and racism, and here's an opportunity for us to stand for something different, and I just felt compelled that that was worth fighting for, and it was worth the risk of going over there to share this story.

David: I'm so glad, and I know our listeners are so glad that you're doing this work. Just before we head to a break, Kate, how can our listeners find out more, or support what you're doing?

Kate: We'd love to have people check out the film at thesecretmarathon.com. That's so you can learn a little bit more about it, see the whole creative team, including my co-directors, Scott Townsend, and everyone that's bringing this story together, and where they can also be part of the community that brings this film forward. We're still in the funding stages, so we'd love to have people that want to get their name in the credits and be part of the community that brings this story to the world.

David: Isn't this an amazing thing that the independent filmmakers are bringing us the films that matter. A few weeks ago, we talked about She Has a Name about human sexual trafficking. Here, we've got The Secret Marathon. So, we're going to take a short break and then we'll be right back with Martin and Kate.

David: We are one. We can be independent and separate from the misogynist, the ignorance, the wall-builders, the people around our planet, whether it's Daish, or whether it's a certain American president, or whomever around the world. We can overcome -- sounds like a song from the '60s. We will overcome. At the end of this segment, we will play our friend, Chuck Rose's, We Are One, and during the break, Kate, Martin and I were just talking about She Has a Name, and the film, and I want to use that as a segue there's some brilliant independent filmmaking happening in a time were Hollywood just seems to want to make action, violent comic book movies, we've got The Secret Marathon and She Has a Name. Kate, can you draw the connection there? I wasn't aware of the connection that you have.

Kate: I'm a huge fan of the film, She Has a Name. I grew up going to school with the Kooman Brothers, who both the writer, Andrew Kooman, and his brothers, Matt and Dan, who could film She Has a Name. I think one of the things that, often, is talked about with film is this idea that there's not as many female filmmakers, and yet, the Koopmans have been a huge part of just mentoring me and bringing me under their wing, so to speak, to help me be able to tell these kinds of stories and to show me an example of how to be able to tell courageous stories and difficult stories. We have a huge amount of respect for the film community in Alberta.

David: Wonderful. Glad to be part of that community and support that community. Now, in She Has a Name, it is a "docufiction". The young woman, the underage woman who's been in slave and prostituted, she's only referred to as 18 because she's in room 18. Tell us a little bit about the women that you were collaborating with in Afghanistan in the Secret Marathon.

Kate: We had the pleasure to meet a whole bunch of women. Martin started off by talking a little bit about some of the women we met, and maybe I'll just let Martin share a little but about meeting Kubra, because that really stood out to both of us.

Martin: For me, it was an amazing trip, because I went there with a goal of supporting women and girls in running is something that I've taken to over the last 14, 15 years. It's a simple act, but it's amazing that there's places where it is despised and attacked, and so it really riled me up. We don't choose where we're born. Again, I was born in England, living in Canada, very fortunate. People around the world, whether it's Afghanistan, or some of the other war-torn countries, they don't choose where they're born, and so they must deal with the cards they're dealt with, and I think we all have a role to do something about that.

When I went there, I wanted to support them. But, what happened is I ended up rather having a goal, I had a purpose, and that was when I met Kubra. Kubra was the young woman living in Kabul, she had been through some very traumatic times and she wanted to run the marathon, but she hadn't trained. She hadn't done enough training due to some issues she had had physically, but she really wanted to run, and I realized that if I work with Kubra, and if I ran with her, we had a chance of her completing the marathon. And my purpose on that day, November the 6th, when we ran the marathon, was to get Kubra across the line before the cut-off. For me, it ended up being my slowest ever marathon, but quite frankly, one of my best.

That was just part of seeing somebody achieve their goal and knowing that you had a hand in it, and that's a really a message I want to share with everyone is see how you can help. There's many little ways, there's different ways, family, friends, but especially people you don't know, and just think about, "How I could help somebody to do something, to make their life better when I don't even know them?" A huge thing for me.

David: I want to come back to nobody gets left behind. We go at the pace of the slowest because we finish together.

Martin: Exactly.

David: Kate?

Kate: Yeah, I think Martin is on to something here, and I mean, not only did he help Kubra get across that finish line, he helped me to even think that running the marathon was even a possibility. A year ago, this time, I'm pretty sure I was saying, "Why would anyone in their right mind want to run a marathon?" I think, oftentimes, we always look to celebrate the leaders, the people that win the races, and I think that's great, but I think there's also a huge role for those of us that are willing to stand alongside someone, run alongside of them, and just help them get a little bit closer to their goal, and Martin has certainly done that for me in coaching me to be able to get through this journey of my own. But, I think, it's really caused me to reflect that I think each of us has a role to play in helping to make this journey that we're all going through a little bit easier.

And so, I think what's been neat is that, along this whole marathon, we've just seen so many people that have come alongside and helped us to achieve this goal, and we're seeing that with the women of Afghanistan. Zainab, the first woman who ran the marathon in Afghanistan, she was the first and only woman in that year, and yet, it had a huge ripple effect, and this past year, there were six Afghan women that came. If you think about where that ripple might go, I think sometimes we don't realize how just taking that first step how much of an impact that could have.

David: Any thoughts, or expectations, or dreams for the 2017 Fall Afghan Marathon?

Martin: I won't be going, unfortunately, but I did hear, and I think this is part of the ripple effect, is that there were number of international runners who ran last year. It's already sold out for the international runners, which is great news, and I can see an even bigger group of Afghan men and women. One thing I want to mention is not only the marathon, but there was a 10k run, and I want to mention that because there were 150 runners, of which, there was almost 100 Afghan girls, and we talk about the ripple effect in the future. There's a group of girls that will become young women, and they're going to be the leaders, and this is the momentum that this race is going to have.

Kate: I think that what Martin is saying has a huge impact, because what we've realized is that, although this is a marathon, it's about so much more than a marathon. It's about so much more than running. This is about everyone feeling safe to be out in the public commons and to be able to have a voice, and have that voice heard. A lot of these women that are participating, they're not elite athletes. They're not super athletes or anything like that, but they've chosen to participate in this run because they see it as an opportunity to speak out about gender inequality. So, I think that's incredible.

David: Yeah, very, very courageous, strong leaders that I'm so thankful that you're celebrating and highlighting, and of course, it's not about Kate, or Martin, or any of the six women that ran. This is an incredible metaphor for freedom and equality.

Martin: Exactly, David.

Kate: We're excited to see how this really starts a full movement, and that by coming and standing together in solidarity with people that are doing something so wonderful, how could we inspire that kind of movement not just in Afghanistan, but also back here in Canada? How do we help to create safe places here? How do we make sure that everywhere in the world, people feel safe to go outside and go for a run?

David: Yes. Now, the theme of this show is Collaboration, The Secret Marathon and Going the Extra Mile. How have you seen the power of collaboration show up in this project?

Kate: We've seen collaboration in so many levels. I mean, the fact that Martin reached out and even invited us at the beginning, that was huge, and I think -- but then to see Biz come alongside us and support us. I think, too, what I've been so impressed by also is my co-director. It's rare that you get to have two people directing a film and collaborating on something together, and I've just seen what a wonderful gift that is. And so being able to co-direct and have a mix gender team co-directing has, I think, brought a unique perspective to this film. I think it really does show that we can bring a stronger perspective when we're doing this together.

David: I, also, want to get back to make sure that we've got some time to talk about how others can get involved with your film, The Secret Marathon.

Kate: Definitely. I think one of the things that is neat about this film is that there wasn't a lot of us that were involve in the actual filming. So, when we thought about the film credits, that usually is there for the cast and crew, but we decided we're going to do something different that we wanted to celebrate the community that's been helping us to take this film across the finish line, and so we received incredible support from so many Canadians, and people that have said, "Yeah, I want to be part of this," so we thought it would be really neat to be able to honor them by putting them in the credits of our film. We're so excited that when we get to finally screen this film, you'll see like hundreds of names, and they'll be all the people that said, "Yeah, we believe in this and we want to be part of that." I think that's the ultimate sign of collaboration is to be able to look at that huge set of names.

David: Yes, celebrating together recognition and gratitude, I'm sure. What's your financial goal? If you make it, then what?

Kate: We're looking to be able to crowdfund $50,000. We are one-tenth of our way there right now, and we are wanting to encourage Canadians to help us get all the way through that marathon-funding goal, and once we're able to achieve that, that means that we will be able to edit this film together and get it ready to bring out for the rest of the world to see. That's one way to get involved, but we're also excited to have more opportunities for partnership. When we started this film, we thought we'd be shooting like a short documentary, maybe 20 minutes long, and then we got over to Afghanistan, and we kept meeting amazing person after amazing person, and we realized that this story was so much larger than we had anticipated. That's opened a whole bunch of new opportunities or partnerships, and for people that say, "Yeah, you know what? I believe in gender equality. I believe in a world where people are free to run," then we want to get them involved, and we want to have a huge community that takes this film across the finish line.

David: This could turn into a franchise. The Secret Marathon of Inuvik, the Secret Marathon of Central Park, New York, the Secret Marathon of Russia. This is such an inspiring story, and it's not going to end with the publication and release of the movie.

Martin: No, David, and I agree. Kate and I have talked about it as a team. The message underlying this film, and we sort of talk about it's not necessarily about the marathon or a specific location. This is a message of freedom, of equality that every woman should have, and man, to a certain degree in different areas, and that's the message we want to get out there is we've got to do this together. We can't do this individually, and that's where traveling with Kate with a film crew and then with the other runners, and now with the community that's supporting the film, this is the momentum that's building will just build and build, and when the film comes out, we want to share it with schools and different groups afterwards, community screenings. We just feel this message will resonate, especially in our current political climate. I think this is crucial. I'm in for the long haul, as I usually am, and I'm super excited about where this is going.

Kate: Yeah, we're excited to be able to take this, especially, to the next generation and just share it, like Martin was saying, in schools because I think that we have this unique opportunity that, one day, I think that our children, or the next generation, they're going to ask us, "What did you do when the world was seeming like there's a whole bunch of negative stories going on?" I think it would be amazing if we can say, "Well, let me show you what we did. Let me show you the film, let me show you the stories that we were able to be part of telling and telling a different kind of story." So, I think this is such an amazing opportunity to be able to tell the next generation, "Hey, these are the kinds of heroes we want to support. These are the kinds of stories that we want to share."

David: Thank you so much, Kate McKenzie, and Martin Parnell for bringing us The Secret Marathon and the invitation to all of us to be part of the credits. Thank you you both, and we're going to go out with Chuck Rose's We Are One.

David: We are going the extra mile with this metaphor of running, walking, hiking, backpacking, and the next great guest that I've got is Shawn Anderson. Shawn is the number one ranked motivational author, unlimited thinker, and lifetime entrepreneur with a history of inspiring others. A six-time author, 75,000-plus books sold. I'm green with envy, Shawn. Shawn is also the creator of Extra Mile Day, a day recognizing the power we each must create positive change when we go the extra mile, and that's November 1st, 2016. 560 cities made the declaration and recognize local extra-mile heroes.

Besides having inspired thousands through his speaking and writing, Shawn has built a million-dollar company, pedaled a bike solo across the Unites States twice, and created adventures in 40-plus countries, including having walked 550 miles across Spain, 450 miles up the coast of Portugal, 750 miles around the island of Shikoku, Japan, and in 2017, Shawn will finish his seventh book, walk across England and Ireland, take his "go the extra mile" message on a speaking tour of Central America, and continue to build on this success, and reach the Extra Mile Day, November 11th. Shawn Anderson, welcome.

Shawn: It's my privilege to talk to you, my Canadian friend. How are you?

David: My privilege to talk to you. Where are you today, Shawn?

Shawn: I'm in Southern California in a place called Marina del Rey just outside of Los Angeles right near the beach.

David: Wonderful. You're resting before this amazing 2017. My son lives in L.A., and I've got lots of friends in that area in San Luis Obispo in Oakland. I trust it's sunny and warm and not raining anymore.

Shawn: For those who love warm weather, you can't beat Southern California. But, you've also got that part you have to sit on the 405 sometimes for 60 minutes to go eight miles. That's the drawback, right?

David: Shawn, when my son moves down to L.A. about a dozen years ago, I rented a Mustang, and he had a motorcycle because, as a student, it's all you can afford to buy, and public transit wasn't very good at that time. I'm just thinking that going the extra mile with my Mustang on the freeways, I didn't go very far in any hour. With his motorcycle, he could go between cars and on shoulders, and go much further, and I'm thinking you can probably run or walk just about as fast as you can drive.

Shawn: Sometimes, you probably can. You can go right and pass above those cars in five lanes and keep on walking and get there before they do.

David: 75,000-plus books. Probably, by this time next year, we'll be talking again, and it'll be over 100,000. Why do you think people are buying Shawn Anderson?

Shawn: Well, you know, I've been an entrepreneur my whole life, David. My first business was when I was 10 years old and I was selling worms to fishermen. I would gather the night crawlers in the evening, place an ad in the papers for fishermen to read on Saturdays and Sundays, and get out there at 6 o'clock in the morning and sell a dozen worms to these guys. I learned a long time ago that if you want to really create a life that you love, if you really have a vision for your world that you got to do more than the status quo, and even though I didn't recognize it at first, is go the extra mile, to do more, to be more, to live more, to give more was really planted on pretty early. I think, throughout my riding, that message starts to resonate with people who really have a dream and a vision for their life and they want to learn how to give that vision legs, and I think that's why my books have resonated, and I hope that they will continue to do so.

David: I could just hear the energy in your voice, and you're not talking about, "Well, when you're really tired, just go the extra mile. I hear a lot of, "Live your dream," and more importantly, "Be the person in your dream."

Shawn: That's right. I believe very strongly. I want to ask people, "What is your intention? What is the intention of your life? What do you want to do?" because that's where living a great life starts. You can never live a great life unless you know what that great life looks like to you. Because, once the dream is established, it allows you to give that dream step-by-step plans, and that allows you to take action daily out of the step-by-step plans, and before you know it, what was once simply an intention, a vision, a goal becomes your reality. I am a firm believer that we can truly live the life we love. We just must take the time to know what that looks like not only in our career, in our financial state, in our relationships, and in our health and our entertainment, where we want to travel. What do you want to do with your life? And then make it happen.

David: Yeah, so it's not easy. Let's be clear about that. You didn't wake up one day a successful entrepreneur. You went a lot of miles to get there. But, people like you, and I believe, people like me, we just don't have any choice. This is our life, the only life we know about, for sure, so let's just do it.

Shawn: That's exactly right. I talk about that first number on my eventual tombstone, or that second number when I was born or when I was dead. But, all those dates in between, those are my dates, those are your dates, those are our dates to make something happen with our life that we choose to make happen. You can sit there and give lip service to a goal all day long and say, "I'm going to take this trip and go to the Greek Islands," but unless you call that travel agency, and unless you set those dates, you're never going to go.

Sure, it's absolutely not easy. Fear knocks and says all off our horse when we start chasing goals. I feel fear every single time that I get onstage and speak. I feel fear every time I read a new book review. But, you know, there's one thing that matters more to me, and maybe to you, and that's the fear of not doing it, of not going after it. That fear is greater than the fear of possible rejection.

David: What was the inspiration behind Extra Mile Day?

Shawn: Extra Mile Day started in 2009 in Canada, like, the United States. We were getting so much bad financial moves: people were losing their homes, businesses were closing everywhere, banks were even closing, divorce rate was at an all-time high. People, I felt, were really starting to lose that sense of, "Man, what's my future going to look like? Do I have any control over it all?" I wanted to remind people that, if you truly want to create positive change, and positive hope in your life, you don't look to the government to create change, you don't look to your spouse and say, "Hey, what are you doing to make our relationship better?" you don't look to your boss and say, "What are you going to do to make sure that I keep my job and make more money in the future?" but you look at the man and the woman in the mirror, and you say to that person, "What are you going to do to make your life better?"

I have that small voice, and I created what was called The Extra Mile America Tour in 2009, and in a Forrest Gump sort of way, I took my non-bicyclist body, at that time, I was 47 years old, and I pedaled 4,000 miles from one ocean to the other ocean just as a symbol of going the extra mile. But, along the way, my staff created events in 21 American cities where we had pre-identified over 200 people who had gone the extra mile in service or volunteers or in fulfilling an amazing dream, and we had a chance to talk to those people. At the end of my tour, I gave away $10,000 of my own money to the stories most inspiring to me, and it was during that tour that I created Extra Mile Day. On November 1st, 2009, 23 American cities, I celebrated the fact that they recognized their local heroes. But, I'm happy to say that in November 1st, 2016, there were 560 American cities.

David: Amazing, just amazing. Share some stories about the Extra Mile people who you've met since 2009.

Shawn: I'm happy to share that, because going the extra mile, for any of us, is when we look at our situation, suddenly, we've lost hope. We don't think that there's any more wind left in our sails and we just can't go anymore. But, some of these stories really are powerful.

I'll take one guy I met in San Francisco. His name was Creighton Wong. Creighton came up to me and he introduced himself. He had two fingers missing on one hand, and he showed me his other hand, he had three fingers missing. I also notice that Creighton, when he walked into the room, was walking with the limb. That was because he was an amputee and had a fake leg. The truth of it is Creighton Wong was born as a congenital amputee. He was born without fingers on both hands, he was born with only one leg. But, Creighton did not let that stop him, and he did not let that kind of physical hindrance prevent him from living the life that he loved, or going the extra mile. Creighton Wong became a tri-athlete. He would run 26 miles, he would bicycle 100 miles, he would swim over a mile without the fingers, without the leg. Life can only stop us when we choose to let it stop us. Sometimes it's just a matter of just saying, "You know what? I want more, and I'm going to go and get more, like Creighton showed me."

David: Wow. What an inspiring man.

Shawn: One more story I'll you. There was a woman in the state of Iowa. When she was introducing to me, she was escorted up on somebody's arm. Sheila Holdsworth was blind. She had two glass eyes. But, it wasn't always like that for Sheila. When she was 10 years old, the orthodontic headgear that she was wearing for her teeth, one day, it snapped, and when it snapped, it gouged out both of her eyes. For the first 10 years of Sheila's life, she was able to see just as clearly as you and I can see right now, but after that, never again.

Now, Sheila Holdsworth could have decided to live her life as a blind person for the rest of her life, but she chose not to. Sheila Holdsworth, when I met her, was considered a world record holder in international downhill skiing and trick water ski jumping. Sheila Holdsworth had ridden a bike tandem across her state of Iowa. Sheila Holdsworth just shows you that even without eyes, you can still put fear behind and you can still do amazing physical things.

All of us in our life have different obstacles that we must overcome. We must decide if we are going to choose and let that obstacle block us or if we're going to find a way to get around it and go the extra mile to get to where we want to go.

David: So inspiring. I'm thinking some people think, "Wow, you need eyes, you need limbs, you need a lot of money." My friend Sean Conklin told me about a Netflix series called The Kindness Diaries where a man left California and motorcycled around the world with no money. He just asks for the kindness of strangers, and he made it all the way around the world. So, everyone, let's get out of our stories and listen more to Shawn and the examples that he has about people that have gone the extra mile, and the incredible collaboration that you generated because of this, Shawn.

Shawn: Absolutely. We can only create something awesome when we bring as many people in it as possible. Not only do we work diligently with all the cities in the mayor's offices trying to identify their local Extra Mile Heroes, they're working with the local organizations of their communities to find people that need to be clapped for or flattered for and said, "Hey, way to go." It's when we plant that idea and we start sharing with others, and we collaborate, and that's when we can just let one seed grow into a hundred seeds, grow into a thousand seeds, and before long, we have a huge forest that we created not by one person, but by all working together.

David: Yeah, we are, together, better. Now, why is this so important to you, Shawn?

Shawn: Why is the whole theme, "going the extra mile" important?

David: Yes. You've committed more than eight years plus. You've probably been this way all the time. What inspires you to do this?

Shawn: We get one life, and I really cherish that mystery, that great adventure that we all have of living this amazing life, and I don't want anybody to, when they take their final long nap, that wish that they had done more things. I want to be that voice right now that reminds people that, "This is our time. This is our time to dream, and to wish, and to do, and to take action." Because, someday, it's not going to be our time, and we will never create the change in our life, David, if we continue to do the same thing we're doing over, and over, and over. We will only create the change we want in our relationships, and in our health and in our financial status, and in our careers when we do more, when we give more, when we become more, when we make the extra two calls, when we do the extra three push-ups, when we run the extra 100 yards, when we bring the extra bouquet of flowers home. That's what's called going the extra mile. It's when we decide that we want to be other people's hero instead of looking for someone to be our hero. It's when we decide that we are going to be the change that we wish to see.

David: I will think everyone can hear the passion in Shawn's voice, and I will say I'm in my early 60s. My wife has shared our commitment. In your 60s, as baby boomers, it's the best decade. We'll never have more resources, more freedom, more health than we do right now, and the flip side is the actuaries will tell us those people that say, "I'll get around to it after I retire," generally, are dead within a few years after retirement. So, get around to it now and make this life wonderful. Go ahead.

Shawn: You know, I agree with that so much. I mean I'm 54 years old, David, and like I said, this June, I'm going to walk across England and Ireland. We can still do things. Just because we go up in age into our 50s, into our 60s, into our 70s, man, if we work daily on improving our health, we can do things like this.

David: Yes. As we close here, Shawn, what's one thing that you'd really encourage our listeners in 32 countries to be aware of change, do, or be?

Shawn: Well, David, I think it's simple, that if you really want to experience your greatest successes, your greatest adventures, your most amazing romances, your best contributions, never stop going the extra mile.

David: Thank you, Shawn Anderson. This has been energetic. I want to walk with you. Let's backpack together someday, and thank you for encouraging all of this. This has been awesome.

Shawn: Thank you for what you do. Thank you for empowering people around the world.

David: Listeners, today, we've had the theme of Collaboration, The Secret Marathon and Going the Extra Mile. What is your extra mile? What's your secret marathon? What are you going to do now that you've heard Shawn, Kate, and Martin? In Collaboration, we're looking to break out of normal, and break through to fresh and exciting insights and possibilities. Now, let's work together better. Talk to you soon.

Chapter 10 Collaboration, Leadership and Disruptive Technologies featuring Jim Gibson

David: Collaboration, Disruptive Technology and Entrepreneurship – that is our theme for this show. We're living in an age of disruption, lies, challenge, economic revolution, fear, alternate facts. How do we navigate our way through?

Along with our great guest today, Jim Gibson, we're going to explore collaboration, disruptive technology and entrepreneurship. I'll introduce Jim more fully after the first break, but as a quick introduction, Jim Gibson provides C-level, that's executive level, consulting services to emerging companies, established enterprises and works with the Alberta Innovation Ecosystem. Jim's in Calgary today and I'm in Cranbrook, British Columbia.

We are now in an age of increasing complexity, challenge, opportunity, risk and separation. We like to quote Albert Einstein, and here's a quote that you may not have heard that's tongue-in-cheek, because I'm sure you've heard this. But it applies to today's collaboration, disruptive technology and entrepreneurship theme.

"We cannot solve our problems with the same thinking we used when we created them." – Albert Einstein

It's much quoted and it's so true, even more today than ever. Think of the rapid change in business. The world's largest taxi company has no cars. Do you know what it is? Uber. The world's largest taxi company has no cars.

The world's largest hotel room company has no rooms. Isn't that strange? Do you know who that is, the world's largest hotel company that provides rooms around the planet, has no rooms? And that's Airbnb.

Think about this podcast as a disruptive technology. Five years ago, ten years ago, we would have never believed this is possible. I have no broadcasting license. I have no $10 million equipment. I have no high price marketing. I have no team of professionals, other than the very few of us creating this podcast for you. Since 2015, we, you, and thousands of people around the planet in, I believe 32 countries across the planet participate by listening and sharing Break Through to Yes with Collaboration. Can you believe that?

The analytics say 32 countries in 2016 and just short of 14,000 listeners. And what do I have? The Internet, professional microphone and headset, laptop, and connections; that's all.

Think of where we're going. What's the speed of business? Is it accelerating? I think so. What's the speed of technological change? What's the speed of change in everything we're doing? It's accelerating. It's wonderful and that creates possibilities that we don't even know exist.

Now some of you have read my book, *Break Through to Yes: Unlocking the Possible within a Culture of Collaboration*. A friend of mine read it a year ago. Kathy is studying at Oxford. She's studying Leadership at Oxford. She read my book and reported to her class, and to me, "David is a disruptive technology. He's challenging us to change the way we collaborate, the way we work together." I like that. Thanks Kathy, and thank you for all those thousands who have listened, all those thousands that have purchased and have read the book.

Thank you, especially my biggest purchaser of Break Through to Yes, is in China. That's pretty cool. I would have never dreamed that when I dreamed the book four years ago, that my biggest listenership on this podcast would be Sweden. My biggest readership for my book would be China. This is pretty cool. And I'm broadcasting from my home in the Kootenay Rockies of British Columbia, Canada.

Let's talk about disruptive technology and what it takes, and entrepreneurship. I'm a serial entrepreneur throughout my 42-year career – oil and gas, renewable energy, healthcare, tourism, mostly getting the right people in the right place, with the right tools at the right time to figure things out for themselves, to innovate for themselves, to solve their own conflict.

So, here's a brief quote from Break Through to Yes that I think applies to our theme today. "A highly functioning team is one where constructive criticism push backs challenges and diverse opinions are highly valued, encouraged and used to build better outcomes. A high functioning team rarely says 'Yes, sir' with conflict avoiders. A key role for me as I work with organizations is to incite insurgency."

I've been told by some of my organizational negotiation and leadership mastery circles, "David, you incite insurgency." You bet I do. I want us to be our best. I don't want us to be comfortable.

I work to re-energize participants to challenge themselves, their teams and their organizations in ways not often seen. I do poke and prod to get the team to respond. Progress is made as team members move from comfort to deeper view, mindfulness and then to challenge, to reflection, to new insights and then better, more sustainable deals and strategies.

In 2008, this is the time where Erica Ariel Fox, David Gould, Emily Gould and I were running the Global Negotiation Insight Institute and we were focusing on helping people around the world negotiate better, negotiate from their values, from their center.

In 2008, I also met Bill Ury. Now, Bill Ury was at the Association for Conflict Resolution Conference in Phoenix, Arizona. As a co-author with Roger Fisher of Getting to Yes and Getting Past No, Ury is widely recognized as the world's thought leader for negotiation, and has been doing so for about 4 years-plus.

As Bill explained to us, he realized that great success in his family, at Harvard University, as a negotiator, and on behalf of the United States and as a business man came largely from saying no. In The Power of a Positive No, he writes, "You are asserting your value. It could be your value as a human being in that commercial context of your product, or service or brand. It could be your ethical and moral values. Ultimately, you are saying yes to what truly matters. By saying no, you're saying yes to what truly matters. You are setting that clear limit, drawing that clear line in creating that firm boundary. Say no more often if you care about the relationship. Counter-propose with something that also benefits you. Say no to normal, Break Through to your yes. Disrupt the patterns, norms and confines of the old paradigms."

This week in Cranbrook, in Mt. Baker High School, I've been working with other Rotarians, leading conversations on values and ethics. What do you say no to? What do you say yes to? And how can that shape your leadership and your future, your entrepreneurship, your leadership? Where do you want to disrupt and change?

So, let's talk for a little bit about the paradigms of business and leadership. One, is your world perfect just the way it is? Two, what is increasingly threatening your world?

If you want to tweet me @davidbsavage or email david@davidbsavage.com, I'll send you all of these questions. I'll be happy to, and I've got an invitation for you at the end of this show as well, to be on this show and Break Through to your yes.

Is your world perfect just the way it is? What is increasingly threatening your world? How innovative is your organization? How agile is your team? Are you doing it by rote? Are they aware and present and able to read and react?

What will your world be in 5 years? What are you planning? What would the world be, looking at the speed of change of business and technology, of life? Where are we going? How can you lead there? What are your possibilities? Most importantly, what are you doing now to create that?

And most importantly, how long with a focus on collaboration, who will you collaborate with? Yeah. Are you working together towards your ideal future? Or are you hauling the coal for somebody else's old future dream, hauling the coal or creating new energy, your own sustainable, renewable energy?

In Break Through to Yes, I talk about compare and contrast the paradigms of business. As we shift from command and control to collaborative leadership, let's also change the standards that we operate under. Where do you fit today? Where do you want to fit tomorrow?

With the old paradigm, in business and many businesses are still stuck here, quarterly reports, short-term economics on capital projects, what's the highest way to return and fastest payout; incentives paid on one-year performance, getting projects built as planned, on-time and on-budget; corporate cultures that see people and resources only as inputs – yeah, only as inputs, us versus them attitudes – and I-don't-have-time-to mindsets, I'll get around to what's important. I've got to do what's easy or expected. Or we're not responsible for blaming, shaming, off-loading. That's not my department.

The new paradigm is more like, seeing bigger opportunities and challenges. This is some of the work that Jim Gibson and I are going to talk about after the next break. Look at the bigger opportunities and challenges. Recognize the impact on our environment, our communities and our economies long term. Yeah, if you can't focus on sustainability, if you are unable to create shared value, you're going to have a tough go of it today and in the future. We can no longer see ourselves as separate.

Capture the opportunity in how you do business every day. The leaders and corporations that do that will outperform those that don't. Those that don't will continue to see their communities, environment and a long term economic health challenged.

What's your paradigm? Why does your future matter? What are the qualities of a collaborative leader? What are he values and ethics of a collaborative leader? What would a leader do? What do you choose?

Lots of questions for you, write these down, email me, tweet me. I'll send you these questions. These can be questions to meditate and be mindful of.

Ask yourself some time each day, maybe as you wake up, what is your ethical code as a collaborative leader: honesty, connection, integrity, excellence, future vision, diversity, inclusion? What behavior will you need to adopt or embrace right now? As that leader, because you're listening to this show, I know that you're that leader and you're in development in evolution just as I am.

There are no experts. We are only sharing and collaborating our wisdom and learning together, awakening together, dreaming together and creating our future. We will not be shut down by fear, walls, uncertainty, risk and the power structure. We will create our future together. We must dream of your children, your grandchildren and their children. What's your legacy?

In Break Through to Yes and on my website davidbsavage.com, you've got my 10 Essential Steps to Collaboration. So, as you think about how you create your future, how you behave, how you design, then look and utilize my 10 Essential Steps to collaboration.

After the break here, we're going to have Jim Gibson join us and we're going to have a brilliant discussion on disruptive technology, the Rainforest Initiative, *Tip of the Spear* and so much more. We'll be right back.

David: Welcome back everyone. I am delighted to interview Jim Gibson. Our theme today is collaboration, disruptive technology and entrepreneurship and Jim is a world leader in exactly these things. I'm excited that we'll be doing some collaborative explorations in person next week in Calgary.

For today, I want to share Jim Gibson, his wisdom and his challenges, insights and experience with you, our listeners in what we believe is 32 countries. So, Jim, I want to give them a little bit of a sense of your background, so give me a moment to introduce you a little more formally.

Jim Gibson has extensive executive leadership experience in the entrepreneurial and innovation area through the 4 startups Jim has built. Those are Kudos Inc., Chaordics Inc., Purist Technologies Inc. and Core Partners.

Now, Jim's firm is JAG YYC and of course some of you will know that YYC is the designation for the Calgary airport, so we use it a lot to designate Calgary, YYC. Jim works in Canada, the United States, the United Kingdom and in the Calgary Innovation Ecosystem. I love to hear that, what a combination of words, Calgary Innovation Ecosystem; including most recently, leading the ongoing Rainforest Initiative.

He's a member of the A 100 and a lead member in the Calgary Innovation Coalition Team. Jim, now this is exciting, you can follow up and buy this book because Jim will soon be publishing his nonfiction book, *Tip of the Spear*. Welcome, Jim. So great to have you, with you and our audience.

Jim: Thank you, David, very much and it's a pleasure to be with a fellow Calgarian here on the world conversation. So, thank you for having me, I appreciate it.

David: Just for our world conversation and our world audience, as we know, sometimes things need to get shaken up and uncomfortable and difficult before people will be motivated to move to a better thing. And certainly, in the city of Calgary, Alberta and in Canada, what had been our number 1 economic driver, that is the oil and gas business, was really, really shaken.

There are by some estimates, 125,000 Albertans that were put out of work in the last 2 ½ years. By some estimates, 30% of the big office towers in downtown Calgary, a city of 1.3 million, 30% of those offices are empty. There's a lot of shifting and there's also people like Jim Gibson, Alice Reimer, David Mitchell, many others in Calgary, Alberta and British Columbia, Canada and around the world that are saying 'Wonderful, let's change. Let's create our future.'

So, Jim, I so appreciate your leadership. I appreciate the conversation that Alice Reimer, our friend, spoke to the Institute of Corporate Directors in Calgary about disruptive technologies.

One of the things I will say in support of what Alice and others on that ICD panel talked about is, if you're on the board of directors, don't spend all your time looking backwards. Don't spend all your time looking at quarterly reports and measurements, and all that stuff. Spend a lot of your time and put a lot of your resources towards creating the future. Look forward.

Jim, any comments generally and then I've got a series of questions I'd like to ask you, but any further comment as a general introduction and start?

Jim: I think framing the conversation as you have centered on the challenge that Calgary is facing as a city is the perfect place to jump off on our conversation and the question that we'll have. I think in this challenge represents all the things that we're going to talk about for disruption and future, to how we work together as individuals.

I think as a city goes through something like this, a couple of things can happen. We can band together and decide that we're going to make things better by understanding what's coming or we can retreat to some of the old ways. And I think I'm very encouraged by what I see around me and the people that I work with.

I think that you set the context perfectly because these challenges are both personal and individual, but they're also organizational, policy, framework, governments and all the people that need to be involved. So, I'm happy to use that as a backdrop for the kind of a more positive future we're looking that we're going to talk about today, so thank you.

David: I'm third-generation Calgarian and for 13 years, I've been a proud resident at Kootenay Rockies in British Columbia, in the city of Cranbrook, so framing also applies. The city of Cranbrook has, for the last 15 years, has been 20,000 and growing for 15 years. Our friends in Toulouse, France, they have challenges. They are so dependent on Airbus.

Wherever we go, there are economic challenges and opportunities. And wherever we go, some of the places we've talked a little bit in the intro about the largest taxi company in the world having no cars. So, it's beyond Calgary, it's beyond Canada, but it's a shared challenge of shifting.

Talking about shifting, Jim, you're one of the experts. You're one of the ones that's been doing this for so long. What are some of the new thinking and collaborative technologies for enterprise?

Jim: Collaboration is something I've studied both as a bit of a social science geek, but also a software engineer and entrepreneur building companies. And I'll date myself a little bit when I say that I watched the first collaborative systems emerge as what we now call email back in the late '80s and early '90s in some of the work I was doing in the multinationals here in Canada.

One of the things that I've observed is this notion that collaboration, as it was embodied by email, was really the idea of moving context, the documents and the things that we care about to people; so, context moving in an email to another person or a group of people. That was really what I call paving the cow path. That was just speeding up the ability of us to send a letter faster, was just packaging context and moving along.

As I've observed and participated and built organizations in collaboration, we flip that a bit on its head, instead of moving context to people or bringing people to context. What that means is the teams that we work with on a both real and virtual way start now coming to places where we share that context, and that is profound implication. And in fact, email starts to get in the way when you move people to context.

The new systems that I see emerging over the last 4 or 5 years, up to a decade in the technologies I was building was about flipping that on its head. So, some of the popular tools today are Slack, Jive and Yammer. Some of those collaboration tools are really flipping this on its head to say, the ability of a team to always know what the latest thinking is about a particular issue or something is critical, whereas if I move things along in an email, I tend to lose the thread. I lose what I was thinking now.

That's a very positive change and it will see a natural and inevitable decline and elimination of email over time, and I think that's a really, really good thing. That's the first trend I see in enterprise collaboration.

David: So just using that, Jim, I'm thinking email as sequential, thinking about cloud folders as collaborative. Is that some of what we've already experienced and what else?

Jim: The cloud is the classic, bring people to a place, bring people to context so that no matter where I am on the planet, I can put a document up and I can say, this is my context on this project, on this thinking, on this piece of music, this whatever it is, and here it is. And it becomes a single source of truth, rather than the game we play when send emails around, where we lose the latest version, we lose the thread. Were you on this, were you copied, and so on and so forth? So, it flips it on the head.

The other thing, David that I'll express that I've seen the change of is this notion of synchronous and asynchronous and let me just maybe talk about that quickly; the idea that asynchronous allows us to move and collaborate over time. So, as I share information in an email or something, I don't have to be in the same place or the same time as you.

What I'm starting to see is the meshing of synchronous collaboration, i.e. what we're doing right now, Skype, some of the tools that you see, are really, interesting. And we're meshing the ability to have same-time conversations, you and me at the same time, just synchronous with these powerful tools of asynchronous, moving context along. I'm really seeing the meshing of these two worlds happening and it's exciting.

And, then, the last thing I'll just say, and then I'll stop, is at the very edge of collaboration, I'm starting to see the creation of a virtual collaboration where I'm able to share context but being able to create virtual spaces where I can bring in any object and for example, I'm an engineer and I want to show you what's happening, what's this valve pipe and I can actually look at it through virtual reality and be able to look at the various physical aspects in a room that is virtually collaborative across the world.

We're seeing some amazing things happen in one of my partner companies up at Edmonton called Serious Labs, that is doing this virtual collaboration in the oil sands business for Halliburton and many other companies; very amazing stuff happening.

David: Yeah, real-time, inclusive and evolves as we proceed as opposed to sequential chain increased complexity, but at the same time, increased inclusion.

Jim: It allows us to increase the complexity, I guess, to teach your work. It really does. So instead of an email message and text to saying, how are you doing, or can you come to this meeting or what have you, I can start to look at the physical properties of an object 5,000 miles away that would weigh 5,000 pounds, but in virtual space, I can skin it and look at it, and create a real knowledge transfer between people across distances and places, and time; some amazing things happening.

But it all comes back to that principle of moving, moving people to context and not context to people. Without getting too deep on it, but that's how I see it.

David: Yes. Virtual reality is about to take off and this is not simply gaming. This is engineering.

Jim, what are some of the key disruptive technologies and combinations emerging on the landscape?

Jim: This is a topic that both in my book and my research, and in my speaking with people, I spend a lot of time on. Probably the best source and the best place for any of our listeners to go to is our friend Peter Diamandis from the Singularity University down in Silicon Valley. And Peter talks about really the 8 technologies that are emerging at the same time.

But what Peter talks about, which is fascinating, is the idea that we have 8 or 9 technologies and I won't list them all, but everything from virtual reality and several things, that they're all tipping at the same time. It's not just the individual technologies and drones and AI, and all those things tipping and moving exponentially. It's the combination.

When I look at some of the changes that are happening and my advice to my client is not look at any one individual technology, but start to combine one, two or three of these together and imagine a new reality. So, the exponential changes and drone technology, combined with AI, with new synthetic materials that are made.

I did exercises with the MBA class here in Calgary to imagine the scenario with 3 or more of these combinations, and they were able to, on the fly, understand brand new businesses and brand-new opportunities right on the fly.

So, it's super exciting stuff, but my message to people is think of combinations, not any one.

David: Yeah, I love that since we're not trying to pick the winning horse. We're creating the culture of imagination.

Jim: Very much.

David: The culture of imagination creates the possibilities, and then we can read, react, innovate, and build our future businesses and not-for-profits.

Jim: Correct.

David: So Jim, we're about to go to break. Any quick comments in the 30 seconds before we go to break?

Jim: I think just quickly, I think that I encourage all of us to appreciate the speed and the depth and scope of the change that's coming. I can't underestimate it enough and I encourage people to spend time and understand, and read about what's coming because the change is unlike anything we've ever seen, and I know you've heard that a lot, but it truly is happening.

David: It's such an exciting opportunity. Now there will be some of our listeners that'll say, I just want to get off that bus. But the bus is taking us anyway, so you might as well jump on.

Jim: Well said.

David: We're going to take a quick break and we'll be right back with Jim Gibson.

David: So what has Jim Gibson said today that's got you thinking about your opportunity and the bus that you want to jump on or drive even better? Jim, let's get back into it. How can leaders prepare their organizations for disruption and innovation?

Jim: I'm asked that a fair bit, and I think that it boils down to two things from my perspective and I'm sure there are others. So, I don't have the monopoly on this.

But they go on two sides of the coin: to continue what I was saying before the break, is what I ask leaders and clients, people I work with, is to pay attention to the changes. Don't download that knowledge about what's coming to others and just get yourself up to speed on the great thinking and research and the work that's being done from outside your industry because it's the combination of technologies from outside your industries that will potentially be the most disruptive.

I encourage you to not become a technical geek, but to certainly do the reading and some of the great publications that I mentioned, Peter Diamandis and the Singularity U. If you spent an hour a week reading that stuff, that would be great. So that's on the one side, keep up-to-date and spend the time and energy learning outside your ecosystem.

The second is more personal, is innovation from my work and research here in the city of Calgary, comes from a culture of trust. And what I mean by that is innovation requires us to step outside of our comfort zone, to reach out to other parts of our world. And that requires us to suspend traditional forms of capitalism, which means I win, you lose. I think we need to rethink that.

I ask leaders to really examine the level of trust and the culture of trust within their organization to absorb new ideas and to understand that failure and the trust in failure is something to be really understood.

In summary, understand what's coming and spend the energy and time, and conversely look inside your organization as human beings around the culture of trust and the culture of fail.

David: Yes. To go back and really underline what Jim's sharing with this, command and control has limitations, especially with rapid change. Collaborative leaders innovate. They play outside their ecosystem. Stop playing with the same toys and the same sandbox. Stop going to the petroleum club and sitting at the same table. Get to old Alberta, lots of great things happening. Get to San Luis Obispo, great, exciting stuff happening there. Go to Revel, France.

This is a global opportunity. Do you want to be on the bus? Do you want to drive the bus, or do you want to get run over by the bus?

I guess the other part of this is, it brings up to my mind when I used to be a chief operating officer, director, VP in business development in various companies in my 41 years. We used to say, maybe we can protect 5% of our budget this year to look at the future and innovation, and change.

That doesn't work anymore. You're putting yourself in a limited opportunity and as Alice shared with the Institute of Corporate Directors, this work that Jim is consulting, leading and writing about and talking about is the way that it will be. Yeah, this needs to be your commitment from the board right to the person at the reception desk.

Now one of the exciting things that I heard about, about 6 weeks ago and really looking forward to hearing more about is the Rainforest Initiative, Jim. What can you tell our listeners about that with respect to disrupted technology, startups, innovation and opportunity?

Jim: David, it's a really great story and it's a long one. I'll get to the shorter version. There's a book called

The Rainforest: The Making of Silicon Valley, built and authored by a gentleman called Victor Wang. Long story short, Victor looked at ecosystems all over the world and basically tried to figure out, from a micro and macroeconomic view point why do some succeed and why do some fail. Why do some areas of the world move faster and move ahead? And he looked at the Valley as a start, but he looked all over the world.

Long and short of it, he created a book called *The Rainforest*, and the rainforest to Victor was really 6 principles of what makes an ecosystem work. But at the center of it, and this is connecting our conversation across this, is at the center of an ecosystem's success and innovation success was the culture of trust and leadership.

He looked at all the factors and features of the Valley for example and he recognized that when I go in, when people in the Valley go in to make a deal, he learned that it wasn't about a win-lose proposition. It was, the venture capitals list of the Valley, believe it or not, look for the fairest deal. They look for a deal that makes everybody win.

That was a shock to him and when he put that together in the book, it was a very, very powerful book. Our assistant deputy minister of innovation read the book and anybody who talked to him for the next 6 months, that you've got to read this book.

One of my colleagues, Brad Zumwalt who is one of the most amazing individuals, successful entrepreneur and social philanthropist read the book as well and he bumped into me and said, Jim let's do something about this. He underwrote it with his financial back. He said, Jim I'll underwrite it if you'll organize it.

Long and short of it is I found 60 of my closest friends and innovation leaders across Alberta. And in September of 2016, just 6 months ago, we brought 60 of them together to the amazing Banff Centre in Alberta and brought the original authors up and walked us through a facilitate session. What does it take to build a rainforest and build a culture of innovation? And it just blew people's socks off. He was humble and frank.

But at the end of the day, David, it was about individuals who didn't necessarily either know each other or even at worst, trust each other. They learned that the number 1 thing to move initiatives, you can put all the capital and all the people and all the activities you want, but if you don't have a culture of trust, nothing will happen.

Out of that session, we built something called the Social Contract, which was 10 principles of how to behave in an innovation ecosystem. We made it explicit. We made people sign it with pen and ink. And then from there, fast forward, we just held our second cohort two days ago in Banff with the Clean Energy Group, the post-secondary institutes across Alberta, governments, entrepreneurs. We had another 60 cohorts with the same group and it was extraordinary.

It's exploded because what it's tapping into David, is this notion that if we understand our frames of reference and we begin with a culture of trust, the velocity of transactions goes through the roof. We're seeing it every day now with the group that we have.

It's a long story, powerful story but I tried to summarize it the best I could. It's so exciting, what's going on.

David: This is so exciting. I hear some exciting things, innovation and culture of collaboration, to pitch my focus again, Jim. Oftentimes, I've been part of forming organizations and we've all been part of forming organizations where people dream but we don't do. Tell me a little bit about, maybe it's within your commitment to each other. How do you hold each other to say, no, this is what we do now; it's not something on the edge of the desk?

Jim: Yeah. I guess the doing part is the individual organizations in an innovation ecosystem for private enterprises, governments and post-secondary, are all basically doing good things. What happens though in the white spaces around them is that we get barriers to moving things forward.

I've had examples in meetings where people who've been a part of the Rainforest Initiative looked at each other in the eye and said, are we being – one of the principles is pay it forward and trust. Are we paying it forward and thinking of the broader ecosystem as we make this decision? And I've seen two organizations that were kind of at each other's throats for years, and kind of go, yeah you know what, let's do it a different way.

There's competition within a rainforest as you can imagine. Trees and birds, and everybody's competing. At the end of the day, it's the overall post.

There's a lot of doing going on in the ecosystem. What we're trying to do in the white space, just make sure that we look at each other in the eye and say, let's get this thing done in the culture and spirit of trust.

David: Thanks for that image. I think that makes a lot of sense and I think to our listeners, you see the increasing complexity and the increasing trust levels to say, okay are we together? Where are we connecting? Where is that white space?

Now before we run out of time, one of the most important things I want to hear about and share is, have you told your listeners about your upcoming book, *Tip of the Spear*, Jim.

Jim: It's my first and probably my last. No, it's been a life's work. The *Tip of the Spear* is this conversation that we're having. The *Tip of the Spear* is a discussion about really three principles and my observation of 30 years in the business.

Number 1 is the exponential curve is increasing at an increasing rate. I've already spoken to that. That's kind of rule number 1.

The second rule that I've observed and I'm talking about it, is the book talks about the genie of technology never goes back in the bottle. You have an exponentially said that technology's changing. The technologies that we invent don't magically go back in if we don't think that they're good.

So that gene slicing technology that allows us to build new organs is all fine and good under certain circumstances, if you can imagine that genie out in the wild in the hands of somebody who has other purposes for it. All the technology that's exponentially changing are out in the wild.

And then the third thing that I talk about is those things are layered against, exponential change is layered again linear institutions. So, at the end of the day, all of this change is happening, but our institutions, governments and education are very linear.

We have this tip of the spear, fast-moving technology, exciting stuff. But that tip is getting too far away from the tail. And what happens is you have inequality. You have distribution of income and these positive results from technology innovation are not being spread across the planet. I look at that as unplannable and unsustainable.

The first part of the book raises that flag and the second part says, what could be done about it. What I do is I talk about the solutions through the eyes of two 12-year olds, a 12-year-old here in North America and a 12-year-old girl in Malawi. And I understand, and I walk them through the next 15 years of our world, through the eyes of a developing nation and the eyes of a developed nation and I think, where are the answers going to come from to solve that problem?

I must get my 60-second pitch a little tighter on the book, but that's what the book's about and it's about understanding how we come up with solutions to solve the tip of the spear problem.

David: Everyone, you can tell that we really need to spend a day, a week, a lifetime of collaboration with people like Jim Gibson. Before we close today Jim, just one takeaway, one thing that you invite our listeners to be aware of, change or do?

Jim: Yeah, I thought about this a lot and I think if I had to boil it down is, look to somebody closest to you. I'm thinking globally, and my advice is very personal. If you're a parent, look to your child. If you're a child or you're a millennial, look to your parents; look to one person you're very close to and have the conversation about what the future of technology should be.

What world do we want to create? And have the conversation with full knowledge that the world's not going to look the same in 10 years. It really isn't. But have a very frank and open conversation about the things you can do as a parent, as a voter – in terms of voting our next cohort of politicians – but have that conversation with somebody you love or somebody you care about and say, what is it that you can do to recognize what's coming and not going to the future naively and with mass optimism or mass pessimism.

I see both, and have that conversation. Make it personal. Make it real. Understand what your kids are going to walk into if you're a parent. Recognize that their school systems, that they're teaching or being taught, are struggling to figure it out.

David: Wonderful. Everyone, that's our call-to-action, is have that conversation with somebody in your first degree of separation, to envision and be part of, and collaborate to creating our own future of disrupt, and build your opportunities. There is so much more to say, Jim. Thank you so much. Thank you, listeners.

I want to make a quick invitation. On my April 20th show, I'm going to invite members of the listening audience, members of Startup Calgary, anyone throughout the world who has a pitch that answers Jim's invitation, my invitation. Email me at david@davidbsavage.com. Make your pitch on how you want to build on this conversation and how you can seek our support. And I'm going to select four people to be on that April 20th show.

Thank you everyone. Thank you, Jim Gibson. Now let's work together better.

Chapter 11 Collaboration, Negotiation and Mediation featuring Jeff Cohen

David: Hey everyone, and welcome back. This is David B. Savage; our theme today is collaboration, negotiation and mediation strategies. I'm delighted to have our special guest today, Jeff Cohen, the mediator leader and chair of the Collaborative Global Initiative from New York State.

Jeff is a good friend. He's a mountain man, passionate about getting the right people to come to their conclusions through mediation and proper negotiation.

In this first segment, I really want to focus on negotiation. I want to talk today about negotiation strategies, personal awareness for negotiation, and I'll give you a checklist. When you hear it, if you want a copy of my negotiation steps to success, just tweet me at @davidbsavage, or email me at davidbsavage.com, and I'll get you that checklist. It's very handy, very useful as you prepare, whether you're just sitting down in a meeting room about to make a phone call, or you really want to plan out your negotiation well in advance with the right people in collaboration. So happy to offer that to you at no charge.

Now, we negotiate every day, and yet we so often fail in our negotiations. Why is that? How do people get in our own way? How do we fail ourselves? What is the cost of being triggered, stuck, enraged, engaged, or just blind, the blind spots? How might we be more mindful and personally aware? These are some of the issues that, in my negotiation success checklist and my personal awareness today, in the first part of the show, we're going to talk about that.

In my life, I've spent a lot of time negotiating that, helping people get to the right place. I bring over 40 years, almost 41 years of experience in oil and gas, renewable energy, healthcare, entrepreneurship, stakeholder engagement, and conflict management. Over a 10-year period, my partners and I, we collaborated to create five companies and sell them within 10 years. Included in that, I also was part of small groups that created four not-for-profit organizations.

Since 2007, I got out of that world and I've been focused on building capacity, innovation, and accountability in people, and in between the organizations and communities. So, that's what I want to do now. I want to help you negotiate, equip you, coach you, focus on where are your strengths, where are your gaps?

As my friend, Erica Ariel Fox, the author of the bestseller, *Winning from Within*, termed it, there is a performance gap between our best potential and what we most often do. My focus, in my entire career and for you right now, is to help you get the right people with the right skills and resources in the right space at the right time to figure things out together. You can do it, we'll do it.

We're faced with rejection, high costs, lack of engagement, limited vision, limited resources. We're constrained. There's that scarcity. How do you Break Through to yes? Well, I offer a bunch of ways of doing that through my coaching and my organizational development consulting and speaking, also my book that you've heard about in the intro several times, and several you have *Break Through to Yes: Unlocking the Possible Within a Culture of Collaboration*.

I also work with a collaborative global initiative. This is six of us in the Netherlands, Canada, and the United

States helping organizations, and communities, and leaders get through conflict and complexity and Break Through to their yes. Since 1999, I've been working on appropriate dispute resolution in the oil and gas industry in Canada. I was one of the co-founders in 1999 of what is now known as the Alberta Energy Regulator, its appropriate dispute resolution program.

After the unfortunate murder of Patrick Kent, an oilman shot by a landowner in 2003, we started a company-to-company resolution council. We created and published a handbook called Let's Talk. Yeah, simple as that. We had 100 volunteers from legal engineering operations, marketing, accounting, all phases coming together to say, "We can do better together."

So, you can Break Through to yes. I want to make this personal. I want to first start you off with my negotiation success checklist. This is the one that I believe -- well, I will send it to you if you contact me, and it's just a great one-pager that you can use, you can develop. But, I think, oftentimes, when we negotiate, we think only about ourselves and what we need. We think about what our companies are demanding, what our boss wants, our positions, our strategies. We need to be far better negotiators.

Here's my guide. I'm going to talk you through it, and again, send me a note at davidbsavage, or David@davidbsavage.com, and I'll get you a copy of this.

Negotiation guide

A) When you're getting ready to negotiate, understand that negotiation starts when the relationship starts. This is the first hello. Negotiation, like collaboration and dispute resolution, is not an event. It's a relationship. Consider what's most important. What is it that you want? What are your fears? What are your interests, your vision, your boundaries? Start to hunch your interests and hunch theirs, their vision, their boundaries, their interests. Remember, interests are what are beneath the positions. So, "I want this," but there's a reason you want that. Focus on that reason.

So, understand it's a relationship is one.

B) really focus on your interests, their interests, and what's most important to you. Is it this particular piece of this particular deal, or is there something much greater?

C) fully evaluate, estimate, and measure, prepare. Get as much data and relevant information as you can. It's so critical. Don't be a lazy negotiator. Come prepared, think it through, and think their side through, and help them win. I'll say that again. Help them win.

D) when you're at the negotiating table, first, money should be the last thing you talk about. Deal with the interest issues, effects, and commitments first. The money part will then be a far more accurate compensation. When you bring money first, you're not building the relationship, and you're setting yourself up for failure, because it's actually not about the money. The money is the final element of the compensation. It's all the terms and conditions and accountabilities that you really want to work through to make sure.

To be blunt, we're not prostitutes. We are business people, we are fathers and mothers, we are leaders, we are community leaders, we're volunteers. Focus on the interest, issues, and effects, and commitments. Money comes later. Money is important, but that's not the reason you're making the deal. You might get a million dollars and be miserable, or you might get very little and be ecstatic. Think about that as a perspective.

E) make time to fully engage and be face-to-face - that's right, face-to-face - as much as possible. Don't use emails and phone conversations. They are so misleading. Increasingly, in the last decade, people have been negotiating by text. Wow, how do you understand each other by text message in 140 characters or less? It is ripe for misunderstanding.

It may seem that avoidance calls, or emails get the deal done, but unless you take the time to meet, you may miss important issues and opportunities. Yeah, that's opportunities. How many conversations or meetings have you been face-to-face where a comment is made and something brand new, a great opportunity, or a great barrier comes up that you would never get by email or by a quick phone call. The keys to getting these opportunities are building respect, trust, and accountability from both parties.

F) at the table, early on, design the negotiation together. In other words, before you get into the bartering and the bargaining, talk about do they have the authority, do you have the authority? What are the resources that you'll need? What are the goals, timing accountability? If this is a D priority for me sometime later next year, and yet it's your number one priority, let's put that on the table, because otherwise, I will frustrate you to death. Make certain you share expectations and understandings. You will be frustrated otherwise.

G) when you're at the table is be persistent, and say no until you're ready to agree. This isn't a time to be nice. Be real, have integrity. If it's not working for you, just

continue to say no. We'll talk about The Power of a
Positive No and *Difficult Conversations* a little later.

H) bring a wide range of wisdoms, personalities, and
possibilities together. Really listen and ask questions if
things are not clear. Especially ask "stupid" questions.
Explore together and with neutral experts when you have
issues that you do not have the resources to evaluate.

I) take great care to serve the other party's interest.
Your work is to also work their side of the deal and to build
trust. Doing that will encourage them to serve your
interests, whether it's in negotiation, mediation, or making
love. If you take care of them, then they'll take care of me.
It works that way. If it's only about me, it's going to be
short-term, and I will get bit somehow. So, take care of
their side of the deal. Make sure that they're proud, they
look good, and they get what they want on the basis that
you also receive the same.

J) It's key important; it's embrace conflicts. Conflict's a
good thing. Look for diversity, seek diversity, and
positively engage challenge. Getting along or being nice
often leads to disappointment. It's going to be fake or
superficial. If there's conflict, go there. If you really
disagree with what I'm saying right now, let me know. I
want to have that conversation. I need to learn.

K) create larger possibilities. What else can be achieved
beyond the immediate short-term objectives? How will our
next negotiation go? So, just think about that. You're
setting yourself for the relationship and negotiations to
come.

L) evaluate and deal, and create mutual
accountabilities. If a party fails to perform, then the
consequences should be agreed up front. Ensure both

parties are accountable, and the consequences are in writing. Yeah, put it in writing, document the deal properly. If there are items that are not in the prepared document, then add them.

So, after the negotiation, so you're done, you're complete, the deal's signed, review what you've learned, gained, lost in the status of the relationship. That's right, whatever you gained, whatever you learned, whatever you lost, how did it go, how can we improve better next time?

Reconnect with the other parties to review and improve the process and outcomes. Prepare for the next deal with this party and others. In other words, sit down with them, design for the next time. And fourth, understand that your negotiations are a complete cycle, a relationship and not an event.

I've dealt with people in oil and gas, in healthcare, in renewable energy, on economic development tribunals where we dealt with each other 30 years ago, and we trust each other, we get it, we're the first point of contact when an opportunity arises.

In my book and on my website, davidbsavage.com, you'll see the realms of negotiation. The world is the outer realm, other organizations or community is next, your organization or company. Inside that is your family, inside that is yourself. Yeah, think about that.

In fact, the most difficult negotiation is with myself. How do I fail myself? Where do we go from here? After the break, I'm going to talk about personal awareness and awareness of others. I'm going to talk about collaboration, negotiation, and mediation, accountability, and vision. Let's take a short break, and I'll be right back, and we'll talk about that awareness. If the most difficult negotiations are with myself, what do I need to become aware of? What do I need to change? What do I need to stand for? We'll be right back.

David: Welcome back. While we're often not aware of it, we do negotiate every day. Our negotiations involve outside organizations, internal teams and ourselves. Negotiation training often targets skills, techniques, and strategies, and dealing with the other. However, there is a performance gap. As I'd mentioned, my friend and co-founder of the Global Negotiation Institute, Erica Fox, I quote Erica, "The performance gap is the distance between your highest potential and what you actually do and practice. There are big differences."

When I coach negotiations, negotiators in their negotiations, I want them to become clear on their interests, boundaries, their flexibility, potential, and relationships. Yes, the most difficult negotiations we have are with ourselves. Let's explore what does that look like. We must recognize this performance gap between our potential and what we do most often. There is a real difference between our intelligences, and we need to access all our intelligences - mental, emotional, physical, spiritual - to Break Through our current and future challenges. When I coach negotiators, that's what I look at. That's what we do together.

Now, if you look at Turning Negotiation into Corporate Capability by Ertel published way back about 20 years ago, the usual way of negotiation is we confirm suspicions and perceptions about each other, we reduce risk-taking and reduce creativity, then we create a low-value deal, and we under-invest in the relationship, then we further restrict information flow, which again, confirms suspicions and perceptions. According to Ertel, and I believe this, a better approach is improving mutual understanding, expand the scope of the discussions, create valuable options, improve trust and communications, and share information about each other's interests.

When we're talking about personal awareness, some of the great books from the Harvard Program on Negotiation, I'll quote here, and I've quoted before, Fisher and Ury's Getting to Yes. It's what? 40 years old now, and they've probably sold 40 million copies. It's a classic. Separate positions from interests, generate options for mutual gain, and most importantly, separate the people from the problem.

My friends, Stone, Patton, and Heen wrote *Difficult Conversations,* which we'll also talk here and a little later. What if the person is the problem? There is more than meets the ear. Do you like that? There is more than meets the ear. In every difficult conversation, there are feelings. Go to the learning conversation.

There's a great ladder in difficult conversations. We often trade only conclusions back and forth without stepping down to where most of the real action is, the information and interpretations that lead each of us to see the world as we do. We've got to come down that ladder of the difficult conversations. Instead of exchanging conclusions, or our perspectives and interpretations, or observations, let's be curious. Let's talk about what's important to us, what are our interests. Let's explore each other.

Now, in the *Power of a Positive No* by William Ury, another great book, we tend to accommodate by saying yes when we really wanted to say no. We attack by saying no poorly or treating a conflict, or most often, we simply avoid. Ury teaches us, and I would share this with you and my negotiation clients, "Say no most often. Say yes to yourself. Be present to what will serve you in the relationship, and counteroffer if you value the relationship, boundaries, and commitments." Set your boundaries, allow the wedge of awareness, assert your interests, be clear and honor yourself, invest yourself. Yeah, truly invest yourself.

Many of you know that one of my favorite quotes is that from Viktor Frankl from his book, *Man's Search for Meaning, From Death-Camp to Existentialism.* You might write this down and put it on your office wall. It's just brilliant. It is a guide for me. It is my reminder. "Between every stimulus and response is a space. In that space is our power to choose our response. In our response lies our growth and our freedom." Yeah, I'll say it again, "Between every stimulus and response is a space." In other words, don't react fast. Don't let the reptilian brain jump in there. "Between every stimulus and response is a space. In that space is our power to choose our response, and in our response, lies our growth and our freedom," Victor Frankl. Speak when you are angry, and you will make the best speech you will ever regret.

Here's a few more things. Not knowing is important. I am a huge fan of the enneagram and Nine Domains, and use those as tools of awareness of yourself, your tendencies under stress, awareness of the other, and really, really look at these opportunities. That's what I want to share with you. Really look at these opportunities.

You know, the dilemma of a difficult conversation, let's get back to Doug and Sheila's book, *Difficult Conversations.* The dilemma is if we avoid the problem, we feel taken advantage of. Our feelings fester, we feel like a coward, we're lost. We've lost an opportunity to improve things. If we confront the problem, things actually might get worse. But, that's the paradigm, the dilemma of a difficult conversation.

What if we looked at it differently? What if we accepted a paradigm shift from proving a point, giving a piece of our mind, get our way, convince, manipulate, or persuade the other to a learning stance. Understand what happened from the other's point of view. In each conversation in negotiations, there are difficult conversations. Stop arguing, start learning together. Separate the people from the problem, and difficult conversations are, at their very core, about feelings. When it comes to understanding our emotions, most of us are lost. Let's just not do that.

Where I want to take you with this is awareness. Use tools, any tools that you like that will help you become more aware of yourself, mindfulness, mindfulness in negotiation, and leadership and collaboration, but let's not deliver our message. Why don't we build the relationship? Why don't we Break Through to our own yes and bring ourselves to understanding the other, focusing on the other, and at the same time, protecting what's most important to us?

After the break, I've got my friend and mentor, Jeff Cohen, from Albany, New York, and he's going to explore with us about dispute resolution, mediation. He's one of the world's leading mediators. He's done so much. I respect him so much. And we will go there after the break with my friend, Jeff Cohen. We'll be right back.

David: Welcome back, everyone. Firstly, I apologize. I've got a bit of a sore throat, and I think my friend, Jeff, who we're about to interview, has the same, so if you hear us a little raw or coughing, [*coughs*] that's what it sounds like. We've talked about my negotiation steps to success, personal awareness, mindfulness, being clear on interests, building the relationship. Now, I really want to introduce you again -- actually, some of you would have heard my friend, Jeff, back in my 2015 podcast radio show series.

Jeff, we can find out more about at jcohenmediation.com, and the collaboraitveglobalinitiative.com. Jeff has been a good friend, confidant, and a mentor of mine for about nine years. He has been an attorney and mediator in private practice since 1984. Jeff's practice is concentrated in the mediation of disputes involving divorce, separation, business, and commercial, organizational, and workplace-related issues.

Jeff is a former director of the Association for Conflict Resolution, ACR. That's acrnet.org, which is the largest mediation organization in the United States. Jeff chaired the ACR ethics committee, which is charged with the creation and promotion of the best ethical practices for mediators and other alternative dispute resolution professionals. He's an advanced practitioner. He's been given that title, earned that title, and has been admitted to the ACR Academy of Family Mediators.

Jeff has accumulated over 500 hours of specific mediation training from many of the finest mediation training programs and trainers around the world, especially Canada and the United States, including Harvard Program on Negotiation and Cornell. Now, Jeff, I could brag about you for a long time --

Jeff: Keep going. I love this.

David: Let me just save our time for your valuable insights. I invite our listeners to connect with Jeff. He is one of the best. Jeff, I've got a series of questions I'd like to ask you, but any remarks that you might want to make, Jeff, before we get into that?

Jeff: Oh my goodness, first of all, thank you so much for having me on your show. You and I go back a very long way, and I think there's a lot of mutual respect, and I think, at this point, a lot of mutual sickness. Both of us are a bit frayed here in terms of our voices, but I will certainly do my best to speak up and answer your questions, and again, I'm honored that you speak so highly of me. So, please proceed.

David: Well, I certainly do. You're a real positive force for business, for families, and for me.

Jeff: Well, thank you.

David: Now, tell us a little bit more about your work, Jeff.

Jeff: Well, the easy way to say it is that I am an in-the-trench mediator. From sun-up to sun-down, to sort of paraphrased Neil Young, I'm waging heavy peace, and I absolutely love the idea that I get up in the morning and I'm helping folks resolve their conflicts. As you say, I do a lot of divorce work, I do a lot of workplace and organizational mediation. I mediate in commercial matters for the U.S. Government, their Department of the Interior, I've done work with Native American groups. I do some facilitation work as well, working with larger groups where there are essential conversations that need to be had. I also teach this stuff up at Syracuse University. Every spring, I lecture on the ethically embraceable model of mediation.

And you mentioned briefly, and I think it's very important is a shout-out for the Association for Conflict Resolution. ACR is an extraordinary organization, and if you are a mediator, facilitator, or other ADR professional, or whether you are just interested in knowing more about it, go to acrnet.org. We are an organization of extraordinary individuals who are doing nothing but trying to promote peaceful, productive conflict resolution, and we have a number of different sections. We have a family section, an environmental and public policy section, we have a state planning section, we have a workplace section. There's a place for you to fit and to get involved, and I ask every one of you that may have an interest, please take a look at us. We are an extraordinary organization, and we'd love to have you.

David: I'm also a member of the ACR. It is an extraordinary organization: powerful people, more important, powerful sense of family and community, and I attribute that, in part at least, to your work on ethics. People might say, "Ethics and law, what's that?" but you have a completely different frame on ethics, and mediation, and dispute resolution.

Jeff: Well, this is what I would say in a nutshell. Any profession is only as good as its ethical underpinnings. Ethics provide structure to a process, ethics provide integrity. Integrity in the context of mediation means that everybody at the table, whether I'm working with divorcing folks, whether I'm working with folks in a workplace or organizational matter, it means that I'm going to provide a level of service that is going to be protective of everyone in the room so that everybody can be ensured that they're only going to make the best possible decisions for themselves, which is the cornerstone of the mediation process, which is uncoerced self-determination. That is very important to me.

David: That's critical. I remember early days when I was getting one of my professional designations. They said, "Well, you got to take an ethics course," and it's like, "Oh my god, it's like pulling teeth. I'm a professional; I don't need this." "Well, I don't think there's anything more important than having that foundation in ethics and values."

What I'll share with you, and I think I've shared this with you in the past, in my local rotary club, that's one of the things I'm most proud of is we go into the local high school in Cranbrook, British Columbia, and we teach half a day on values, and we teach another half a day on ethics, and all of a sudden, these high school students, it becomes real to them. This is their guide, this is their boundaries. This is where I will say no. Simple approaches that make it real for their interests and their world, all of a sudden, gives them the guidance on how to behave.

Jeff: Absolutely, and in my practice, I tell folks right up front, "Ethics first, money second." So, if I will never breach one of the ethical rules or ethical principles of our organization, then I will always have a good reason for why I won't do that in a particular instance. Some people will say, "Oh, come on, you can do this, that, or the other thing," and I'll say, "No, I can't," and I give a reason for that. So, for me, if you uphold the ethics of the process, the process will uphold you.

David: I like it. It's a beautiful phrase. Is it rules of engagement then, Jeff?

Jeff: Well, there are a number of different aspects of this. Back in 2005, the Association for Conflict Resolution,

ACR, along with the American Bar Association and the American Arbitration Association co-adopted, if you will, or approved -- there were specific ways that they either approved or adopted a set of practice standards. I have them on my website if anybody's interested. I've posted them there and I make sure all of my clients read them, and then a number of years later, I co-authored the ethical principles of our organization, and if you're a professional, you understand there are practice standards and principles, and the principles are really the lens through which we interpret those standards.

So, when in doubt, you go to those standards and they will tell you what it is that you need to know about professionalism, about competency, about how you hold yourself out to the public, about the ethics of the process itself, the ethics of what is, in fact, a mediator. These are so important, and I make sure that every new set of clients that comes in the door has a copy of those ethical principles and ethical standards in their hands. Where a practitioner may have a difficulty with it, not sure about something, they can call myself or my co-chair on the ethics committee, and we'll have a conversation with everyone about what is ethical, and what isn't, and give our perspectives. Yes, I guess, is the short answer, and I just gave you the long answer

David: Oftentimes, we get into conflict, we fail to negotiate effectively when the values and ethics of the two parties, or three parties, are so different. Would it be important for us to actually talk about that up front?

Jeff: Rephrase that for me in some way just so I can really focus in on that in my drugged-up state here, as you perhaps are.

David: No drugs here, and it's interesting, everyone. Jeff, I think you're in your office in Albany, New York, and I'm in my office in Cranbrook, British Columbia. We didn't share this, but I think the weather system seems to go across the Rockies, all across the plains, to the Great Lakes, and to New York. So, we are one. I want to get back to the --

Jeff: What you're saying is I caught this illness from you?

David: Yes, three days ago, I coughed, and being playful a bit, that coughing and sharing the sickness, or raspiness, or lack of ethical standards, it can be a metaphor for -- why don't we start with the basics about ethics? Oftentimes, we will look at even our political leaders and our community leaders are activists these days and say, "Wow, where are they coming from?" I talked earlier in the show about the boundaries, about designing the negotiation, about really being clear about what's most important. That's where I come back is at sometimes in my career as a negotiator and collaborator, there are very few, but there are a few people that I just cannot deal with. They are just aliens to me and I need to find that I need to simply say no and shut down. Is there a way that we can gauge? You take care with your clients, and then in your teaching, you help them create those understandings and those ethical approaches and awareness, how do you deal with it when at least one party just doesn't act that way?

Jeff: Well, it's funny you say that because I'm springing this on you. As much as we're good friends, I don't think you know that I'm actually writing a book about conflict awareness, and I only start out with folks that are seemingly intractable by explaining to them my role in very simple terms, and I'm not sure if you're familiar with - I'm sure many of our readers are - Viktor Frankl, who wrote the book, *Man's Search for Meaning*. That's one of those books that's on every top 10 list on the planet, and he says that, "Between the stimulus and the response, there is a space. And in that space, is our power to choose our response. In our response lies our growth and freedom." So, I set the stage. It's a very powerful statement, and then I follow up with and say, "Ethically, my role is to occupy that space between the stimulus and the response and to use the various interventions and techniques that I have to make sure that, in that space, we are working towards a proactive, positive, mutually acceptable outcome.

David: Why would I do that?

Jeff: Well, why would you do that? Well, you've got to get things done, right? If people are in my office and they're having a conflict, they need to resolve it because the conflict is either disruptive to their private lives, or they're losing money in their businesses because of it, or their job is at stake, or any number of reasons why a conflict may be negative. And my theory is, in this book that I'm writing, that the more aware we are of why we are in conflict, the more likely we are to be able to transcend the conflict and create options for positive outcomes.

And I truly believe that there are conflicts of the mind, conflicts of the body, and conflicts of the spirit. Our unconscious mind creates automatic behaviors, which we all have, our body can also hijack us, our amygdala, our fight-or-flight response can hijack us and make us less amenable to a cognitive process. And conflicts of the spirit, really, are about what we individually believe to be just, what our own deeply-held beliefs are without necessarily wanting to understand, or discounting what other people's deeply-held beliefs are, and what other people feel are just.

So, I believe that by talking about these things with my clients and making them self-aware of why they are conflicting, and these are things that everybody relates to. I don't care how obstinate a person is. People will say in the beginning, "Well, I don't really need a lesson in psychology, or physiology, or in what is just," and I'm not doing that at all. I'm just simply making them aware of their own behaviors and why they may be stuck in conflict.

David: This is going to be a brilliant book, and I know that I need that. I need that on a daily basis when my reptilian brain starts to get triggered. Most of the time - not all of the time - I remind myself of, "Okay, notice the emotion, notice the reaction, what's underneath there, why am I responding this way, what value is it crossing, what are my interests? How would I choose to react now that I've given myself that space between stimulus and response?"

Jeff: Well, here's the problem. When we have a problem with our body, we try to treat it ourselves, and there comes a point where we say, "Uncle! I've got to go see a doctor," right? When we have these kinds of issues, often, we try to self-justify our behaviors rather than say, "Hey, we may actually need a professional to get us through this," and I can say the same thing. As a conflict resolver, I'm not really good at my own conflict because it's very difficult when it is you experiencing it for all of these reasons.

So, the whole idea is, A, we must be aware that we are being automatic. Automatic behaviors, let's face it, every morning, when we get up, folks, I guarantee that very little different happens every morning from the time you touch the floor with your first toe until the time you have your first cup of coffee. At least me, I'm a coffee addict. I go through my morning ablutions in a similar pattern every day. Much depends upon us being automatic. But, if you're really honest with yourself, the way you conflict with somebody now is the way you've always conflicted, because we create automatic behaviors around how we conflict as well, and you need a professional that's able to take you out of those behaviors, those circular patterns that keep you stuck and mired in your own backwash.

The same thing with that -- and those are the conflicts created by the mind, the conflicts created by the body. You talked about your lizard brain, which is what Carl Sagan talked about, our amygdala is our fight-or-flight response, and as Peter Diamandis said in his book, *Abundance*, he said, "The amygdala, once activated, doesn't easily turn off," and he ends with the idea that the amygdala is always looking for something to fear. So, if you're going through a divorce, if you're going through a conflict, the amygdala gets fired up and hijacks you, and makes you rely more on your automatic behaviors, and lets you rely more on what your own deeply-held beliefs are without having the capacity to look beyond those beliefs to understand, compassionately, that someone else may think differently. Just look at our election in this country.

David: Yeah, I'm just hesitating. I'm not an American, but I keep on thinking of certain politicians where you look at it and say, "Well, certain politicians," and I don't relay this only to the President of the United States, I relay to many politicians, and many leaders, coaches of sporting teams where they simply lead by fear, lead by isolation, lead by shutting down the other as opposed to what you're helping us to understand is to be more aware of ourselves and more aware and respectful of the others, of the people who are in conflict.

Jeff: And to tell you the truth, I'm not trying to plug CGI here, folks, but if there's anyone out there who has the resources to hire someone like a CGI, to go throughout North America, and to not be political, but to hold these kinds of conversations, to help stakeholders on both sides actually compassionately understand why they voted one way or another, we can create a new center in this country, a new center that will allow everyone to be heard, everybody to be respected, as opposed to us continually being polarized. I apologize; I tripped over my tongue there.

But, that's really what we need at this point. We need an organization, we need to have town hall meetings where we're listening to Trump voters, where we're listening to Hillary voters, where we're listening to people who didn't vote at all, and to create deeper understandings as opposed to simply dispensing with someone who didn't hold your world view. There are a lot of reasons to be compassionate on both sides, but it's not happening.

David: Yeah, I'm really proud as a Canadian to say many people around the world think Canada and Prime Minister "Joe" Trudeau, according to Sean Spicer, Justin Trudeau in actual fact, is a great thing. Now, many Canadians think he's a horrible thing, and none of that really matters. Justin Trudeau, Donald Trump, whomever, they're just people. And as Margaret Wheatley taught us a long time ago, we set up these heroes for failure. Through work in mediation, negotiation, collaboration, we're actually trying to set up teams to work together better.

So, Jeff, we've only got about a minute left here, but what I'd really like to have our listeners understand is what does a mediation look like when you help people guide them past their amygdala, and their fears, and their hearts.

Can you just say a little bit about what it is that you do in the room with them?

Jeff: Well, the training is in literally hundreds of psychologically-based interventions and techniques that are used never to manipulate folks to a result, but to manipulate folks to a place of objectivity, emotional safety, as I just said, conflict awareness, why you may be holding onto this conflict, all of the things that I talked about. And then my job, on top of that, is to impose a frame. I like to say that I own -- I don't remember who said this, but I'm going to quote whoever it is, and thank you if you're listening, "A mediator owns the structure of your conversation; you own the outcome."

And the structure can be interest-based negotiation through the Harvard Program on Negotiation, it can be one of your countrymen, and someone who lives around the corner from you. Larry Fong's version of the Milan, the hypothetical model, it could be a narrative approach. There are all these various approaches.

My job is to help everybody by imposing a structure on the conversation, and to impose the structure of realizing we're not here to talk about what's wrong. You already know what's wrong. We're here to talk about what's possible and how to implement it. So, that's very important because courts are interested in justifying what happened in the past in order to hang their legal peg on an outcome.

We don't worry about the past. We're not interested in proving what happened three years ago, because people have evolved beyond that. My job is to help people move forward and to build their new future, to help them to collaborate in the purest sense of the term, and to help them build something, and to preserve the relationship rather than destroy it.

David: And to stay in control. They are the ones that create that outcome.

Jeff: Yes.

David: So, Jeff, thank you so much for joining us in our show today. We've explored our steps to negotiation success, personal awareness for negotiators, and mediation and dispute resolution in the structure in ethics. So, our call to action to you is reach out to three key people in your family, in your business, your clients, or your community, and talk about the structure of your collaboration, how you wish to negotiate, innovate, resolve your conflicts. Be open, listen deeply, and design it, and decide together. Thanks, everyone, and thank you, Jeff. Let's work together better.

Jeff: We will.

Chapter 12 Collaborative Global Initiative Tool Kit featuring Barry Wilson, Doreen Liberto, and Jeff Cohen

David: Welcome everyone. Today we talk about these challenging times and our Collaborative Global Initiative. Today, we're joined by my friends, my mentors Barry Wilson, Doreen Liberto, Kathy Porter, Jeff Cohen and myself. I guess I'll join us myself. We're going to explore the movement and solutions to the increasing complexity, frustration, lies, environmental collapse and separation and segregation in the world today.

Now this is a live show. Tweet me at @davidbsavage or email me at david@davidbsavage.com and we will respond.

We're going to do this in four segments, so I'll have a change not only to facilitate this great group of people we have here today, but also respond and engage you because that's what our hope is. We're looking for a way to work together better.

Some questions just to set this up. Isn't there a better way? Are you worn out fighting? How costly are your conflicts? And how long are the delays in getting your projects built and your visions realized? Where do you find the help? How do I deal with cumulative effects in such a positive way, as opposed to a negative? Sometimes, do you feel like an outlier? You don't need to. We're here and there's hundreds and thousands of us around the world.

So today, we're going to have an open discussion. We're going to have each one of us make a few statements, put some things on the table and make some offers. Then we'll just have an open discussion amongst us, and if you call in, tweet, whatever, you'll be part of it as well.

In this age of complexity, conflict, there are potential massive risks, risks to our future as well. Who's the Collaborative Global Initiative? Go to collaborativeglobalinitiative.com. Our focus is training, coaching and accessing a global network. We're planning online courses and in-person workshops throughout North America, including New York, California, British Columbia and Alberta in the next 18 months.

We will get you to the networks, to innovation and success. We can do this way more efficiently and effectively than in the past. Now one of the things that I'm really delighted that Barry is going to share with us a little later on, he's got a cumulative effects playbook that he's bringing out, an online series on cumulative effects. Go to ceanalytic.com for more.

Doreen and I, on May 25th, we're going to be hosting a dialogue in San Luis Obispo, California. July 5th, Doreen and I will be in Vancouver, British Columbia doing the same. That one's around our upcoming book, Learn to Talk, Talk to Learn.

What do you need? I think you need a lot of things, but I think you need collaboration to succeed.

Jeff Cohen is writing a reframing conflicts series. There are lots of resources. If we don't have them, you probably have them and if we don't have them, we can connect you to the solution providers.

Now before we get into the guests, I just want to talk about something that Rod McKay, the chair of the Canadian Heart and Stroke Foundation and a friend of mine, said "Leadership is difficult. Leadership that depends on collaboration is very difficult. And yet, we all think we know how to collaborate. We try to build capacity, decide things, but we actually do not collaborate very well."

I've sought out professional development as a coach, mediator, facilitator, negotiator. These are powerful positions from around our world and great skills for leaders like you. But like collaboration, too often I hear leaders state, 'I coached her', 'I mentored him', 'I mediated that conflict', 'We collaborated'.

These statements are disingenuous, ignorant and diminish professionals in those fields. Collaboration, to many, is getting together to work on something. That's not collaboration. That's a meeting and sometimes manipulation.

Let's make a joint proclamation that we value collaboration as a powerful way of leading. Collaboration isn't an act. It's the way we are together. To collaborate isn't simply to work together. It's an organizational culture, and that's what I talk about, unlocking the possible within a culture of collaboration in my book Break Through to Yes.

A quick introduction of my friends and my mentors, and people you will all soon listen to. Barry Wilson of British Columbia is a systems ecologist and BC-registered professional forester, and a principal at CE Analytic Ltd, as well as associate of ALCES Landscape and Land Use Ltd.

Barry is an expert in holistic, cumulative effects analysis with 27 years of experience in integrated land management in North America. And Barry was just in California, speaking at a conference on these issues.

CE Analytic is a 1% For the Planet member and a proud donor to the Columbia Mountains Institute and so much more.

We're hoping that from an airport lounge somewhere in the world, Kathy Porter's going to join us. Kathy is also part of our Collaborative Global Initiative. Kathy's intention is to engage in dialogue, not only to those practicing professionals but also those individuals and enterprises curious enough to move in new and even novel directions.

How can we reframe our experiences in our preferred way of thinking? Some of this work that Kathy does so brilliantly. Kathy is most of the time in Toronto, Ontario these days.

I move on to Doreen Liberto. Doreen, her experience includes collaboration of program management, land use, environmental transportation, climate change and resource management sustainability and communication strategies. Sustainable land use planning, resource management, transportation, greenhouse gas reduction; she has just a great CV as well. And she received her graduate degree from Pepperdine in the School of Law and Dispute Resolution.

And our president, Mr. President, Jeff Cohen, who if you're listening was with me last week and did a beautiful interview discussion on dispute resolution mediation. Jeff is a conflict engagement specialist, concentrating in mediation, facilitation and stakeholder engagement. And he's done it almost as long as I have, for 26 years-plus.

He does divorce and family, commercial employment and business, stakeholder engagement, environmental, public policy issues, workplace, conflicts, organizational conflicts, facilitation. He is a proud member and part of the center of Jeff's heart is values and he does that work with the Association for Conflict Resolution.

We are the Collaborative Global Initiative. I'm David Savage. I know stuff too, I guess. Over the last 18 months, you've heard a lot about my interests and my offerings. I will now turn it over, pardon me as I get a sore throat here. Doreen, can you start us off to talk about dialogue and some of your ideas behind our upcoming book?

Doreen: Sure, thank you David for inviting me to be on your program. And I look forward to hearing from everybody on the program today. I think what I want to do, first of all, is frame what's going on and the changes that are happening from a cultural standpoint.

Unfortunately, we've developed a culture of debating and not listening to understand the other side. We only have to watch the events in the 2016 U.S. Presidential Elections to see the attitude of I'm right and you're wrong, to know that there's, at any time, there can be debating, violence and collaborations put aside.

We no longer dialogue. When I started my planning career in land use and environmental planning years ago, people would agree to disagree on the evidence or the facts that were presented. Shortly after that, we'd get together to determine, look at the situation to determine where we differed, try to get the evidence and then attempt to go ahead and rectify that or work together or collaborate, where we could find common ground.

But what happened over probably I'd say the last 5 to 10 years is that we've become, we'd look at it and we become like sporting teams. We are on each side of the football team and we are rooting for our side and booing the other side, and not willing to speak with them. We, essentially, have taken on the mentality of sporting teams and fans.

Given the fake news stories that we now have, our value changes, people accepting lies because the lies reflect their emotional support system, it's become a very challenging situation.

And it's not just something that I'm speaking about. There's actually a study that was done by Robb Willer, Professor of Psychology at Stanford. And what he found was that indeed, the divisions of opinions are becoming wider and that social media is part of this and how it's used, that people essentially only look at news, they look at social media that reflects their views, not opposing views. They have an echo chamber and they're not willing to dialogue. They want animosity.

And I'm finding more and more workshops that people are attending on how to be an advocate, how to be an activist and get your way from fighting. That's unfortunate. I feel like we're going backwards and what we need to do is start dialoguing, listening to one another. But I think we first have to have this dialogue to talk about the need for it. What's really happening in our society? But not only what is currently happening. If we continue down this path, what will happen? Where are we going with this?

Society has begun to stereotype positions, blame the other side when something goes wrong and we take a group think behavior. And what we're going to try to do in our book is talk about basically how we need to start talking, listening and not dehumanizing the other side. Once you dehumanize the other side, it's okay to say what you want about them. It's okay not to listen to them.

You need to go ahead and start talking again, and get small groups of opposing positions together and teach them how to listen, teach them how to dialogue and then hopefully they can continue that on into their community.

David: We've heard so much about the post-truth era. We've heard so much about castigation and judgments. What I'm going to suggest now, everyone, is let's just take our short break now and then we will come back and discuss the dialogue making. How do we get out of judgment?

Everyone, let's take the break now and we'll be right back.

David: Even during the break, we had some great conversations and Jeff has reminded me that while Doreen and I are hosting some dialogue events in California and British Columbia in the next two months, Jeff and Kathy, and Barry I hope will join us virtually. We really want this to be a collaborative, global initiative.

Doreen, you were talking about dialogue and the importance of breaking through to intelligent conversation and learning conversations. Let's pick it up again.

Doreen: I want to give another example. I was giving community presentations on climate change recently and I mentioned the conversation about whether people believed the climate's changing due to human activity or due to natural patterns. And one person took offense at my statement and said, there's no doubt that humans are causing the climate change. How can I even make, have a question that bad?

And then I went to another event where there were different people and somebody, a man stood up and very sternly told me that what is happening to the planet has happened many times before and it's a natural pattern, and why didn't I understand that?

I think that shows a good example where people are coming from different positions and they need to, rather than shout out their positions, what we need to do I think as collaborators is say okay, let's put your positions aside. Let's listen and dialogue. Can we all agree that there is a change that's taking place? Certainly, climate patterns are changing. Sea levels are rising, and because of the significant economic damage is and will continue to occur.

And I think what happened was we did get both sides to say, yeah there are some changes. Can we then take a step further and say we can agree on that, and what do we do about that? What do we do because there's some economic issues that are developing?

I think what's important is that we put our egos aside and we start collaborating on solutions. I think – is it important that we're right all the time? Is it important that we shout the loudest and we demand that, I'm right and you're wrong, I don't want to hear anything else you had to say?

It's really important that we really sit down and begin listening to one another, getting beyond our talking points and coming together with the common solution.

David: Yeah. That's so important, to go to the, instead of the debate and the adversarial approach, go to the learning, go to the learning conversation. Talk to learn.

Doreen: Right. I'd like to call that, David, collaborative learning. That is that everybody gets together and learning how to dialogue, is collaborative learning, how to listen is part of it. So that's part of what we'll be working on in our series of books.

David: That's great.

Jeff: I have to totally agree. And I just wanted to relay an experience of mine, that Kathy Porter and I had actually in working in a very complex landscape in the Alberta oil sands region, between about 2005 and 2008. We were working with a group up there. We're trying to figure out a path forward on a 10 million-hectare landscape, 50 stakeholders including all levels of government NGOs, indigenous people, big oil and other heavy industry, and a range of local citizens who were trying to collaboratively plan for sustainable environment, economy and society in this area that was experiencing and still is experiencing hyper growth in the resource extraction sector.

When we started the process with all of these stakeholders in the room, they sort of lined up on opposite sides of the room glaring at each other. We went through a process, first of all Kathy laid out some ground rules and said, we're going to spend the next little while here just learning. And we're not going to in with our positions on.

So, we did that, and we went through an exploration phase of understanding what this landscape could produce, and if we pushed it hard in different directions, what the outcomes might be. Another important part that comes out of the dialogue is being able to understand where other people are coming from.

By the end of this process, you had NGOs being able to very eloquently describe the business requirement of the oil industry. And you had a representative from oil and gas being able to speak very conclusively on the need for long-term biodiversity. And once they were able to fully understand each other's position, I think that's the learning that Doreen was talking about. Then solutions emerge from the group very quickly.

Doreen: Right.

Jeff: Yeah, that makes perfect sense.

David: I want to check in. I think we've got Kathy Porter join us. Kathy, are you on yet? Okay, sorry we'll continue on. There is so much to talk about this and this is very much in kind of this whole career is collaboration as a way to drive innovation.

Let's move on at this time to Barry and you're an expert. You've got so many resources and tools and expertise in cumulative effects. Let's go there now, Barry.

Barry: Thank you David, and as Doreen said, thank you very much for this terrific opportunity to join you on your show and to share some of the things that we love to talk about.

Cumulative effects, it's quickly becoming a buzzword. I have been working on this for a couple of decades. I guess before, it was super popular. The fact that we're growing at a rapid rate on this planet as humans and the planet isn't getting any bigger. It's becoming more and more of an issue.

And as Doreen talked about, this idea of getting into a debate versus dialogue seems to hamstring us a lot. From my perspective and my business, I work with clients all over North America and too often it seems to me that business as usual, sort of the standard way of going about our business gets us stuck pretty quickly in a tug of war between the environment and the economy.

David: Yeah.

Barry: And yet, we know that we need community and stakeholder support for this development and I think we all understand that that then requires both economic and environmental success in ways that we measure the outcomes. And oftentimes though, it can seem just too complicated to deal with the multiple overlapping land uses, and now combined with uncertainty like climate change. But we do have tools and processes that allow us to do just that, and I wanted to share a little bit about that today.

David: Yeah.

Barry: And as you mentioned, the CE playbook, I do teach people how to go through this process. You can go to the website, as you mentioned, or also ceplaybook.com. And I'll come back to that a little bit later, but it's a resource that folks could follow up on a little bit later.

I just think that if we all sort of think a little bit deep down inside, each one of us knows that we're going to have to deal with this complexity, even though it's difficult. And I think we all also understand that we have to find this right balance in order to survive and prosper, or some people say to find a safe operating space on earth. And I think our planning success will come easier when we view the world holistically as an integration of systems.

You've probably heard John Muir's quote, "When we try to pick out anything by itself, we find it hitched to everything else in the universe." I think understanding this is critical to our planning success.

Very simply, it just isn't good enough to look at only one land use in isolation. We need to understand the cumulative effects of all human activity, and Mother Nature acting together. And we found ourselves into this, what's been described as this geologic epoch, the Anthropocene, which is a period in time where basically from the industrial revolution, in which human activities have had a significant global impact on your ecosystems.

And we're right now in this period called The Great Acceleration of Unprecedented World Population Growth. That increasing population is bringing, it's actually increasing many simultaneous pressures on our natural systems, all the way from primary resource extraction like timber and minerals, the service industries, settlement, agriculture, transportation, energy, tourism, recreation.

And the effects that happened to us at home, like where I am here in the Shuswap in British Columbia are affected by what happens in other areas of the world. Certainly, growth in the oil and gas sector in Alberta brings lots of tourism to our little watershed here. But we also feel it from the Pacific Northwest in the United States and even offshore in Asia.

We're in this large, global connectedness and yet we're still managing maybe individually, different sectors individually.

And I think where some of this comes from is it's embedded in the legislation and we tend to encounter cumulative effects in things like environmental impact assessments, and there's wording in those that basically says there are cumulative impacts, there are negative things that must be mitigated. And what we're trying to do is develop a project while we minimize the harm from that project.

Where I really hope we're going is that we'll switch this around to a more holistic approach to managing growth and development. We'll look at our activity in combination with natural disturbance. We'll look across the triple bottom-line of environmental, social and economic outcomes at a range of scales beyond individual developments; because when we don't, we end up with this big tangle of issue-specific policy responses, not well-connected.

And it leads us to this debate rather than dialogue, and quite frankly from my perspective, I think it's time we stopped admiring the problem and started working on it, rethink this tug-of-war. Really, it's a delicate balance that we're striving for. We need to imagine our future, write our own story, plan for what we want rather than minimizing the harm.

And this is where collaboration becomes absolutely crucial, because as our landscapes continue to get busier and we're bumping into each other and overlapping, the collaboration becomes more and more important because if we don't, we're working at cross purposes or we're trying to compete and there's winners and losers, and it doesn't really need to be like that.

David: So we're going to again go to a quick break. Tweet or call in @davidbsavage for example. Barry's placed a very critical and complex issue and opportunity in front of us. We'll be right back.

David: So just before the break, we had Barry Wilson from Cumulative Effects or CE Analytics talking about the challenge and complexity, the positions and opportunity and during the break, Jeff made some great points. Jeff, can you join in now?

Jeff: I'd love to. And like everyone else, David, thank you. It's an honor to be on the show. And I think this is critically important for everybody. I think anyone listening, whether you believe there is climate change or whether you don't, our group is here to help you to try to find answers so that you can do your business, move on and work across the table from everyone else.

The other day I was watching a M*A*S*H episode and I'm a little old M*A*S*H junkie. And B.J. Honeycutt said in this episode, "we can't even have a fight in peace anymore." And it really struck me because that's really where we are right now.

It used to be that we were deeply divided, but you could sit down and have a conversation. We can't talk about climate change or global warming, or environmental issues without either getting a deep hooray from someone or a punch in the nose. And I want to offer something a little different to those of you who may be skeptical that may be listening to us.

I'm sort of the Swiss army knife of the Collaborative Global Initiative. I do facilitation. I do mediation. I do stakeholder engagement. But I'm going to talk about mediation as a way that all of us can come to the table and feel comfortable and safe coming to the table, whether you're someone who believes or is in disbelief that there is anything happening to our planet.

The reason why it works that way is that my job as a mediator is to be neutral and impartial. I'm not here to give opinions. My job is to own the process while my parties own their own outcome. You've heard it said in many ways here today by other folks. My job is to create the dialogue and not the debate so that everybody can learn from one another.

How does that happen? How does that happen and how do we work when we're doing more of a mediative role in our work rather than a role that takes on, hey we've got people that understand that this is an issue and we're all trying to collaborate.

The first thing that we do is we try to design a safe way for folks to communicate. Everyone in this group has background in conflict systems design. Our job is to meet with everyone, find out the best way to create a dialogue, whether it's a public facilitation, whether it's working with small groups, whether it's breaking people out into work groups. But the first thing that we do is design the safe haven, the safe place where everyone with all different opinions and ideas can come to the table and feel that they're going to safely be able to express their views.

Again, are we facilitating? Are we mitigating? Is it a public dialogue? Whatever it is and however we do it is based specifically on the circumstances.

The whole idea of communicating is to create understanding. And David, you and I have talked about this in a previous show, is that there is a thread that we talk about and that is, is that having a safe environment where everyone can have their dialogue facilitated by someone like myself, helps us to understand each other.

Once we have understanding, we can then develop trust in one another, even if we're on opposite sides of the table. I can't tell you how many times people come away saying, I don't necessarily agree with you, but I trust you now. And understanding and trust is what allows folks to start working on creative outcomes. Sometimes each side may be acquiescing to the other in some way for the purpose of moving forward, but relationships have been built. And that's really a very important part of what I do.

When I'm facilitating or mediating a conflict or a disagreement between stakeholders, everybody knows I'm coming in to coerce anyone into a final decision. In fact, the whole idea of mediation is uncoerced self-determination of all issues.

David: I was just thinking, I really want to stress this point that has been raised here, about embracing conflict. Yes that's one of my 10 Essential Steps to collaboration, but as long as I'm certain that I know it all, I'm a pretty useless leader because I don't need you. As probably the oldest guy in the table here, the older I get, the more I realize a.) I'll never know it all, and b.) if I pretend I know it all, it excludes everyone else.

I just want to give a quote before we go back to Barry here. But here's a quote from our friends Doug Stone and Sheila Heen, "Remind yourself that if you think you already understand how someone feels or what they're trying to say, it is a delusion. Remember a time when you were sure you were right and then discovered one little fact that changed everything. There are hours more to learn." That's a quote from Difficult Conversations, How To Discuss What Matters Most.

Jeff: Another quick quote that may be very helpful to this, from a dear friend of mine. Dr. Charlie Kennedy. It says, "We must embrace our impotence. We must embrace the fact that we don't know it all, and that is how we create the humility necessary to begin to understand."

And if I may just punctuate this for a moment, is that the magic of my process is when parties who are at odds with one another, we'll say to one another, 'I never understood that'; 'I've learned something'. That's when shifts begin to happen. Basically, you're changing the culture of how folks are communicating with one another in a proactive way.

It promotes understanding. It promotes trust. You can't have a collaboration without first having an understanding and trust. My job is always to focus on those things, to bring peace into the world.

David: And why on earth would you want group think? I want to bring it back to Barry, because cumulative impacts, cumulative effects are so critical in my time long ago in oil and gas in Canada. As I go, no I'm not responsible for everybody else's problems, let me just do my thing. We can't get away with that anymore. It might mean shutting down old facilities that don't protect the environment, the community as well as the like. But it's such a complex issue and great opportunity.

Barry, I mentioned at the top of the show that you're offering a playbook. Can you tell us a little bit more about that to help us get through this complexity and collaborate better?

Barry: Yeah, absolutely. Thank you. Basically, the CE Playbook is a sure-fire approach to help people build that understanding and trust that we're just talking about. It's actually a set of exercises, lessons that allow individual practitioners, decision-makers, land use planners, a credible way to create a safe and productive arena for conversation and collaboration to get to those solutions.

I realize that there's not enough people with access to the tools that they need. One of the things I thought was to deliver this online to people. They could be more cost-effective. They could do it at their own time, their own speed and it'll be better.

Develop the CE Playbook. It's a 4-volume online course that you can access on any of your digital devices. And each module is designed with your own individual productivity in mind. So right from the start, the lesson and exercises get you to apply your new knowledge to the plan or opportunity that you're working on right away, so you can get to using it.

And I would say that the CE Playbook is for you if you're involved in land use planning in any way; if you're working on an environmental impact assessment for sure; if you're a project manager or developer who has to deliver, on-time, on-target and on-budget, I totally get that, I've been in that seat a few times; then the CE Playbook is for you. If you're a subject matter expert, like a biologist, engineer, economist, sociologist, forester, healthcare practitioner, anybody who's been asked to provide guidance on balancing development and conservation; and I guess maybe most of all, if you're in a nonprofit working in a watershed to preserve or develop certain important values, whether they're education or salmon or anything like that, this is definitely for you. I'm a co-founder and president of a nonprofit, and I think I have a pretty good idea of what they need.

I guess I wanted to also say thank you to you and your guests for the time today, and offer a special discount to ceplaybook.com, you can get 50%.

David: Thanks Barry. This is such a critical thing. And one of the things that I learned when I first met Barry probably a year and a half ago is some of the things that just aren't true, some of the things that we don't know can hurt us. Barry's got some incredible technology where he can go over cumulative impacts over the last hundred years within his database, and I've seen him display it with respect to British Columbia and Alberta.

But things that surprise us, where we think even little things like how we recreate when we use ATVs or what's the impact of that? Why do we spend so much time on pipelines and not worry about ATVs? Why do we spend so much time with respect to nuclear and not worry about gravel pits?

Nobody's getting out of here alive. Let's really make this better. Doreen, any comments? I struck a laugh there.

Doreen: You did because it reminded me of a bumper sticker back in the '80s that said, 'The person who has the most assets wins when they die', or something along those lines. And of course, we know that that's not true.

But I feel like we've gotten a situation whereas the person who believes they've won the most arguments is the superior. And I think that's when things – we need to change that thinking and one way is to I think again, dialogue and teach people how to dialogue because I'm not quite sure that a lot of people know the difference between dialoguing and debating.

And I think getting people to be empathetic towards another person's position, and I have a short quote since Jeff had one, and you had one, and I had one. And that is, "Empathy is seeing with the eyes of another, listening with the ears of another, and feeling with the heart of another."

It doesn't mean that you are going to agree with somebody with an opposite opinion. But at least empathize, understand how they got there and by doing that and getting that way is by asking some critical questions, and really not dehumanizing the other side.

David: All right.

Barry: I think there's something else that we should also, it's on-point and it's off-point. I think the problem that we have today where we are working with electronics, where we are so focused on our work, fewer and fewer are getting out and have any understanding of what the wilderness is.

I know for a fact that I have friends, they don't know the difference between a loon and a duck. They don't understand what mercury does to a loon and how mercury even gets into a loon through acid rain.

And sometimes, I think to all of our listeners, if you're skeptical, get out of the woods. You're going to want to protect it. You're going to want to hedge your bets and I think we need to find a way to make people more aware of the natural world and then you're more apt to want to protect it.

David: So in the couple minutes of this break, just go outside and take a deep breath. If you can't have a nature bath, have a nature shower for a moment. We'll be right back.

David: We're having some fun and some laughs here. Welcome back everyone, I'm just delighted that we have listeners from around the world in this conversation. I wish everybody could be more a part of it and that's our intention here, to build this cumulative impact to collective intelligence.

Where I want to go with this is let's make this fully holistic, fully rounded. For example, the oil sands industry in Canada, for far too long wanted to debate whether they were a bad guy or a good guy in climate change and all this stuff. And they're realizing that now that they're fully engaged and as we talked about earlier, not having to be right or wrong but looking for the knowledge and the innovation that Kathy Porter is an expert at building collaboration to drive innovation, I just want to honor Kathy in that way.

The Canadian oil sands industry is now saying, when we focus on CO_2 emissions, when we deal with that with a collaborative wisdom, with the Canadian Oil Sands Innovation Alliance and other groups that are working on these significant challenges, they're actually finding opportunities. They're finding that by capturing greenhouse gas emissions, they are actually becoming even more cost-effective and more efficient at it.

It's a business advantage that was unrealized. There are so many opportunities in life, whether it's energy, whether it's dealing with your teenage kids. So often we get surprised when we realize that there's a real opportunity.

One of the things we've had some fun with today is everybody came up with a favorite quote around our challenges. Barry's got to have his time. Barry, jump in.

Barry: Thanks. Thanks David. John Muir is one of my favorites and I really appreciate his work. But another one of my favorites that I think is so relevant to our conversation today is by Dr. Alan Edwards and I use it in so many of my talks and presentations. The quote is, "No innovator works alone. And the most innovative of all collaborate not only within their institutions, but also with others across the country and around the world."

I just think that that's so salient to this, is that we also not be limited by our near circle and we have this opportunity to reach out to the world and share knowledge now in the digital age. It can be very powerful for us.

Jeff: Absolutely. What comes to mind is a number of years ago, I worked with a really wonderful environmental and public policy mediator and facilitator by the name of Cindy Cook up in Vermont and we worked together on a collaborative project, where the Chippewa and the U.S. Forest Service needed to get together to try to collaborate on forest replanting rules every 7 or so years. The federal government comes out with new rules and the reason why they do that here in the U.S. is because there are all kinds of issues of invasive species and because of climate change, the landscape is changing.

Each side was relatively resistance, at least initially, to the suggestions of the other. At the end of the day, to make the long story very short, the federal government agreed to adopt some of the anecdotal agent land management ways of the Chippewa. And the Chippewa, in exchange, would work with the wildlife biologists of the U.S. government. It was put into the forestry planning rule that way.

It was a wonderful example of everybody sitting at the table, listening to everyone else around the table; we were listening to medicine men and tribal biologists, and federal biologists, and forest rangers. And at the end of the day, there was such – there were many days of work – slowly but surely, everybody understood that they had differing ideas, but they finally had a very similar goal. At the end of the day, it was really a magnificent piece of work on both sides to come up with this very, very important set of rules.

So that was just a good example for everybody to know that this works, and it works so effectively, and it preserves relationships. It doesn't destroy relationships and makes relationships stronger between adversaries.

David: I'll jump in and tell a little bit of a story while the bird sings the song. Today, I chaired a meeting in Cranbrook, British Columbia, my home. I've been asked over the last 14 years to help create the non-motorized trail network in British Columbia.

I'll shorten this to say July 1st, 2017 is my nation's 150th birthday. It's a big deal. We're very proud. The TransCanada trail now connects in a largely non-motorized, I think it's about 90% that goes from the Atlantic to the Pacific, to the Artic Oceans; non-motorized trail, fantastic, whether you're cross-country skiing, whether you're hiking, biking, whatever it is.

When we started to look at a celebration for Canada Day 2017, our 150th birthday, we realized we want to make this a big deal. We want to celebrate this new 42 ½-kilometer trail from Cranbrook to Warner, about 30 miles. Then we realized, oh my god everybody's doing a celebration. Oh my god, how are we even going to get noticed?

And then the local first nations, the Ktunaxa and the ?aq'am band said, we're not really into celebrating Canada Day. That's really not our thing. We've been here for about 10,000 years. How about 10,000-year day? How about that? Instead of getting into this competition with the city, with the regional district, with the Columbia Basin Trust, the Tanaka, with anybody, we said, you're right. Let's do them both.

Doreen: Right.

David: And I was just delighted today, we came to an understanding where we've got a series of events, June 21st on National Aboriginal Day, June 30th, July 1st. We are so much better together, and we are seeking international media for this. So, we could've fought, and all had small attendance, or we could've really built this thing, which looks like we're going to.

I want to give – we've only got about a minute left. I'm going to give just a chance for a quick last word. Doreen?

Doreen: My last words, all right; I hope the people can join us at our workshops in San Luis Obispo and Vancouver; May 25th at San Luis Obispo and July 5th in Vancouver. More details will be coming out. It's an opportunity to form a dialogue about...

David: We're running out of time. Barry, and then Jeff, quickly?

Barry: Just thank you very much, reminder to go to ceplaybook.com and use the coupon code to get your 50% discount. And share the indigenous lesson I got this morning, that cumulative effects are really understanding our relationships with other living and nonliving things.

David: Thank you. And Jeff?

Jeff: If anybody's interested, folks we are here, the Collaborative Global Initiative. We are the international network and mediators, facilitators and systems design professionals that are here to assist you in working with others to collaborate on your projects. We're here to help you achieve common goals and if you are interested in any way, give us a call. Take a look at collaborativeglobalinitiative.com and we'll be happy to talk to you and help you to find a way.

David: Wonderful. Thank you everyone. In these challenging times, we've got a way.

Chapter 13 One Yes, One Thing, One Dream featuring Deva Premal and Miten, Klara Fenlof, Robert Stewart, Sara Amos and Quinn Amos

Klara: Hello people, planet Earth. I am Klara Fenlof with you today from the youngest town of Sweden called Skellefteå. Today, I've been asked to tell you a few words that mean collaboration in different languages around the world.

The ones that I know are Swedish, which is *samarbeta*. I have got Icelandic, which is *samstarf*; Dutch, *samenwerking;* Danish, *samarbejde*. I've got German, which is *die mitarbeit*. I've got Spanish, *la colaboración*; Norwegian, *samarbeid* and Swedish, *samarbeta*.

Have a nice day, bye.

David: One Yes, One Thing, One Dream. That's our conversation for today for collaboration. And thanks Klara for all of those linguistic experiences of the word collaboration. I really appreciate that. Klara is from Sweden and a delightful young leader who happens to be on an exchange with Rotary in Cranbrook, British Columbia, my club.

Today, I'm also very, very thrilled to have Robert Stewart, to have my grandkids Quinn and Sara Amos, and the wonderful Deva Premal and Miten as my feature guests.

Deva and Miten have tapped into an apparently unending stream of uplifting, inspirational music; 21 albums, sales of about 1½ million copies. So here are some testimonials. You might know Eckhart Tolle. "Pure magic," he's talking about Deva Premal and Miten and Manose. "Passionate and powerful," Tony Robbins. You might know this fellow by His Highness Dalai Lama,

"Beautiful, beautiful music." And of course, Cher, "My favorite album for yoga."

Deva and Miten and Manose have become my friends over the last dozen years. They're fantastic, beautiful people. When we talk about one yes, get it.

Recently, Miten recorded Temple at Midnight, a soulful no-frills, lots of thrills, all-acoustic tale of love and redemption. And today, Miten has allowed me to share with you his version of the Beatle's Norwegian Wood.

Now between September 2015 and today, April 2017, I've hosted and been the guest on at least 40 podcasts, sharing the wisdom of my life and most probably that of 75 guest experts from Canada, America, France, England, Spain, Australia, Sweden and Germany. Yeah, I'm proud of that. We do have a global network. We are a global network.

According to our analytics, these shows have attracted people like you in 32 countries and the show's been downloaded more than 30,000 times. I am so honored.

We've talked about collaborative leadership, 360 assessments, critical thinking, disruptive technology, aboriginal economic development, next generation leaders, Rotary Heart and Stroke leadership, dispute resolution, why collaboration fails, curiosity, how to find your own truth. We've talked about zombies and of course, my 10 Essential Steps to collaboration. We are seeking better ways of working together. We are seeking our dreams by collaboration.

We are in challenging times and we are in amazing times; Peter Diamandis, abundance; it's very, very exciting times on so many factors. The world is getting better, education-wise, most every nation in some way or another.

But how do we work together better? As part of my book Break Through to Yes, the characteristics of boundless collaborations, dream big and you will be great. You will create great. Here are the characteristics. Our intentions must be authentic. We build relationship trust and trust first. We respect and invite diversity of opinion, no group think. We establish key questions that matter, the powerful questions. We listen. We seek new ideas from the collective wisdom. We are open to unexpected outcomes and it takes as long as it takes. If you want to go fast, go alone. If you want to go far, go together. Let's also hold accountability.

Doreen Liberto and I are writing a book we're calling Learn to Talk and Talk to Learn, about dialogue, about intelligent dialogue. There's another great book that's just been released that I'm reading right now, and think about it, it's called The Knowledge Illusion: Why We Never Think Alone. It's by Sloman and Fernbach. And here's a piece of it.

"Humans have built hugely complex societies and technologies, but most of us don't even know how a pen or a toilet works. How we achieve so much despite understanding so little?" Cognitive scientists Sloman and Fernbach argue that we survive and thrive, despite our mental shortcomings because we live in a rich community of knowledge. The key to our intelligence lies in the people and things around us. We're constantly drawing on information and expertise stored outside of our heads, in our bodies, our environment, our possessions and the communities with which we interact. And we don't even realize we're doing it.

In my career, professional career, 42-plus years, I co-founded Synergy Alberta, West Central Saskatchewan Surface Rights Owners, Global Negotiation Insight Institute, the Collaborative Global Initiative, Company to Company Dispute Resolution Council. I volunteer a lot of my time for Trans Canada Trail, Heart and Stroke Foundation Rotary, ?aq'am Economic Development. I've even had a bunch of lines and a good part in Prime Cut with Gene Hackman, Sissy Spacek, Lee Marvin. And just recently, I had a minor part on Hard Powder with Liam Neeson. I've had a great life.

So, we've got a great idea. I've got a great idea and I think it's your idea. We are one. We are all interconnected in our spirit, in our hearts, in our intelligence. The more we learn to let go of our hero story, the greater we become. Our hero story is when we think we must be great as a solo or a leader. We don't have to be great. We have to have great outcomes, and whether you actually are a hero or not, if you're on your own, you're not going to get much done.

Through judgment, through segregations, through isolation, I don't know, but consider that all the expertise and experience we have may not be enough to effectively deal with great challenges that we face today in organizations, families and nations. We see it on the news, on social media and conversations. Consider the collective wisdom that is possible from a circle of listening, speaking, understanding and co-creating.

I want to talk to you about is; let's get out of the group think. Let's get out of us versus them, Americans versus Russians, Muslims versus – within the Muslim community, the youth versus the old folks. Let's invite the youth. Let's invite the future. Let's invite the crones, the wise women and our elders. We are one. We will create shared value that respects the environment, the community and business. We are one. Let's just simply be that. Let's understand that this is the way we are.

In my 40 segments, go back over them. There's a rich treasure trove of insight and advice there. We will talk about the one thing I often ask my guests, what's in this moment? What one thing that you would think about, ask our listeners to become aware of? And that one thing is often so brilliant, that one thing is often so good.

So here, my friend Charlie Graydon who's living in Spain, an excellent intelligent woman, collaborator, author, facilitator, here's her one thing. "Understanding that all people of the world are neighbors, I encourage your listeners to enjoy every moment of the day." Yeah, think about that. There is so much here, so much possible.

Here's something from my friend Ken Cloke of Los Angeles, California; author of *The Dance of Opposites and the Conflict Revolution.* "If we are to evolve and survive as a species, we need to learn how to collaborate and resolve conflicts with each other, both personally and globally. Doing so will require us to build skills in conflict resolution, strength in our capacity for empathy and compassion, and recognize that in the end, there is no 'them', there is no 'us'. There is just 'one'. There is 'us', together."

Now, Ken says that I've written a powerful and insightful book. I won't go into that, but can you only imagine what's possible? That was the focus. That was the focus of all the interviews, all the insight.

When we come back, we will play for you Norwegian Wood and then go into our interview with Deva Premal and Miten.

{Miten's recording of Norwegian Wood playing}

David: You'll be performing in Los Angeles on May 27th and I will be bringing my son and his girlfriend, Jamie.

Deva: Oh, great. Miten's right here with me. We're all together.

David: Good afternoon, Miten. It's so nice to reconnect.

Miten: Nice to hear your voice. You're coming through very clean and clear. Are you doing good? Life is good?

David: Life is in transition, as I shared. I'm largely taking the next 7 months simply to let go of everything and see what comes up and see how I can be childlike and learn again.

Miten: Fantastic. Every blessing with that; you can't really go wrong, David, when you step out like that, with that heart full of intention. You only will be supported to very magical, mysterious adventures. Good luck on that. It's going to be great, fantastic.

David: I believe that and I'm so thankful because in a time where many people have told me, including myself, David you put out so much energy into the world, it's time to get back in balance. And when I reach out to friends like the two of you, it's like wow, they're here.

Miten: Yeah.

David: Thank you.

Miten: That's the great gift of the spiritual family, that we are all a part of, and that's the blast from me and Deva. Wherever we are, we have this feeling of meeting you in a different body, but the same energy, the same beauty, the same sincerity. There's a lot of us around on the planet now, David. That's good news.

David: Yeah. And thank you, one of the things I was thinking about this morning as I woke up is that the story you told me, told Lise and I and Lise says hello.

Miten: Hi Lise.

David: She's not in the room. She just went to boot camp to exercise.

Miten: Good, that's good.

David: But you told us in Tulum, at Tantra Mantra – I believe maybe it was in Calgary when you did your workshop and you shared that the first workshop that you did in Germany, only one woman showed up.

Miten: Yeah.

David: And you believed that therefore, she was the right one and if you hadn't done that, then you wouldn't have shown up for others. That really is a strong message to the world, I think, and in the world today.

Deva: I remember that.

Miten: It reminds me of the Dalai Lama, I think. He was quoted in saying, never give up. Because that can be taken in many different ways, but on the spiritual understanding, there is no other way to approach your spirituality. You have to brave or courageous, and you just have to never give up. I think that's the great teaching.

David: Yeah, thank you. I'm feeling that we need to start recording this because so much of the magic...

Deva: We have already.

David: Okay. let's proceed. What I would like to do is start off with an introduction of you and then I've suggested that I've got a few questions of you, but let's take it wherever you want to go and for however long you're prepared to be with my listeners. I know I've asked for 16 minutes and we can go from there, and I'll leave it up to the two of you because I expect that you're in Berlin tonight and you're probably performing tonight.

Miten: No, not quite. Almost. No, we actually, Deva – first thing you have to know about me and Deva is that we can't call what we do when we share the music a performance. It's not that we're performing anywhere. We don't perform because if you try and perform mantras, the actual essential energy of the mantra gets distorted.

So, the only way you can share these mantras is by being exactly the opposite of a performance, a real openness to the moment. If you stay in there as musicians, to share the music then something of the power of the mantras will be shown.

David: Yes. That is certainly my experience. When we first met, it was the fall of 2004, Liz had taken me to Knox United Church in Calgary and I'd never been in an experience like you host; when you ask the audience, please don't clap, this is for you and for us. And the second thing I've never seen before is during the break, you actually came to greet the audience as opposed to going back off-stage. That is consistent, powerful one-ness, one yes. Thank you for that.

So, our listeners can get a sense of the both of you and the spirit that you offer, our show today is One Yes, One Thing, One Dream. Friends sometimes do you wonder who is out there in your heart and in theirs? Sometimes, do you reach out not knowing what will come back?

Sometimes, do you wonder? Sometimes, do you notice who is actually with you?

Friends, we have wonderful friends as our feature guests today, Deva Premal and Miten. Here's a little bit of insight from my knowledge of them and insight as to how hundreds of thousands, millions of people around our beautiful planet see them.

And I'm quoting, "Flame carriers of a 5,000-year-old tradition, Deva and Miten are at the forefront of the bourgeoning worldwide chant phenomena. Bridging ancient mantras of Indian Tibet with contemporary musical settings, their debut album, The Essence, introduced a unique musical genre. The album rocked to the top of the world and new-age charts where it still remains."

Deva Premal, The Essence 1999. If you don't have it, get it. They have released 21 albums since and their sales, I believe they're about 1 ½ million copies sold. It's just such beautiful, centering, one spirit, one planet, one us.

Here's some quotes of some of their other fans. Some of you might know Anthony Robbins. Anthony says, "They're passionate and powerful." His Highness, the Dalai Lama, "Beautiful, beautiful music." Eckhart Tolle, "Pure magic." Cher, "My favorite album of yoga."

And just wonderful stuff, I invite you to go to devapremalmiten.com, find out more. My friend, Miten with Deva has recently released Temple at Midnight. It's a collection of songs, all acoustic, of love and redemption, celebrates many dimensions of love and meditation he has explored in his journeys, from his hedonistic days in London's rock scene in the 1970s to a voyage of self-discovery in mystic India and that's where the two of you met, and then on the 20 years of world tours with Deva Premal, diving deeper and deeper into himself. It's a beautiful album.

Go see them. Find where they are not performing, when they are with you in spirit, close to your home. I am delighted that the next experience for me and Dan and Jamie will be in Los Angeles on May 27th.

So Miten, let's start with your new album. This is going back to the 1970s, with songs like Norwegian Wood, that I played earlier by that other British band. Yet it's so you. Tell us about Temple at Midnight.

Miten: Okay, okay David. The thing about Temple at Midnight for me is it's not really a feeling of going back. It's more a feeling of arriving. I felt that I was ready to make that album. I was encouraged to do it by Deva and our producer Joby Baker.

I called it Temple at Midnight because I wanted to give myself the feeling when I was singing and playing the music, that I was actually in a small temple somewhere in India or Tibet, and the temple had been filled with chant all day long. And it was empty now, and the vibration was strong and present, and beautiful. I could be in that temple at midnight, and just play my favorite songs with my favorite musicians. We're in a very intimate and sacred place for those songs to be heard and to be played.

Yeah, of course the Norwegian Wood is just a homage to one of my great gurus and John was definitely, I count him as one of my three gurus in my life. John Lennon is one, Osho is the other and the one that I will take with me because we'll never actually leave its body is music itself, the spirit of music. So those three elements make up my life. So, they make up that album. That's just who I am and I'm glad you like it.

David: I love it because it is coming together so many forms. May I read to you our friends online, one verse from All is Welcome Here that's really meaningful to me, Miten?

Miten: Sure, you can. Thank you, sure.

David: Here are just four lines of this beautiful song, and it's the theme of one yes.

"All is welcome here.

I stood alone at the gateless gate,

too drunk on love to hesitate.

To the winds I cast my fate,

and the remnants of my fear."

I just want to let people pause for that. Think about that. To the winds I cast my fate, and the remnants of my fear.

Miten: Yeah. That's a great place to find yourself, David.

David: I'm finding.

Miten: I know. I can feel it. I can feel it.

David: Deva Premal, tell our friends, our listeners today more about your journey and purpose, please.

Deva: I'm so happy that I don't have to figure that one out, because it's really just happening and it's happening beyond my dreams, beyond my possibility to imagine. I've been with Miten now for 26 years, 24/7 almost really hardly ever apart. We're travelling. We've been travelling for 23 years constantly. We've been only doing what we love to do most, which is live in this world and this community, share our music, meditate together with the people who come to be with us and be with each other. We are actually living in this heaven on earth that I couldn't have imagined. I feel so blessed and so grateful, and also humbled and mystified.

Yeah, I had it kind of put into, in German we say, I had put it in my cradle when I was a kid. My father brought me up with mantras and meditation, and that kind of looking to the east feeling. This is the continuation of it, but I would've never imagined that it would unfold this way or that I would be singing, or there would be people who want to come and sing with us, and that it will be so supported and most of all, that it really seems to bring healing and transformation, and peace and joy to people.

We receive emails or Facebook messages from people, how the music or mantras affected them, and it's happened more than once that somebody wrote us a strong message, like I was at the brink of taking my life because nothing made sense. And the mantras came, and I saw a ray of light again that made me just consider going on and it started a journey to light again. I feel like, okay if this one person was touched or was helped with our music, then my life had a purpose.

I can already die happy, basically that's what I'm saying. I'm really very fulfilled and every day, I ask myself, are you ready to die? And every day, so far, the answer is yes. If it comes, I'm ready because I feel just very, very fulfilled.

David: Beautiful. And if I may, I am not a singer. I've never felt I wanted to sing anywhere other than in the car or in the shower. And yet with you and your workshops in the retreats and in your concerts, and even alone listening to your music, I feel that I can join a global chorus and I feel the power of one through your music. Thank you for that.

Miten: Yes. That's what sustains us all, I think David, is the sense of community that we feel we belong to in a global dimension. By singing and chanting, we actually, it feels like we strengthen the sense of community. That's really important, not just for me and Deva of course but for everyone.

We were thinking we should do some kind of flash mob Gayatri all over the planet, something where everybody would chant the Gayatri at the same time. But we haven't really figured out a way to do that yet.

David: Yeah.

Miten: But the sense of community is essential, I think, to our survival.

David: I would love to be part of that global Gayatri chant, and I think it's very possible. You just pick the time and the context. You remind me of that famous experiment by the Japanese scientists, I believe, on water. When they had World Meditation Day, they could see under high resolution, big microscopes, they could see the difference in water once meditation and the love was in the air. It's beautiful, and we do need that.

Miten: That's a good idea. We planted the seed right now, so let's see how it manifests.

David: So I encourage friends who are listening to us today to engage with Deva Premal and Miten, with respect to whatever you think you wish to communicate with them

This is our journey. This is the time where fear, walls, ignorance and warfare are a place that we want to reduce and minimize, and lead from love.

Miten and Deva, how do you collaborate? That's my focus. Tell me how collaboration shows up in your world.

Miten: I just do what she tells me.

David: That's the way...

Miten: It's that easy. That's great collaboration. But...

Deva: Apart from that.

Miten: Apart from that, I don't know really. We have a flow that just...

Deva: Works most of the time.

Miten: It just kind of works most of the time, David. We never had really had to delve too deeply into explaining what's happening with us. It's just, like David was saying, we're just rolling on it. It's like we're riding a wave and we caught the wave, and as a result, we are in a very open-hearted place in ourselves, with ourselves and with the world.

So, in that kind of dimension, creativity just bubbles up and it's just something that's there. We just share it as it comes and then we just trust whatever we're doing. So far, that's the wave. It's been very, like I was saying, it's not about performance. If we can stay in a place of awareness, of gratitude, that we can actually be here and share in the music, then that's what I now understand to be the place where real music comes from, because there's no other reason to play it.

It's not for ambition. It's not for financial gain. It has nothing to do with the worldly perception of reality. It's a totally different dimension. That's where the music is born, down there.

If we stay true to that and there's nothing else we can do anyway, this is what we do in our lives, then you can only count your blessings and let the music come, let the collaborations happen. And we have Manose, the great flute player from Nepal. We have great producer Joby Baker from Canada. We have a great drummer from Copenhagen, Rishi.

We collaborate in the understanding that we are playing for the higher good. We all know that our egos are not important and that we all understand that, and we all understand that the only way to play music is from a place of participation and compassion, and forgiveness. These kind of real, strong attitudes, once you play from this place then you can't turn off the creativity.

David: Thank you. Some people have called that the collective unconscious. Some people have called it collective intelligence. I call it collaborative intelligence, and probably most of us would call it spirit.

Miten: Yeah.

David: From both of you, share just part of your dream for our shared future on this planet.

Deva: Personally, I never really think about the future very much. If I do think about the future of this planet, it doesn't look very bright to me at this point. I think the more that we can stay in the moment and choose every moment, the past that is the most loving and the most kind to the best of our abilities, whatever that means, it starts with big things, our diet, how much can we do without meat, how much can we do without dairy; all these choices that we can make, every moment to help this planet basically survive and us on top of it.

And the mantras and the meditation help us find the peaceful place within that make those right choices and those peaceful choices. So, it's really a moment to moment affair and whatever we dream into the future doesn't really have that much importance right now, personally for myself. But with Miten, I don't know...

Miten: I don't know. I don't know, really. I came to a point a few months ago where I realized that the only way I could live a perfect life was to accept my imperfection. I started to just accept my imperfection and since then, I don't look very far out. I'm kind of interested in the journey I'm going on inside and the people that I'm with.

I don't project too far out. The most important thing for me is honesty, that every time I play and every time I sing, I'm being as true as I can be, and I feel at service to the muse, to the great spirit of music, just as its humble devotee. I just go to the feet of music and surrender myself. That's what I encourage Deva to do and that's the understanding that we have as an ensemble.

We're not kind of messing around, David. We're not trying to entertain anyone. It's more, another dimension.

David: You reminded me, this is not a performance as you said a couple of times. This is you. This is a reminder to all the rest of us on being, on being present and being in the moment, not in the past or the future. And also, a reminder that actually, this isn't about worshipping Deva and Miten and Manose and others. It's their invitation to ourselves.

As we close and thank you for giving me far more time than I even hoped for, but as we close, I'd love to hear one thing that you would encourage our listeners to be, do or become aware of.

Miten: David, maybe the way to answer that is for Deva and I to chant a universal piece mantra for you and your listeners. Would you like that?

David: Beautiful, thank you.

Miten: Okay.

[4-minute Gayatri Mantra chant]

David: Thank you so much. Thank you. I love you both.

Miten: Thank you David. We'll see you soon.

David: Yes.

Deva: Namaste.

David: Namaste.

David: Now we invite Robert Stewart into our podcast.

Robert: Hi. My name is Robert Stewart, a father, peace educator and Rotarian. And I have a dream. In my dream, I see Rotary International, in collaboration with all the other service organizations and cultural creatives, step into the peace leadership and education gap in the world.

Imagine, 2 million-plus peace leaders, educators and ambassadors around the world, connecting and helping to build global peace and cooperation; 70,000-plus organizations modeling a culture of peace and balance; $1 billion dollars annually invested in raising peace literacy and consciousness levels around the world; focusing our immense resources, human, technological and financial on the greatest hindrances to peace.

We can and will transform the world to a culture of peace, to bring lasting peace in our homes, communities, countries and world for our children and future generations. I can be reached at stewart@peace.ca.

David: Welcome back everyone. I just love Miten and Deva Premal. They are so generous with their time and with their heart. You can get a sense of how they are in this moment. I love their reminder that there is only a now. There is only a what's here now, so let's be here now.

I admire Robert for his lifelong commitment to building peace networks, skills and commitments across the world.

Let's not focus on some distant future or some distant past.

In the last few months, I've been feeling really depleted, really exhausted, too much energy going out. And I've decided that I would go on a walkabout, really pull back, write some more, hike some more, bike some more, fish some more and really refine my balance, do some travelling, do some conversations. We're doing some dialogues in British Columbia, California, New York with the Collaborative Global Initiative.

I really wanted to let go, let go of everything, realizing that as long as I'm putting stuff out there, it's all about my ego as opposed to what spirit or what you really want from me. I'm listening. I'm becoming more present. I am in the world.

So, every episode of Break Through to Yes, every podcast and many pages in my books include one thing. Look at them. Pick one thing. Act now.

My challenge to you, as a leader in your community, in your family, in your organization, in your not-for-profit, take time every moment, every day, every month, every year. Reflect on the ways and behaviors that your leadership integrates the whole. Reflect on the ways and behaviors of business leaders that do not integrate the whole, that isolate, that condemn, that separate, that build walls.

Then reflect on your beliefs on what the outcomes of both approaches most often create. This is getting away from the hero leader, going to the successful collaborative leader. What are you mindful of based on these reflections? How might you change the outcomes of your business decisions and initiatives by utilizing a more holistic approach to collaboration, including more perspectives, including greater accountability, including Muslims in Turkey, including Tea Party members from Washington, including even the odd Canadian and there are a few odd Canadians?

So just notice in every moment, you've got this opportunity, and go on your own walkabout, get into nature. Go for that backpacking trip. Just get outside. I have noticed that when I get outside, when I am in the mountains hiking, biking, backpacking, whatever it is, kayaking, it just recreates my energy, fills me up, connects me with what's real.

Early in my podcast, I've asked you, invited you, encouraged you to lead from love, lead from your heart, not your wallet or your to-do list. Let go. Notice what's actually called of you. Be kind to yourself.

I want to express my gratitude to all 75 guests in the 41 podcasts, and to Robert, Charlie, Klara.

We're going to close with my grandkids, my 7-year-old granddaughter Sara and my 9-year-old grandson Quinn. I asked them, what is your dream, your one dream for their happy future? And you're going to hear them.

Namaste. We are one. We have one yes. There is one dream. Thank you. And now we go to our future leaders, Sara and Quinn Amos.

Sara: My dream is for world peace. People can't build walls. They can't hurt animals. We need to take care of the earth. And most of all, people need to be nice to everyone, not just their friends.

Quinn: My dream for the future is that we save our planet by stopping pollution. So, we don't have to find another planet to live on. People need to spend more time outside in nature because it makes you healthy and happy. People need to stop bullying each other. We need to say nice things and help each other, and make much as possible. Most of all, I think the world needs less war and more hope.

Chapter 14 Unlocking the Possible featuring Ken Cloke and Duncan Autrey

David: Make it so, unlock the possible. Today, the leader of America has little knowledge of the world or of leadership. The leader of Russia is a gangster. The leaders of the world are under great pressure to be self-centered, to be the heroes and too often do not have the skills to collaborate.

Leaders in business today around the world are increasingly hostile to their employees and their customers, pulling in tens of millions of dollars in compensation, in some cases hundreds, while others struggle on minimum wage. The next generation of leaders in business, not-for-profits and government are also generally inexperienced. They don't know what they don't know.

That came up again and again when I do workshops and coaching. We'll be working on one thing and then you realize we must step back. We don't know what we don't know. And when we collaborate, we can know more together.

There are many of the most popular people in the world and they're not yet powerful, but we include them because they will find a voice, who don't have the skills to lead for a better future. There are many that lead or are led by fear and ignorance. Fear and ignorance, it just seems far too often.

Today, we have the most educated, most connected, most wealthy and most healthy population in history. Today we can access collector of intelligence like never before, and yet they don't know what they don't know.

A couple of months ago, I was providing a workshop for about a hundred business professionals. It was a great early morning session. Most of the people in the audience that I was working with were in the 30 to 45-year-old range. Negotiators, accountants, joint-venture, human resources, operations, finance, those were their responsibilities at work. We were focusing on negotiation and collaboration skills and techniques, and processes.

At the end of the workshop, it was painfully apparent that the attendees didn't know the expertise, precedence, templates, forms and forums that are available to them to do their work, to do their work even better. They just didn't know what they didn't know.

I proposed slowing down and hosting a once-a-month workshop to explore topics that cause real friction, wasted time and resources from them and identify better practices together. Let's collaborate. Let's design a better process.

Everyone liked the idea, yet we are all so busy. We're having a hard time finding even 2-hour spots that we can commit to every month to get away from our to-do lists. Too often, we are too busy to be more effective. This is serious. These professionals are already putting in 10 to 14-hour days.

With some guidance, coaching, mentoring and education, I know they will work more productively and get it done in less time. We need to collaborate. By working together better, we can create business Break Throughs, political Break Throughs, environmental Break Throughs and social Break Throughs. Break Through to Yes: Unlocking the Possible Within a Culture of Collaboration.

Why? Why not? Why not now? Why not us? Why not you? How can we work together and collaborate more powerfully? What are the 10 Essential Steps to collaboration? You know them. They're in my book. They're in these podcasts. Work them. Refine them. Make them work for you. Change them.

How might I get access to the great leaders in this new field of true and visionary leadership on Break Through to Yes? Yes, you can. So welcome to our brighter future. Unlock your possible. Make it so, which is step number 10 of my 10 Essential Steps to collaboration.

This is my invitation to change and learn together. Yes, it is. It is time. Check out the videos, podcasts, books, etc. in my Collaborative Leadership 360 Assessment. There's so much available to you at davidbsavage.com.

Today, we also have great collaborative leaders, visionaries Ken Cloke and Duncan Autrey on our show. We also have a brief taste of Miten, with Deva Premal performing All is Welcome Here from Miten's new album, Temple at Midnight.

Linda Matthie, I love this woman. She's a good, great visionary, living in Mexico, mentoring around the world. I've asked her, what's one thing that she'd like to share with you? And Linda shared, "I would wish for our audience that people be present, do what's right and become aware of the reality that each and every one of us makes a difference in the world." Yes, each and every one of us makes a difference in the world.

I also asked Linda, what's her dream, one dream? That was last week's podcast. Linda shared with me, "The one dream that I have for our shared future is that people always do their best and live every day as they would wish to be remembered. If everyone did this, we would live in a world filled with honesty, integrity, love, respect and we would without ego, naturally collaborate to create a better world."

So, what do you think? Do people matter? Do they matter to your effectiveness, to your efficiency, to your sales, to your bottom-line, to your future? Why do they matter to you? Why, why, why?

Now according to Alex Gray of the World Economic Forum, "Change won't wait for us. Business leaders, educators and government all need to be proactive in upscaling and retraining people, so everyone can benefit from the 4th industrial revolution." That's from his article, The 10 Skills You Need to Thrive in the 4th Industrial Revolution.

Those skills are;

1) Complex problem solving. Yeah, we live in a very complex time. We need to collaborate. It's not simple. It's not black and white. Complexity demands collaboration and collective wisdom.

2) Critical thinking. We've done a show on that. It's so important, not just to eat what you're fed. Examine it yourself.

3) Creativity. I can go on and the list includes decision-making, negotiation, flexibility, coordinating with others. I can go on. There is so much to be done. Are you ready? Is your company ready?

What are the skills, gaps and collaborative characteristics? Take a look. Consider my 360 Collaborative Leadership Assessment. Do you hold meetings that are purpose-driven and focus on the end results? Are you highly regarded? Are you able to be open to new ideas and new realizations? Do you distribute power and leadership in a process of collaboration and change? Is it a culture or is it just an event?

So, after the break, we're going to hear from short replays of two of my favorite podcast interviews with Duncan Autrey and then Ken Cloke. Then another song from Miten's Temple At Midnight. So please, Listen Deeply. That's number 6, step number 6 of my 10 Essential Steps. I'll talk to you after the break.

David: Welcome back, listeners. I'm really excited about my next guest, Duncan Autrey. Duncan is a kindred spirit. He is a conflict transformation consultant with experience in both North and South America. To find out more about Duncan Autrey, go to duncanautry.com.

Now Duncan and I first met I think it was 6 or 7 years ago at the Omega Institute in Upstate New York. We were working with our mutual friend and best-selling author Erica Ariel Fox. She's penned and promoting and doing great work with Winning from Within. And we were also working with great people like Emily Gould and David Gould and others.

We've evolved ourselves, Duncan and I have stayed very close. We've collaborated, coached one another and dreamed together. Duncan works with Mediators Beyond Borders and has worked in the United States, Argentina, Ecuador, Turkey and other places. Duncan's now back in California doing great work there.

Duncan, thank you so much for joining us. What else might you say about your introduction and your vision around collaboration?

Duncan: Thank you David. Thank you for the introduction and it's a pleasure to be speaking with you. I wanted to actually just touch on that transition, that I've recently returned to the United States after many years abroad. It's been interesting to realize the importance of building networks, both locally and internationally. It's really important.

It's been really interesting to connect with conflicts that are more local, whether they'd be conflicts with the local drought in California or to be in attention to conflicts that are happening in collective houses, or just between neighbors. It's been interesting to connect on a community-level again.

But yeah, I think that's a great introduction, so thank you.

David: One of the things that I will tell our listeners, then you can correct me Duncan.

Duncan: Sure.

David: One of your most recent contracts has been in Ecuador, dealing with boundary disputes, dealing with what happens when satellites give you different boundaries than 20 steps from the old oak tree type of survey system. It's my recollection, my judgment that while you were really initially focused on resolving boundary disputes, the majority of your success there was actually building skills and capacity within the people that you're working with. It's a teach a man to fish, type of metaphor.

Duncan: Yeah.

David: Can you tell us a little more about that experience?

Duncan: Absolutely. Yeah, so I was working in Ecuador with the provincial government to help them resolve a series of border disputes. They were basically just historical accidents based on maps that were done in the 1500s, not corresponding to the maps done in the 1980s.

It was interesting, the idea of the work was to help the communities really communicate with each other to help decide where the borders will be. But what ended up becoming more and more important was the realization – because of the political situation in Ecuador, where it's just very divisive politics, the work of getting people to work with each other and realize just the value of including the voice of the other side became I would say the main focus of the work.

It was always easy to say we don't want to include the voices of our enemies, we just want to include the voices that agree with us. Unfortunately, I would say a rule of conflict is if you try to not include someone, then they're going to find a way to be included later.

David: Whether it's positive or otherwise.

Duncan: Whether it's positive or otherwise, whether you have any control over the situation or not. When you're in a culture that's people like protesting and so forth, it becomes a very relevant situation.

Yeah, but it was really interesting also, just the importance of working with the team, coordinating, people who are taking legal perspectives, who are taking a geological perspective, people who a retaking a cultural perspective and a historical perspective and a political perspective, those are 4 very different ways to try and decide where a border is going to be. And getting those voices to communicate with each other is also very interesting.

It's very easy for us to sort of focus on whatever our sort of field of work is and say, this is the main focus. I think that a lawyer's job is to defend the law but in the same way, a scientist's job is to defend science, and someone who's working with people's job is to defend the voices of the people.

David: So in that situation, what's your job, Duncan?

Duncan: I think one part of the job is to make sure that each of those voices actually recognize that they have a voice that they're trying to communicate, and then from there, helping them to communicate that to each other. It can be even as simple as, it sounds like you're trying to say x and helping the person realize that what they're trying to say and realize the importance of what they're trying to say, and then they could just be even a little coaching about how can you communicate that. It definitely almost became personal work with just co-workers and colleagues.

But I would say on a bigger level, I think that you need to create spaces where all those voices have a space or that are acknowledged as being important. I think that that's just something you build into the system, you build into the way you present the concept.

David: In another way, I'm thinking nobody gets to be wrong and your right doesn't have to be my right. But together, we can figure out what works better.

Duncan: Yeah. I loved the example or the example that Kathy Porter brought of the Apollo 13 because oftentimes, that's what happens. You can say, look we have this bit of law that says, this. We have this historical practice that says this. We have this request, that is this. We have to figure out how to move forward from here.

I think just a reminder of that was always important. Oftentimes, people will say wait a minute, we don't agree. We're stuck. And we'll say, of course we don't agree. That's why we're here in the first place. That's why we came together. The question is, how do we find an agreement.

I think another thing that was always really important was to help people realize that they are the ones that get to make the decisions. It's very often that people feel like when we get stuck in conflict, that we want to hand that decision up to a higher power. I think that's why we like to go to the police or going to a judge or whatever.

But with the realization that those of us who were in the situation are the ones that are going to have to come to the solution or help people come to that realization, I think is super important. There's no way they can move forward without moving forward with the other.

David: And moving forward means buy-in and it's theirs, not the mediators or the lawyers or the governments.

Duncan: Absolutely.

David: I wanted to spend some of our time talking about the Collaborative Global Initiative that you and Kathy, and Jeff Cohen, Charlie Graydon, Sarah Daitch and I have been working on. I'll just read a little bit of our text for our listeners.

We live in an increasingly complex and interconnected world. Humanity faces global and environmental economic and human-based challenges of all kinds. Lasting solutions to these challenges require effective communication and learning across perspectives, cultures and sectors.

At CGI, we believe humans are by nature collaborative. When people work together, allowing space to capture collective wisdom, we achieve great things. Forward-thinking people and communities recognize the need for widespread collaboration. They will need a unique toolbox, a tool kit and skills to collaboratively navigate the future of our increasingly complex and diverse world and work.

Tell me more about that, Duncan.

Duncan: I would say that the greater complexity that we started seeing in the world, and I would say just as the process of globalization and interconnectedness moves forward, that things will always be more complex. As we become more complex, our need for greater collaboration increases in pace.

And the reason for that is, in a way, the best way we can find true solutions or...I guess the best solutions will always come from the most perspectives. But this only is true if those perspectives are working collaboratively toward a shared goal or a shared understanding.

Of course, the trick is turning people from enemies into people who are willing to collaborate with each other. It's that new vision of the world that's going to get us through this next stage.

David: Yeah. And oftentimes, as facilitators, coaches, mediators, we can help people get unstuck by focusing on the future. Where do we want to end up together?

Duncan: Yeah.

David: In the intro to this show, I mentioned my grandchildren and this show and my book, and our work with CGI as being for them. How does that work for you? How do you bring that in to your clients?

Duncan: This is a work around affirmation. It's an affirmation of the world that we want to move towards, and the choice to be collaborative is also an affirmation. It's an affirmation that our collective wisdom is greater than our individual perspectives.

When we ask, what is the world we want to live in, almost all of us start finding the same answer at that point.

David: And it's different than the world we live in today. Listeners, you can find out more about Duncan Autrey at duncanautrey.com.

Duncan, if there was one thing in this moment that you'd like to challenge our listeners to do or be aware of, or think about, what would it be?

Duncan: Right. I would say, conflict is a normal thing. It happens to everyone, at all scales. It can either be positive or negative and there are people who can help you with it. Reach out to them.

David: Thank you so much, my friend. Listeners, this has been Duncan Autrey. Thank you.

David: This is David Savage, author of Break Through to Yes, with a good friend and a mentor, somebody I highly recommend and respect, Kenneth Cloke. Ken is the director of the Center for Dispute Resolution. He's a founder of Mediators Beyond Borders. He's a mediator, an arbitrator, a facilitator, coach, consultant, trainer. He specializes in communication, resolving complex multiparty disputes of all sorts.

The most recent book that I read of Ken's is *The Dance of Opposites*. If you go to Ken's website or Google him, you will find this is a very wise and great spirit for our world. But enough of me, trying to tell you how much I love you Ken. Can you introduce yourself to our listeners?

Ken: Thank you very much, David. It was very kind and generous. I have been working in the fields of collaboration and conflict resolution for I think nearly all my life, but professionally, certainly for the last 35 years. And I think what's most interesting about it is that it has a variety of different forms that activity assumes. But beneath that activity, there's a lot that's in common between all the different things that you mentioned, between mediation, facilitation, coaching, dialogue, and various of what I think of as the collaborative arts and sciences. So that's my passion and my work.

David: Yeah. Wonderful. What is it about what people call collaboration that is so often misleading?

Ken: I think the first thing that's misleading is that there is a single thing that is known as collaboration. We can certainly think of it as singular, but we can also think of it as having a kind of infinite number of manifestations.

There are small-scale collaborations, which we engage in every time we have a conversation. There are larger collaborations that we engage in, in communities and families.

And what we have a hard time, I think imagining is how far exactly this could go. What is the deepest level of our collaboration? What's the highest achievement that we can make in this field? And I think when we begin to think in those terms, we begin to see all of life completely differently. What we then, I think see, is that the collaborative project, if we can call it that, is one that has been building over the course of human history and has yet to realize complete fruition.

David: Do you see this, Ken, as a building evolutionary, positive progression then towards collaborative leadership and a collaborative culture?

Ken: I do. However, we have to talk a little bit for a moment about what progress means in this context. The reality is that there are two fundamental forces that drive us and it's the conflict between those forces that end up creating a kind of two steps forward, one step back outcome when it comes to collaboration.

The first of those forces is the force that unites us, that brings us together, that touches us in our hearts, that allows us to connect in a deep, fundamental level. We can think of this as the force of love, the force of spirituality, the force of heart. There are a number of different ways that we can describe it but essentially, they're all the same.

They're the thing that brings us together. But when we come together, we don't just come together in a single unit. We have unity and we have diversity. And the most wonderful thing about diversity is not just that it's a nice thing to have but that it allows us to achieve higher orders of unity.

So, diversity, on the one hand, creates the basis for conflict and unity creates the basis for resolution. And that's why it's a dance, it's always been a dance. It will always be a dance. What we want to do is to learn how to dance and to do it with the greatest style that we possibly can bring to it, to become, if you will the freight of stairs of our conflicts.

David: Wonderful and so well stated in *The Dance of Opposites*. We've talked about the progress and the big dream of collaborative culture and leadership, and the spirit. Let's get a little more tangible. What's the value of collaboration? Why do it?

Ken: I think if we imagine collaboration on a large scale, it becomes a little difficult to manage. Whereas if we think of it on the smallest possible scale and ask the question slightly differently, what do we get, each individual one of us, what do I get from the collaborations that I engage in?

And the answer is, I get myself. The self isn't just a thing that stands alone as philosophers have said, the smallest human unit isn't one, it's two. And in South Africa, they have a concept called Ubuntu, and Ubuntu means I am who I am because you are who you are, that you create me just as I create you. And together, we create each other.

That's what collaboration is. It's actually a road to the self. It's not a denial of the self. It's not an elimination of the self. It's actually the highest road to the self, just as the self is the highest road to collaboration. So, it doesn't mean denying who you are or not having desires or wishes. It means adding your desires and wishes to other people's desires and wishes in a way that's constructive and produces a higher order of outcome.

David: Yeah. The sum is truly greater than all the parts. Collaboration is not compromised. It's actually creation, part of what I'm hearing.

Ken: Beautifully said.

David: Ken, as we close this interview, how do people find out more about your work, how to connect with you? How do they connect into your network?

Ken: Probably the first way doing it would be to check out my website, which needs a little work. It's not quite up the snuff yet, but it's kennethcloke.com or check out any of the books that I've written. The one that you mentioned, *The Dance of Opposites* is a good way to start. Those will all be very nice.

David: I hear an airplane in the background, that must be collaboration is taking off.

Ken: Must be.

David: Any last comments, Ken?

Ken: The last comment is really kind of an aphorism. The aphorism is this, it doesn't matter whose end of the boat is sinking. We're all in this together, and so we have to realize, take responsibility for it and start working on our problems together. It doesn't mean it's easy. It just means it's the truth.

David: Thank you so much, Ken; kennethcloke.com. Thank you for your wisdom.

Ken: Thank you very much.

David: This is the Break Through to Yes Collaborative Podcast Series. Welcome. Let's learn together. You matter. We are good enough. We can stop the madness. We will make the necessary changes. We can do it based on our values, to create shared value.

First step in my 10 Essential Steps to Collaboration is Set Intention. The last step, number 10 is Make It So. So that's why we need to set our intention. Welcome, set your intention. As you listen, learn. Disrupt. Challenge and evolve what you're listening to now. All is welcome here. Make it so. Unlock the possible within your culture of collaboration.

There are many, from the most powerful in the world to the not yet powerful who do not yet have the skills to lead for a better future. There are many that lead or are led by fear, ignorance or just simple ideas, black and white.

Today, we do have the most educated, most connected, most wealthy and most healthy population in history. Today, we can access collective intelligence like never before. Break down those walls. It's more than Mr. Gorbachev; it's all of us. Break down those walls.

As you lead, as you vision, as you play, as you design, realize the world is your playground, not just your organization. By working together better, we can create business Break Throughs, political Break Throughs, environmental Break Throughs and social Break Throughs. *Break Through to Yes: Unlock Your Possible Within a Culture of Collaboration.*

Our world and challenges are more complex than ever before. The world demands skilled collaborators. Collaboration is a culture. It's not an event or a meeting. Think of meetings, bloody meetings, I still want to make that movie Collaboration Bloody Collaboration, it's misunderstood, misused and yet the most important tool we have yet to really capitalize on.

Collaboration unlocks the possible. Collaboration builds collective intelligence. Are you ready to build your awareness, your skills, your network and your success? Why not? Why not now? Why not us?

Welcome to your brighter future. This is my invitation to this podcast series and to learn together. I don't know it all, but we've got people like Ken Cloke saying we are only at the very beginning of knowing the possibilities that will come through real collaboration. We have Duncan Autrey, the first rule of conflict is that the people who are not allowed to have their voice will find a way to have their voice. They will find a way. Invite them in.

In my podcast series, has a total of 41 episodes from 2015 and 2017 so far. I've got 75 guests from Canada, America, France, Germany, Spain, the Netherlands, Sweden, Australia, Argentina and another hundred visionaries and experts in my book, Break Through to Yes. I don't have all the answers. We have all the answers we need now. And now, you are part of the network. You are part of the opportunity.

Here are the resources in this podcast series, 41 different episodes. Here are a few of the podcasts;

- ✓ Finding Your Truth,
- ✓ Critical Thinking,
- ✓ The 10 Essential Steps to Collaboration,
- ✓ Great leaders know that they don't know.
- ✓ Egos, yeah look at the cover of my book, the letters shaded in the title make "egos" and that's what threatens true, successful, brilliant collaboration.
- ✓ How collaborative is my organization?
- ✓ Collaborative Leadership Assessment.

- ✓ Collaboration is the way; Creating Shared Value is the Destination. In Creating Shared Value, we put the environment first. And the community informs business, what they want and what they will buy. Then business succeeds and profits.

- ✓ How to build your collaborative culture?

- ✓ One of my favorite podcasts and one of my favorite human beings is Duncan Autrey. We share our conversation on Fractal Friends.

- ✓ Mastery Leadership with Bob Acton.

- ✓ Why Collaborate?

- ✓ Collaboration gone bad – yeah, that's one of my most popular. The good, the bad and the ugly.

- ✓ Our Global Campfire, we talk about this is a global movement. Rotary International is one of the organizations at the center of it.

- ✓ Then I get into the 10 Essential Steps, each podcast reviews one step. Set intention. Be aware. Embrace conflict. Seek diversity. Design the collaboration. Come together. Listen deeply. Collaborate with vision. Now lead. Make it so. There is so much in each one of these episodes, I'm very proud of it and very proud of the 75 guests.

- ✓ Then we go into team leadership awareness, next generation leaders and our future. We present some of the younger generation, brilliant connectors from across the planet talk about collaboration and their work.

✓ Then we talk about collaboration in leadership, collaboration in sports, collaboration in organizational culture. There's collaboration everywhere. Think of any sport. There is no sport, no business, no group, no family that you can simply be on your own. I guess you can, but it'll be a lonely, unfulfilled life. That's my view. That's my judgment.

✓ What is your organizational culture?

✓ Collaboration, company to company dispute resolution and mindfulness; slow down before you go too fast, really listen. What's not being said but needs to be heard?

✓ Collaboration and critical thinking in this age of lies.

✓ Collaboration Europe and Rotary International, we go to Germany and France.

✓ Collaboration in the end of human sexual trafficking; yeah, we're dealing with some great subjects in this series, important subjects. How do we work together to end human sexual trafficking?

✓ We also have an episode on human resources and global networks. The secret marathon and going the extra mile, including the secret marathon for women in Afghanistan.

✓ Leadership and disruptive technologies, talking about the disruptive technologies. What's required by a board of directors, by a management team and by you to create a better future where you profit, you gain, you succeed, and others don't have to fail. Negotiation and mediation, and global initiative tool kit.

✓ Then we bring One Yes, One Thing, One Dream, with the beautiful wisdom of Miten and Deva Premal, and my grandchildren Quinn and Sara Amos, and others.

✓ Unlocking the Possible is the latest podcast.

So, these are the tools, the ideas and the people around our planet that are breaking down walls. We can do this. We are doing this. Let's do this. Let's understand what is possible.

When we hear from people like Robert Stewart on his peace initiative for Rotary, Rotary has almost eliminated Polio globally. Now, Robert Stewart has been working for probably 30 years on Peace Plus for Rotary. Julie Murray gives us the resources of mindfulness. Bob Acton and David Mitchell show us leadership. What does leadership really require?

There are just so much here. What I want to share with everyone is, gratitude. Yes, just gratitude for what we're doing together. This is an opportunity. This is my offering, my 41 podcasts, my book, my books to come. But mostly, it's because I want to learn, and I want to learn with you. These are the tools and ideas and people. What can you bring?

Thank you for being part of this. Let's collaborate. Let's learn and resolve together. Let's co-create our better future. Let's create a world that is inclusive. Let's invite everyone. All are welcome here. Invest in our shared future for our grandchildren, your grandchildren, the great-grandchildren.

Email me at david@davidbsavage.com and let's build together. Let's make this so. There is so, so much.

My 10th step in my 10 Essential Steps is Make It So. What about let's make it so, let's make it sew, sowing the seeds? We're sowing the seeds right now. This won't happen overnight. We won't create the intelligent leaders, the intelligent bosses, the intelligent staff that we so seek overnight.

And many of us will not have the time, our lives and legacy will end before we do it. Wouldn't that be a shame? What's your legacy? What is your legacy?

I think, I don't know. I don't know it all. I don't know much. And after 42 years in business as a negotiator, as a collaborator, as a team builder, as a connector, I think I know even less.

The future does matter. Let's build this system. Let's make Ken Cloke's statement true, that we can only dream of what's possible. Let's Unlock our Possible. Let us Make It So.

Now thank you for setting your intention. Thank you for listening to me. And mostly, I want to learn from you. Send me a note. Give me a call, whatever works because this is just one step in our many steps of collaboration. You matter. We matter. And there's got to be a better way. There's just got to be a better way. Unlock our possible.

I'm David B. Savage. I hope that you enjoyed this, and I hope that you will step in. I know you will. This is brilliant. This is the way of collective intelligence, innovation and future-making, and inclusion no matter what. We all matter. No heroes here, just evolution.

Thank you for listening. Thank you for leading. In the end, we must lead from love. Inclusion, listening deeply, designing a culture, vision, innovation, collaboration, and accountability create great leadership opportunities that create a better future.

Now, let's work together better.

Lead from love not fear.

Break Through To Yes: The Collaborative Podcast Series
by David B. Savage

Book 1: The Foundations for Collaboration
includes eight 15-minute podcasts originally aired on the
Tenacious Living Network. The chapters are;

Finding Your Truth
10 Essential Steps to Collaboration
Great Leaders Know That They Don't Know
Global Book Release Celebration
EGOS
How Collaborative is my organization?
Collaboration is the Way; Shared Value is the Destination
Building Your Collaborative Culture
Thank you to Tenacious Living Radio for originally
producing these episodes.

Book 2: The Collaborative Guest Podcasts
offers three podcasts where David B. Savage was a guest on
Barry Wilson, Bob Acton and Duncan Autrey's podcasts.
The chapters are;

Fractal Friends Duncan Autrey,
        -talking about conflict resolution, communities,
        activists and collaboration
Mastering Leadership with Bob Acton,
        -exploring negotiation, collaboration and leadership
Collaboration and Cumulative Effects on our Land with
Barry Wilson,
        -sharing ideas on how we collaborate on the true
        cumulative effects of our construction, capital
        projects and communities.

Book 3: The 10 Essential Steps of Collaboration
provides you with 16 podcasts originally aired on Voice
America in 2015 and 2016. The chapters and guests are;

Book 4: Unlocking the Possible with Collaboration provides you with 14 podcasts originally aired on Voice America in 2017. The chapters and guests are;

Collaboration and Leadership
     Bob Acton, David Mitchell
Collaboration and Sports
     Tristen Chernove, Martin Parnell
Collaboration and Organizational Culture
     Mike Thompson, Stephen Hobbs
Collaboration, Company Dispute Resolution and Mindfulness
     Julie Murray
Collaboration and Critical Thinking in This Age of Lies
     Doreen Liberto, Chuck Rose
Collaboration, Europe and Rotary International
     Elisabeth Delaygue Bevan, Florian Wackermann
Collaboration and Human Sexual Trafficking
     Lance Kadatz, Cliff Wiebe
Collaboration, Human Resources and Global Networks
     Amy Schabacker Dufrane, Japman Bajaj
Collaboration, The Secret Marathon and Going the Extra Mile
     Kate McKenzie, Shawn Anderson, Martin Parnell
Collaboration, Leadership and Disruptive Technologies
     Jim Gibson
Collaboration, Negotiation and Mediation
     Jeff Cohen
Collaborative Global Initiative Tool Kit
     Barry Wilson, Doreen Liberto, Jeff Cohen
One Yes, One Thing, One Dream
     Deva Premal and Miten, Klara Fenlof, Robert Stewart, Sara and Quinn Amos
Unlocking the Possible
     Ken Cloke, Duncan Autrey

I hope you enjoy the Break Through To Yes: The Collaborative Podcast Series

"David B. Savage's *Break Through to Yes* provides the key for real success – collaboration!"
Marshall Goldsmith, *Thinkers 50* #1 Leadership Thinker in the World and Top 5 Management Thinker 2015

"Written in a manner that illustrates collaboration in action, *Break Through to Yes* shares decade's worth of knowledge and a structure that outlines what true collaboration looks like."
David L. Milia, MBA, CET, Associate Director, Centre for Corporate Sustainability/Energy Initiatives
Haskayne School of Business

"David Savage is deeply insightful and highly intuitive. He is a skilled and highly regarded practitioner with a strong sense of ethics and values. He has a profound commitment to personal and organizational transformation and can be counted on to be honest, resourceful and supportive. I recommend him highly." **Ken Cloke, Founder Mediators Beyond Borders**

"David is a brilliant leader who is the expert when it comes to understanding the power of collaboration and creating an open culture/ open door environment for all. His ability to share information, target the needs of the audience, and engage their perspective was seamless.
Denise Baril, Founder, Workplace Speaker Network

"Savage reminds us of who we are and what is most called for in our organizations. He brings qualities, values and intentions to the core of our professional work." **Gloria Boogmans, Independent Business Woman.**

Acknowledgements

Thanks to;

a) every one of my guests from around the world on my 2015, 2016 and 2017 podcasts.

b) VoiceAmerica (Book 3 and 4),

c) Tenacious Living Radio (Book 1),

d) Obair, CE Analytic and Autrey (Book 2) for originally producing these podcasts.

e) Dawood Taiwo for editing and cover.

f) Vladimir Krstic and Pete Stover for audio production on the audio books.

g) Ginger Wilmot for transcribing the podcasts.

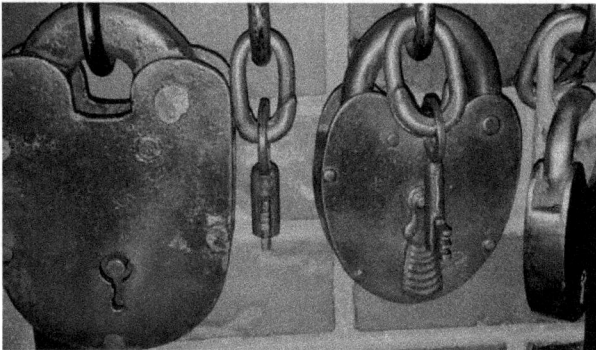

Unlock the Possible within a Culture of Collaboration

SAVAGE
MANAGEMENT Ltd.

About the Author;

David B. Savage, BA (Econ), PLand, CPCC
Collaboration, Business Development and Negotiation Specialist
Savage Management Ltd.

Savage brings over 42-years expertise, experience and leadership in oil and gas, renewable energy, health care, entrepreneurship, stakeholder engagement and conflict management. Over a ten-year period, David and partners, collaborated to develop 5 companies and 4 not for profits. Since 2007, Savage Management has focused on build capacity, innovation and accountability in people and in and between organizations and communities.

David Savage works with leaders and organizations to advance their success through collaboration, negotiation and business development.

CORE COMPETENCIES:

Negotiations and Agreement Building, Business Development, Acquisitions, Management Consulting, plus Strategic Planning & Execution, Sustainability Engagement and Organizational Development, Management Leadership and Team Building, Stakeholder Engagement, Business Development, Conflict Management, Executive and Team Coaching plus 360 Leadership Assessments.

KEY CORPORATE EXPERIENCE:

➤ Savage Management, President, (founder, 1993 to present, private, consulting, oil and gas management, coaching, leadership and negotiation training, negotiation mastery circles and leader round tables, conflict resolution and collaboration assessments),

> Prior to 2007, David held executive positions with BXL Energy, Marmac Mines Ltd., Sebring Energy, TriQuest Energy, Sommer Energy, Westar Petroleum, Total Petroleum, Ashland Oil, Bank of Montreal, and CIBC.

PUBLICATIONS

2003: David's Company to Company Dispute Resolution Council published the Let's Talk Handbook.

2011: Think Sustain Ability published Sustain Magazine.

2012: Ready Aim Excel: 52 Leadership Lessons

2016: Break Through to Yes: Unlocking the Possible within a Culture of Collaboration

2017: The Collaborative Podcast Series (print, eBook and Audible) is now available. The Books, which include 75 guests from eight nations) are;

Book 1: The Foundations For Collaboration

Book 2: The Collaborative Guest Podcasts

Book 3: The 10 Essential Steps

Book 4: Unlocking the Possible

Break Through To Yes Updated and Revised edition

2018: Break Through To Yes: Generating More Value with Collaborative Negotiation.

PURPOSE

Getting the right people, in the right places, with the right systems and the right resources to collaborate, innovate and figure out challenges together is the best way. And, if that is not possible, then guiding the parties to the right people, principles, processes and systems to ensure everyone's interests are heard and considered is my goal.